Complete Book of Crochet Border Designs

Linda P. Schapper

Sterling Publishing Co., Inc.   New York

Edited by Barbara Busch

Library of Congress Cataloging-in-Publication Data

Schäpper, Linda.
  Complete book of crochet border designs.

  1. Crocheting—Patterns.   2. Borders, Ornamental
(Decorative arts) I. Title.
TT820.S278 1987   746.43′4041   86-30155
ISBN 0-8069-6428-6
ISBN 0-8069-6430-8 (pbk.)

1   3   5   7   9   10   8   6   4   2

Copyright © 1987 by Sterling Publishing Co., Inc.
Two Park Avenue, New York, N.Y. 10016
Distributed in Canada by Oak Tree Press Ltd.
% Canadian Manda Group, P.O. Box 920, Station U
Toronto, Ontario, Canada M8Z 5P9
Distributed in the United Kingdom by Blandford Press
Link House, West Street, Poole, Dorset BH15 1LL, England
Distributed in Australia by Capricorn Ltd.
P.O. Box 665, Lane Cove, NSW 2066
Manufactured in the United States of America

◆ Contents ◆

ACKNOWLEDGMENTS
I would like to thank David Thane Tegethoff of Orlando, Florida, whose wisdom and kindness helped me to start this book, and Barbara Busch, my editor in New York, whose enthusiasm and sense of humor helped me to finish it.

• Introduction •

There is not much of a written record about the history of crochet. Like so many handcrafts, it grew and flourished and no one thought it important enough to write about.

Crochet is believed to have originated as early as the Stone Age, as a rough hook used to join clothing. It seems likely that we have adopted the French word for hook, *crochet*, as the name of the craft because the French did more than any other group to record crochet patterns.

Without written instructions available, patterns survived by being passed down through families. New patterns were copied by examining the design with a magnifying glass. In the last century, written instruction became more popular as the reading level of women improved. Instructions, however, can be long and tedious, and although perfectly clear to the writer, can be unintelligible to the crocheter.

This book introduces, in more extensive form, the international crochet symbol system. It is easy to read after you have worked out a few of the basic stitches. By using this system, it is easier to see the whole pattern in proportion, and it is a nice experience to be able to pick up a crochet book in Russian, French or Japanese and understand the crochet symbols. The symbols themselves look a great deal like the crochet stitches, and are not difficult to follow.

Crochet is based on a few simple stitches used in endless variation. It begins with a chain, and the way the stitches are formed determines the pattern. You only need a crochet hook, your hand and the thread. It is easy to carry with you and do anywhere. Unlike knitting and weaving, it is difficult to make a mistake which cannot be corrected immediately.

Crochet is versatile. It can make generous lace patterns, mimic knitting, patchwork or weaving, and it can form any number of textile patterns. I found the challenge of making 501 different patterns with the same off-white thread to be exhilarating and never-ending.

This book focusses on bands and borders. Patterns range from small in size to large flamboyant lace designs. Crocheted borders can be used to finish projects in weaving, knitting, sewing or many other handcrafts. Bands can be used to decorate clothing, household textiles or any type of sewing. In Switzerland crocheted filet bands were used to piece together sheets and tablecloths before the looms were wide enough to make one whole piece. Borders can be used for blankets, place mats, towels or sheets. They could decorate handkerchiefs, altar cloths, curtains or children's clothing. They could be used as curtains, collars or doll clothes. There is no limit to the amount of ideas and uses for crocheted borders. All you have to do is vary the size of your needle, the material you use and the way you use it.

Stitches

Starting

Make a slip knot.

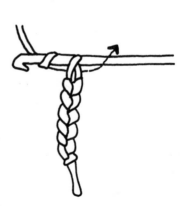

Pass the hook through the loop, under the thread, and catch the thread with the hook.

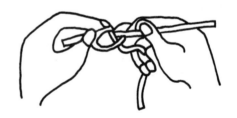

Place the thread over the hook and put it back through the first loop.

Slip Stitch   <

< < <

Make a chain the desired length. Place thread over the hook and insert it into the 2nd chain from the hook.

Repeat this procedure of catching the thread on the hook and pulling it through the hole until you make the desired number of chains.

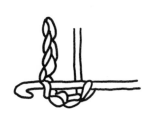

Single Crochet   +

+++

This is a short tight stitch. Make the chain the desired length. Insert the hook into the 2nd chain on the hook and wrap the thread around the hook.

Pull the thread through the 2 loops, leaving 1 loop on the hook.

Continue the process by inserting the hook into the next chain desired.

Wrap the yarn around the hook and draw up a loop through both the chain and the loop on the hook.

Triple Crochet

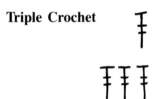

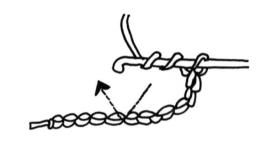

Work a chain to the desired length. Wrap the thread around the hook twice and insert the hook into the desired chain.

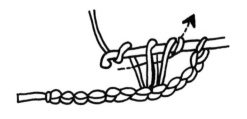

Place the thread around the hook and pull it through 1 loop, leaving 4 loops on the needle. Wrap the thread around the hook and pull it through 2 loops on the hook, leaving 3 loops on the hook. Wrap the thread around the hook and pull it through 2 loops on the hook. Place the thread on the hook and pull it through the last 2 loops.

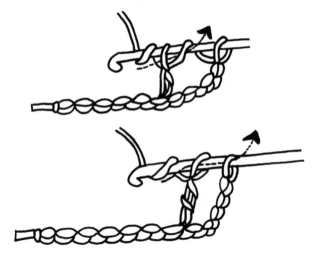

Popcorn Stitch

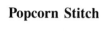

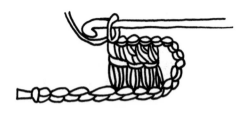

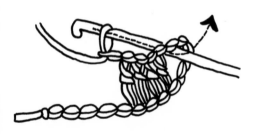

Chain to the length needed. Make 3 or more double crochet as desired, in the same chain, turn and chain 1. Slip stitch into the chain after the last double crochet, chain 1 and turn. Can be worked with 2 to 6 loops.

V-stitch or Shell Stitch

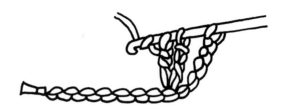

This is a very easy stitch, but when several double crochets are used, looks very intricate.
Work 1 double crochet. Work another double crochet, using the same chain or space.

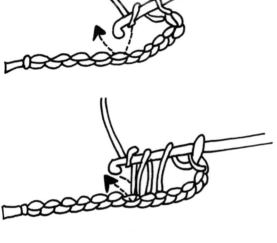

Puff Stitch

Chain to the length needed. Insert the hook into the desired chain, yarn over, insert hook again, yarn over, as many times as desired, only pulling the yarn through all the loops once at the end. A puff stitch can be made with 2–6 loops.

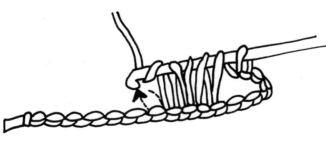

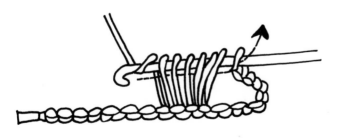

Picot

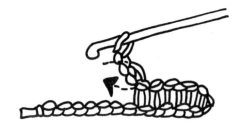

Chain 3 and slip stitch in the base stitch.

Double Crochet

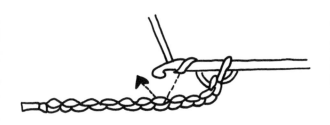

This is perhaps the most popular and frequently used crochet stitch. Make the chain the desired length. Wrap the thread over the hook, and insert the hook into the chain.

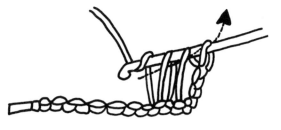

Wrap the thread over again and pull the thread through. Wrap the thread around the hook again and pull the thread through 2 loops, leaving 2 loops on the hook. Wrap the thread around the hook and pull the thread through the 2 loops on the hook.

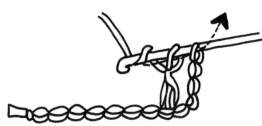

Half Double Crochet

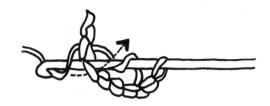

This stitch gives a lot of body and structure and resembles knitting.

Make the chain the length you want. Wrap the thread around the hook and insert into the chain and pull it through.

There should be 3 loops on the hook now. Wrap the thread over the hook and pull the thread through the 3 loops on the hook.

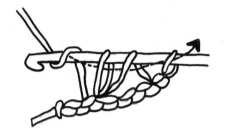

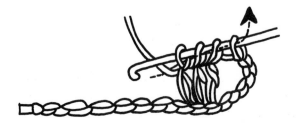

Cluster Stitch

Chain the row to the desired length. Wrap the thread around the hook towards you. Insert hook, wrap thread around and pull through 2 loops, leaving 2 on the hook. Wrap thread around the hook, insert it into the same chain, draw it through 2 loops, leaving 3 on the hook, until you have the number of stitches on the hook that you need. Then wrap thread around the hook towards you and pull it through all the loops, leaving 1 on the hook. Can be worked with 2 to 6 loops.

Triple X-stitch

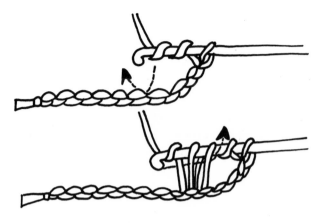

Wrap thread around the needle towards you twice. Begin 1 triple crochet, pull yarn through 2 loops, leaving 3 on the hook. Begin 2nd triple crochet in the 2nd chain, and pull the yarn through 2 loops, 3 times. Chain 1 and work 1 double crochet in the joint of the base of the 2 triple crochet.

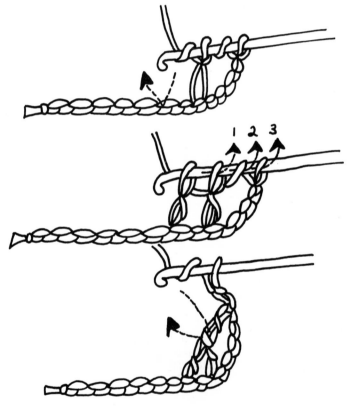

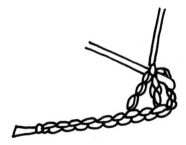

Small X-stitch

Work 1 double crochet in the 2nd or 3rd double crochet, chain 1 or 2, depending on the pattern. Work 1 double crochet backwards 1 or 2 stitches.

Y-stitch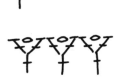

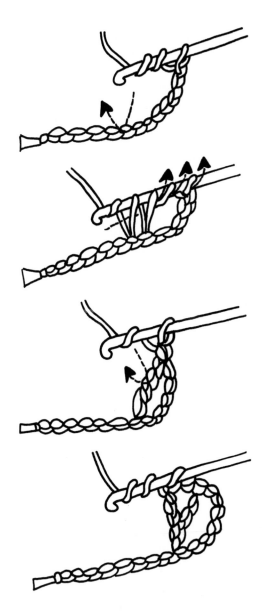

Wrap around needle twice, as if doing a triple crochet. Pull yarn through 3 times. Wrap yarn around hook once. Insert in the middle of the triple crochet, and make a double crochet in the middle of the stitch. Begin next stitch.

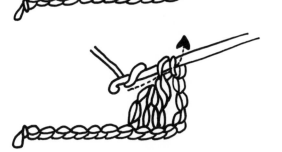

Inverted V-stitch or Inverted Shell

Work chain to needed length. Begin double crochet in desired chain, yarn over and pull yarn through 2 loops, yarn over. Begin 2nd double crochet, pull yarn through 2 loops and continue until necessary number of double crochet are made, then yarn over and pull through all the loops on the hook.

Relief Double Crochet

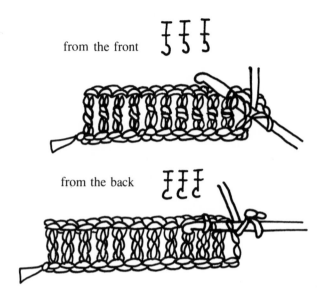

Same as the double crochet, except that instead of the hook being inserted in the hole, the crochet is formed by circling the post of the crochet stitch below, either from the front and out again or from the back and out again.

from the front

from the back

Borders with jagged or irregular edges look very difficult, but by using the following few simple tricks of adding on to the ends of rows, are very easy and very rewarding.

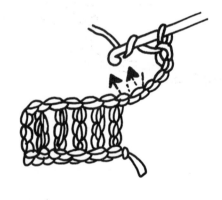

Increasing at the Beginning of the Row

After the last stitch, chain the specified amount and turn. Work double crochet in the specified chain afterwards, until the pattern returns to the previously completed stitches.

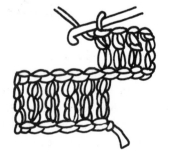

Increasing Space at the Beginning of the Row

After last stitch of row, chain amount specified and turn. Make normal double crochet in the next double crochet and continue.

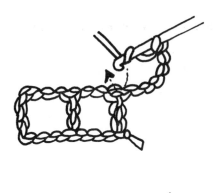

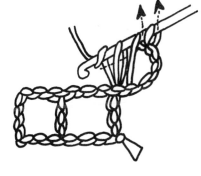

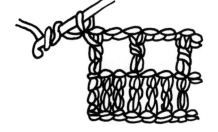

Adding to the End of the Row

After the last double crochet, work a triple crochet back into the bottom of the double crochet just completed, work additional triple crochet as required.

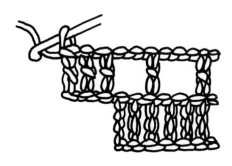

Adding on to the End of the Row

After last stitch, chain 2 and work double triple crochet into the end of the row.

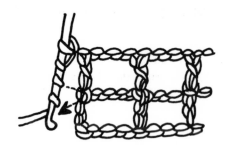

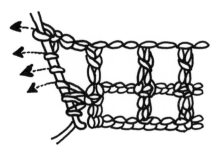

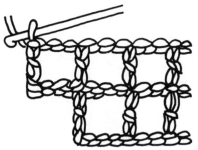

Borders may be crocheted directly onto the material or finished first and then stitched onto the finished piece.

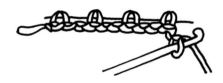

◆ International Crochet Symbols ◆

chain stitch	○	∞∞∞∞∞
slip stitch	<	< < < < <
single crochet	+	+ + + + +
half double crochet	T	T T T T T
double crochet	Ŧ	ŦŦŦŦŦ
triple crochet	Ŧ	ŦŦŦŦŦ
double triple crochet	Ŧ	ŦŦŦŦŦ
relief double crochet from the front	Ƨ	ƧƧƧƧƧ
relief double crochet from the back	Ƭ	ƬƬƬƬƬ
3-chain picot	⊕	⊕ ⊕ ⊕ ⊕
4-chain picot	⊛	⊛ ⊛⊛ ⊛ ⊛
3-looped popcorn stitch	⊎	⊎⊎⊎⊎⊎

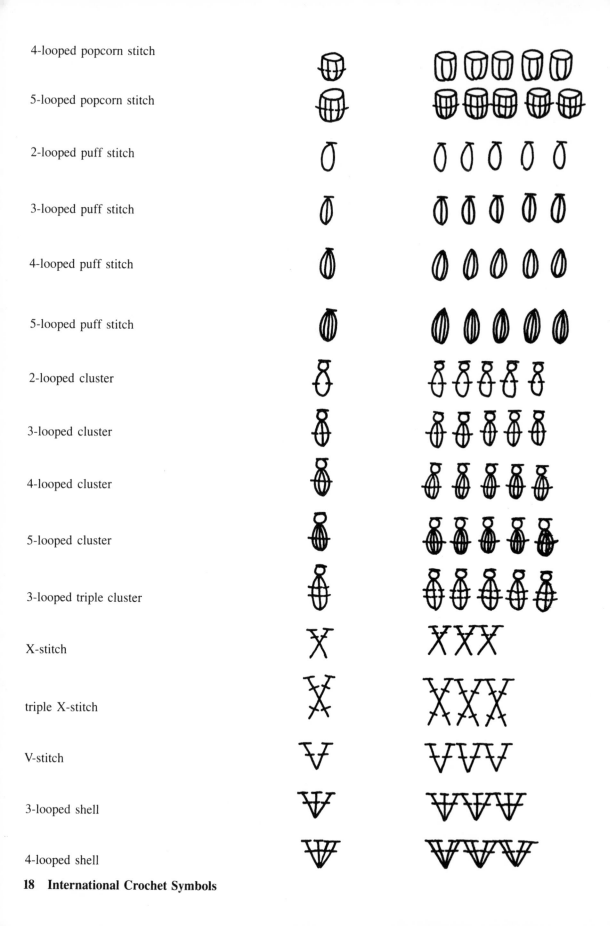

4-looped popcorn stitch

5-looped popcorn stitch

2-looped puff stitch

3-looped puff stitch

4-looped puff stitch

5-looped puff stitch

2-looped cluster

3-looped cluster

4-looped cluster

5-looped cluster

3-looped triple cluster

X-stitch

triple X-stitch

V-stitch

3-looped shell

4-looped shell

18   International Crochet Symbols

5-looped shell

inverted 3-looped V-stitch (shell)

inverted 4-looped V-stitch (shell)

inverted 5-looped V-stitch (shell)

shell with chains

shell with chains

examples of 1-chain

dropped stitch, dropped double crochet

wraparound stitch

Y-stitch (3-looped, 2-looped, 4-looped)

Abbreviations

ch(s)	chain(s)
dc	double crochet
sc	single crochet
hdc	half double crochet
trc	triple crochet
rep	repeat(ing)
sk	skip
sl st	slip stitch(es)

*used to mark the beginning of a set of instructions that are to be repeated.

Notes for those using the written instructions

1. Stitch is always counted from the last stitch used, unless otherwise specified.

2. The abbreviations are the American ones. British readers should keep this in mind since a few British abbreviations differ.

3. It's best to allow a few extra chains in the beginning. Since borders may often require set lengths, learn to count the pattern and then calculate how many extra chains you might need to complete the pattern.

4. Learn to read the diagrams. Any new behavior is uncomfortable in the beginning, but it is much easier than the written explanation. When in doubt about the written explanations, check them against the drawings.

5. Although the instructions for the vertical bands begin with row 1, instructions for repetition usually begin with row 2. The first row is not standard because it is all worked on a base row of chains.

6. The division of stitches into chapters was difficult because many of the patterns could fit into several chapters. I tried to place them where they were most typical.

•1•
Single Crochet and Chain

1. Chain multiples of 2 plus 2.

Row 1: Sc in the 2nd ch and in each ch all across the row, ch 1 and turn.

Row 2: Sc in the 1st sc, *ch 1 and sc in the 2nd sc, rep from *, ending row with last sc, ch 1 and turn.

Row 3: Sc in the 1st sc and sc in the 1-ch, *ch 1 and sc in the next 1-ch, rep from *, ending row with sc in the last sc, ch 1 and turn.

Row 4: Sc in the 1st sc, *ch 1 and sc in the next 1-ch, rep from *, ending row with sc in the last sc, ch 1 and turn.

Row 5: Sc in the 1st sc and sc in the next 1-ch, *ch 2 and sc in the next 1-ch, rep from *, ending row with sc in the last set, sc in the last sc.

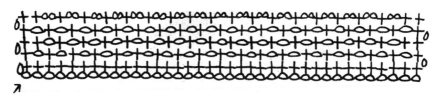

2. Chain multiples of 9 plus 6.

Row 1: 1 sc in the 2nd ch and 1 sc in each of the next 4 chs, * ch 4, 1 sc in the 5th ch and in each of the next 4 chs, rep from *, ending row with last set, ch 1 and turn.

Row 2: *sc in each sc, ch 5, rep from *, ending row with last set of 5 sc, ch 1 and turn.

Rows 3–4: Same as row 2, ch 1 and turn.

Row 5: *sc in each sc, ch 6, rep from *, ending row with last set of sc, ch 1 and turn.

Row 6: *sc in each sc, ch 7, rep from *, ending row with last set of sc, ch 1 and turn.

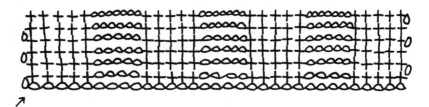

3. Chain multiples of 4 plus 2.

Row 1: Sc in the 2nd ch and in each ch all across the row, ch 1 and turn.
Row 2: Sc in the 1st sc, * ch 5 and sc in the 4th sc, rep from *, ending row with sc in the last sc, ch 1 and turn.
Row 3: * sl st in the sc, ch 7 and rep from *, ending row with sl st in the last sc.

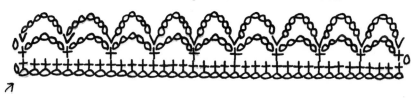

4. Chain multiples of 4 plus 2.

Row 1: Sc in the 2nd sc and in each sc all across the row, ch 1 and turn.
Row 2: Sc in the 1st sc, *ch 5, sc in the 4th sc, rep from *, ending row with sc in the last sc, ch 1 and turn.
Row 3: *sc in the sc, ch 7 and rep from *, ending row with sc in the last sc, ch 1 and turn.
Row 4: *sl st in sc, ch 9 and rep from *, ending row with sl st in the last sc.

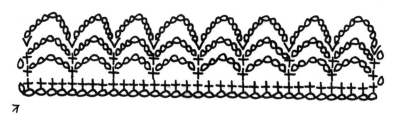

5. Chain multiples of 7 plus 2.

Row 1: Sc in the 2nd ch and in each of the next 4 chs, * ch 6 and sc in the 3rd ch and sc in each of the next 4 chs, rep from *, ending row with sc in each of the last 5 chs, ch 1 and turn.
Row 2: Sc in each of the next 3 sc, * ch 8, sl st into the end of the 6-ch, sc in the 2nd sc and the next sc, rep from *, ending row with sc in each of the last 4 sc.

6. Chain multiples of 6 plus 2.

Row 1: Sc in the 2nd ch, * ch 5, sc in the 4th ch, ch 3, sc in the next ch, rep from *, ending row with sc in the last ch, ch 5 and turn.
Row 2: *sc in the middle of the 5-ch, ch 5, rep from *, ending row with last sc, ch 2 and 1 dc in the last sc, ch 1 and turn.
Row 3: Sc in the dc, * ch 5, sc in the middle of the 5-ch, ch 3, sc in the middle of the same 5-ch, rep from *, ending row with sc in the turning ch, ch 5 and turn.
Row 4: *sc in the middle of the 5-ch, ch 5, rep from *, ending row with dc in the last sc.

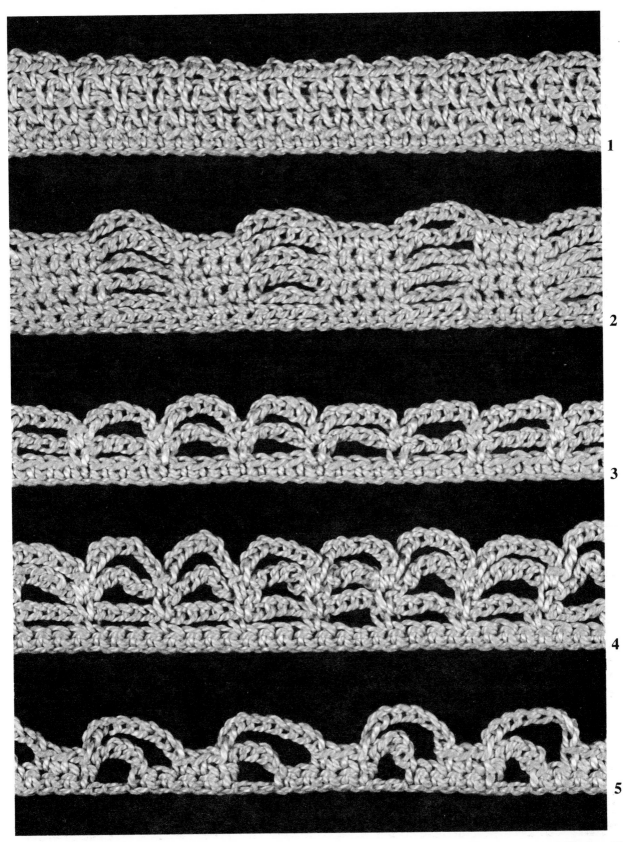

1

2

3

4

5

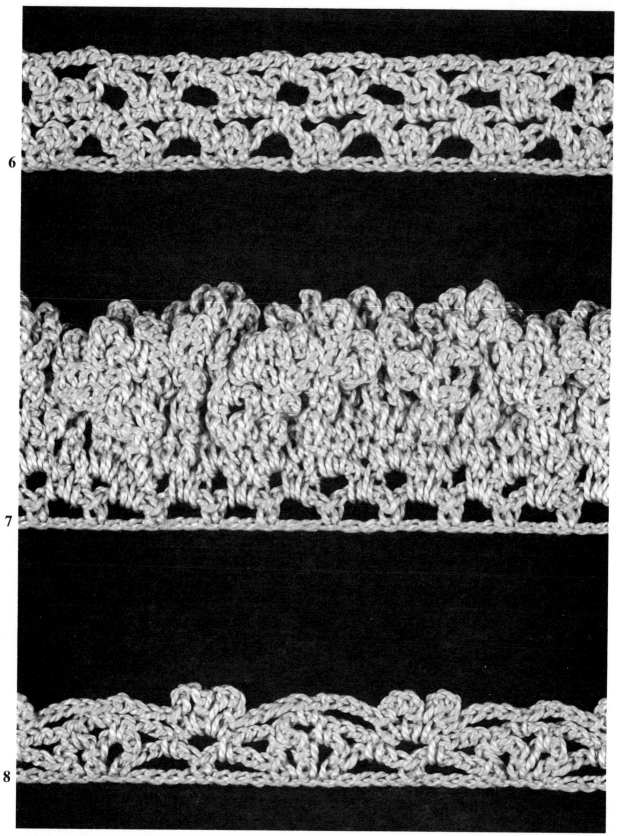

6

7

8

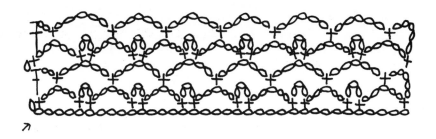

7. Chain multiples of 3 plus 7.

Row 1: Sc in the 7th ch, * ch 4 and sc in the 3rd ch, rep from *, ending row with last sc, ch 2 and dc in the last ch, ch 5 and turn.

Row 2: Sc in the 2-ch, *ch 4, and sc in the 4-ch, ch 4 and sc in the same 4-ch, ch 4, sc in the next 4-ch, ch 4, sc in same ch, and rep from *, ending row with sc in the turning ch, ch 2 and dc in the turning ch, ch 1 and turn.

Row 3: Sc in the dc, *ch 5 and sc in the 4-ch, ch 5 and sc in the same 4-ch, ch 5 and sc in the next 4-ch, and rep from *, ending row with sc in the turning ch, ch 4 and turn.

Row 4: * sc in the 5-ch and ch 5, rep from *, ending row with last sc, ch 2 and trc in the last sc, ch 1 and turn.

Row 5: Sc in the trc, *ch 5 and sc in the 5-ch, rep from *, ending row with sc, ch 4 and turn.

Row 6: *sc in the 5-ch, ch 5 and sc in the same 5-ch, ch 5 and rep from *, ending row with sc in the 5-ch, ch 2 and trc in the last sc.

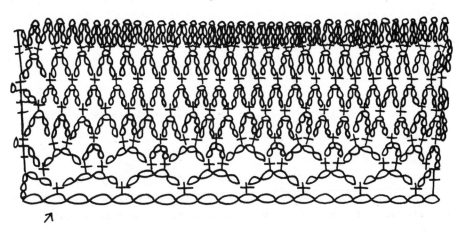

8. Chain multiples of 12 plus 2.

Row 1: Sc in the 2nd ch, *ch 5, sc in the 5th ch, ch 5, sc in the 5th ch, ch 5 and sc in the next ch, ch 5, sc in the next ch, rep from *, ending row with last sc, ch 6 and turn.

Row 2: *sc around the 5-ch, ch 3, sc in the middle of the next 5-ch, ch 3, sc in the middle of the next 5-ch, ch 3, sc in the middle of the next 5-ch, ch 3, rep from *, ending row with last sc, ch 3 and dc in the sc, ch 1 and turn.

Row 3: Sc in the dc, *ch 5, sc in the beginning of the 2nd 3-ch, ch 5, sc in the middle of the same 3-ch, ch 5, sc in the middle of the same 3-ch, ch 5, sc in the middle of the 2nd 3-ch, rep from *, ending row with sc in the turning ch.

9. Chain multiples of 7 plus 7.

Row 1: Sc in the 10th ch, *ch 7, sc in the 6th ch, rep from *, ending row with last sc, ch 3 and dc in the 3rd ch, ch 1 and turn.

Row 2: Sc in the dc, ch 3, sc in the 3-ch, ch 3, sc in the 3-ch, * sc in the 7-ch, and 3 chs 3 times, and 1 more sc in the same 7-ch, rep from *, ending row with sc in the turning ch, ch 3, sc in the same ch, ch 3 and 1 more sc in the turning ch, ch 1 and turn.

Row 3: Sc in the 1st sc, ch 7, sc in the 4th 3-ch, *ch 7, sc in the 3rd 3-ch, rep from *, ending row with sc in the last sc, ch 7 and turn.

Row 4: * sc around the 7-ch, ch 7 and rep from *, ending row with last sc, ch 3 and 1 double trc in the last sc.

10. Chain multiples of 4 plus 2.

Row 1: Sc in the 2nd ch, * ch 5, sc in the 4th ch, rep from *, ending row with sc in the last ch, ch 5 and turn.

Row 2: *sc around the 5-ch, ch 5, rep from *, ending row with sc, ch 2 and dc in the last sc, ch 1 and turn.

Row 3: Sc in the 1st dc, * ch 5, sc around the 5-ch, rep from *, ending row with sc in the turning ch, ch 5 and turn.

Row 4: * sc around the 5-ch, ch 5, and rep from *, ending row with sc, ch 2 and 1 dc in the last sc, ch 1 and turn.

Row 5: Sc in the 1st dc, *ch 5, sc around the 5-ch, rep from *, ending row with sc in the turning ch.

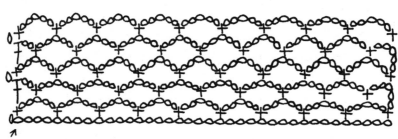

11. Chain multiples of 4 plus 2.

Row 1: Sc in the 2nd ch, *ch 3 and sc in the ch just used, ch 3 and sc in the 4th ch, rep from *, ending row with sc, ch 3 and sc in the last ch, ch 2 and turn.

Row 2: *sc in the next 3-ch, ch 3 and sc in the same 3-ch, ch 3 and rep from *, ending row with last set, ch 2 and turn.

Rows 3–5: Same as row 2.

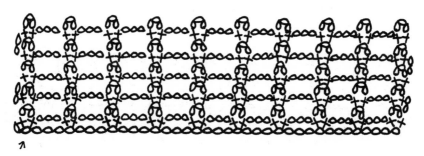

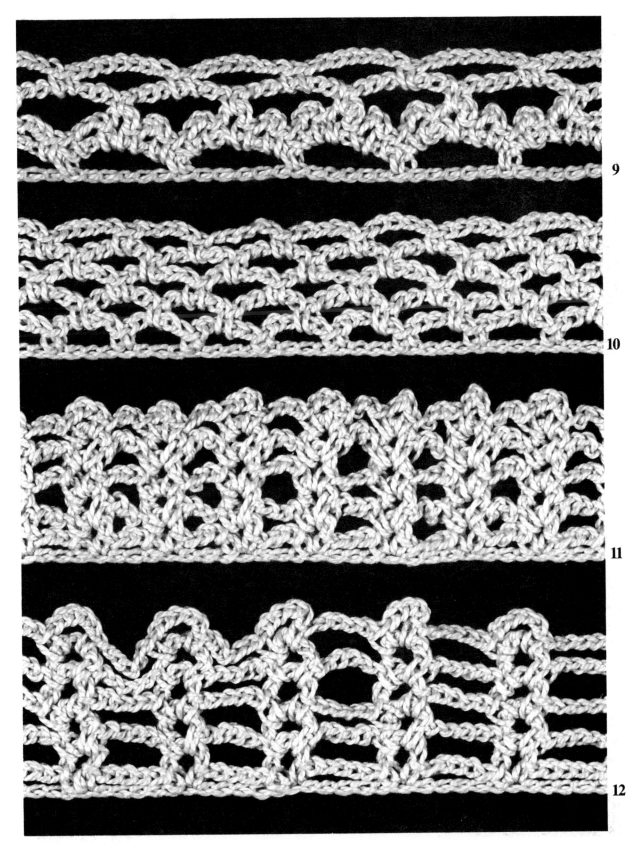

9

10

11

12

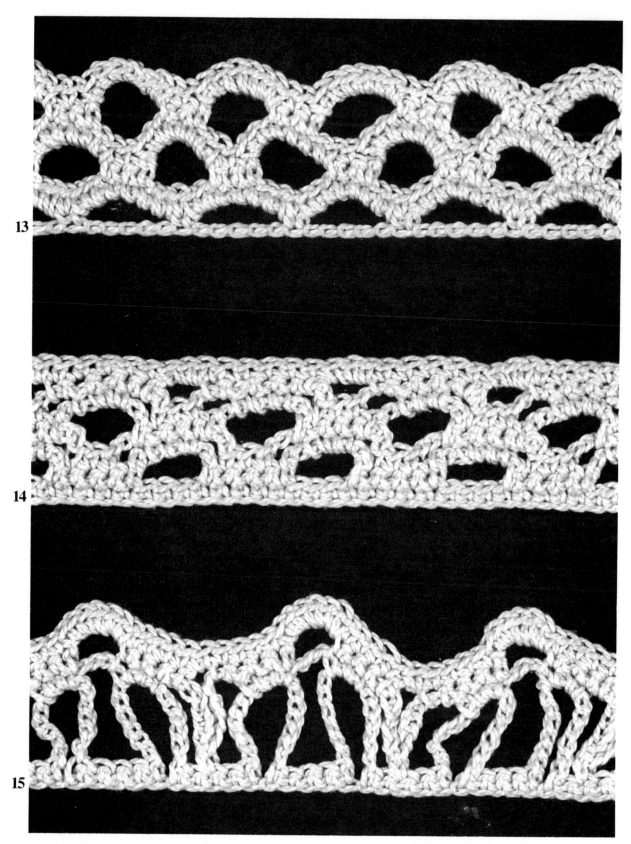

13

14

15

28   Single Crochet and Chain

12. Chain multiples of 6 plus 6.

Row 1: Sc in the 6th ch, *ch 5, sc in the 6th ch, ch 5, sc in the ch just used, rep from *, ending row with 5 chs and 1 dc in the 6th ch, ch 3 and turn.
Row 2: Dc in the 1st dc, *ch 5, sc in the loop of the 2nd 5-ch, ch 5, sc in the same loop, rep from *, ending row with dc in the last sc, ch 3 and turn.
For pattern, rep row 2. Can be any width. Sample shown here consists of 5 pattern rows.

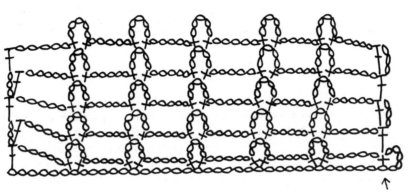

13. Chain multiples of 6 plus 2.

Row 1: Sc in the 2nd ch, * ch 6, sc in the 6th ch, rep from *, ending row with sc in the last ch, ch 1 and turn.
Row 2: * sc in the sc, 7 sc around the 6-ch, rep from *, ending row with sc in last sc, ch 7 and turn.
Row 3: Sc in 4th sc, *sc in each of next 2 sc, ch 6, sc in the 6th sc, rep from *, ending row with sc, 3 chs and 1 trc in the last sc, ch 1 and turn.
Row 4: Sc in trc, 1 sc in each of the 3-chs, *sc in the 2nd sc, 7 sc around the 6-ch, rep from *, ending row with 4 sc in the turning ch, ch 1 and turn.
Row 5: Sc in each of the 1st 2 sc, *ch 6, sc in the 6th sc and in the next 2 sc, rep from *, ending row with sc in the last sc, ch 1 and turn.
Row 6: Sc in the 1st sc, *7 sc around the 6-ch, sc in the 2nd sc, rep from *, ending row with sc in the last sc.

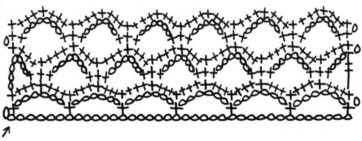

14. Chain multiples of 8 plus 4.

Row 1: Sc in the 2nd ch and in each ch all across the row, ch 1 and turn.
Row 2: Sc in the 1st sc and in each of the next 2 sc, * ch 7, sc in the 4th sc, and sc in each of the next 4 sc, rep from *, ending row with sc in each of the last 3 sc, ch 1 and turn.
Row 3: Sc in the 1st sc and the next sc, *ch 3 and work 3 sc around the middle of the 7-ch, ch 3, sc in the 2nd sc and sc in each of the next 2 sc, rep from *, ending row with sc in each of the last 2 sc, ch 8 and turn.
Row 4: *sc in the last of the 3-ch, sc in each of the next 3 sc, sc in the beginning of the next 3-ch, ch 7, rep from *, ending row with 4 chs and 1 double trc in the last sc, ch 1 and turn.
Row 5: Sc in the 1st double trc, sc in the beginning of the 4-ch, ch 3, * sc in the 2nd sc and each of the next 2 sc, ch 3, work 3 sc around the middle of the 7-ch, ch 3 and rep from *, ending row with 2 sc in the turning ch, ch 1 and turn.
Row 6: Sc in the 1st sc and sc in the next sc, sc in beginning of 3-ch, *ch 3, sc in the end of the next 3-ch, sc in each of the next 3 sc, sc in the beginning of the next 3-ch, rep from *, ending row with sc in the last ch and sc in each of the last 2 sc, ch 1 and turn.
Row 7: Sc in each sc and in each ch all across the row.

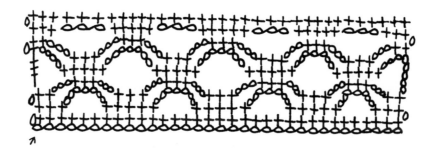

15. Chain multiples of 12 plus 3.

Row 1: Sc in the 2nd ch, *ch 15, sc in each of the next 6 chs, and rep from *, ending row with 15 chs and sc in the last ch, break thread.

Row 2: Attach thread, *work 3 sc around the middle of the 15-ch, ch 8 and sc in the middle of the 4-sc between the 2 sets of 15-chs, ch 8 and rep from *, ending row with 3 sc in the top of the last 15-ch, ch 1 and turn.

Row 3: Sc in each of the 3 sc, *ch 5, sc in each of the 3 sc and sc in the 1st sc after the 3 sc, ch 2, sc in the last of the next 8-ch, sc in each of the next 3 sc, rep from *, ending row with last 4 sc, ch 1 and turn.

Row 4: *sc in each sc, work 1 sc in the 2-ch, sc in each sc, work 7 sc in next 5-ch and rep from *, ending row with sc in the last sc.

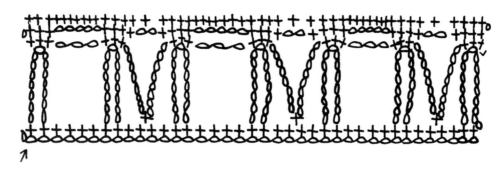

·2·
Single Crochet, Chain and Picot

16. Chain multiples of 8 plus 2.

Row 1: Sc in the 2nd ch and in each ch all across the row, ch 1 and turn.

Row 2: Sc in the 1st sc and in each sc all across the row, ch 1 and turn.

Row 3: Sc in the 1st and next sc, *work 4-ch picot, sc in the next sc and the next 7 sc, rep from *, ending row with 8 sc.

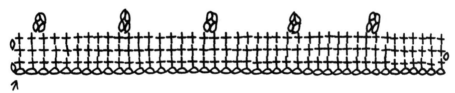

17. Chain multiples of 3 plus 2.

Row 1: Sc in the 2nd ch, *ch 5, sc in the 3rd ch, rep from *, ending row with last sc, ch 3 and dc in the 2nd ch, ch 1 and turn.

Row 2: Sc in the dc, *ch 2, work 3-ch picot, ch 2, sc around the middle of the 5-ch, rep from *, ending row with last sc, ch 1 and dc in the last sc.

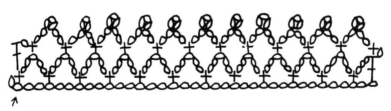

18. Chain multiples of 4 plus 2.

Row 1: Sc in 2nd ch, *ch 5, sc in the 4th ch, rep from *, ending row with last sc, ch 5 and turn.

Row 2: *sc in 5-ch, ch 5, rep from *, ending row with sc in last 5-ch, ch 2, dc in last sc, ch 1 and turn.

Row 3: Sc in dc, *ch 5, sc in 5-ch, rep from *, ending row with sc in turning ch, ch 5 and turn.

Row 4: *sc in the middle of the 5-ch, ch 5, rep from *, ending row with 2 chs and 1 dc in the last sc, ch 1 and turn.

Row 5: *ch 5 and sc in the middle of the 5-ch, rep from *, ending row with sc in the turning ch, ch 4 and turn.

Row 6: *work 3-ch picot, ch 3, sc in the middle of the 5-ch, ch 3, rep from *, ending row with last sc, ch 3 and 1 dc in the last sc.

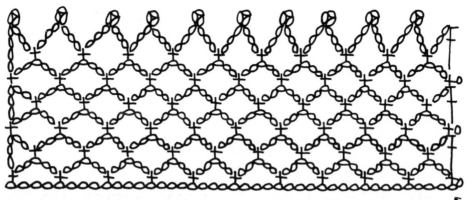

19. Chain multiples of 8 plus 4.

Row 1: Sc in the 2nd ch and in each of the next 2 chs, *ch 7 and sc in the 6th ch, sc in each of the next 2 chs, rep from *, ending row with sc in each of the last 3 chs, ch 1 and turn.

Row 2: Sc in the 1st sc and the next sc, *ch 4, work sc in the middle of the 7-ch, work 4-ch picot, ch 4, sc in the 2nd sc, rep from *, ending row with sc in each of the last 2 sc.

20. Chain multiples of 5 plus 2.

Row 1: 1 sc in the 2nd ch and in each ch all across the row.

Row 2: 1 sc in the 1st sc, *ch 2, work 1 3-ch picot, ch 2, 1 sc in the 5th sc, rep from *, ending row with sc, ch 1 and turn.

Row 3: *sc in the sc, ch 3, work 3-ch picot, ch 3, rep from *, ending row after last set.

21.

Row 1: *work 6-ch picot, work another 6-ch picot and sl st to bottom of 1st picot, work another 6-ch picot and sl st in same place, ch 8, rep from *, ending row with 2 picot, ch 4 and turn.

Row 2: Sc in the top of the 6-ch picot, * ch 8, work 6-ch picot, work another 6-ch picot and sl st to bottom of 1st picot in the same place, work another 6-ch picot and sl st, ch 7, sc in middle of 2nd picot of set, rep from *, ending row with sc in the middle of the middle picot on last set.

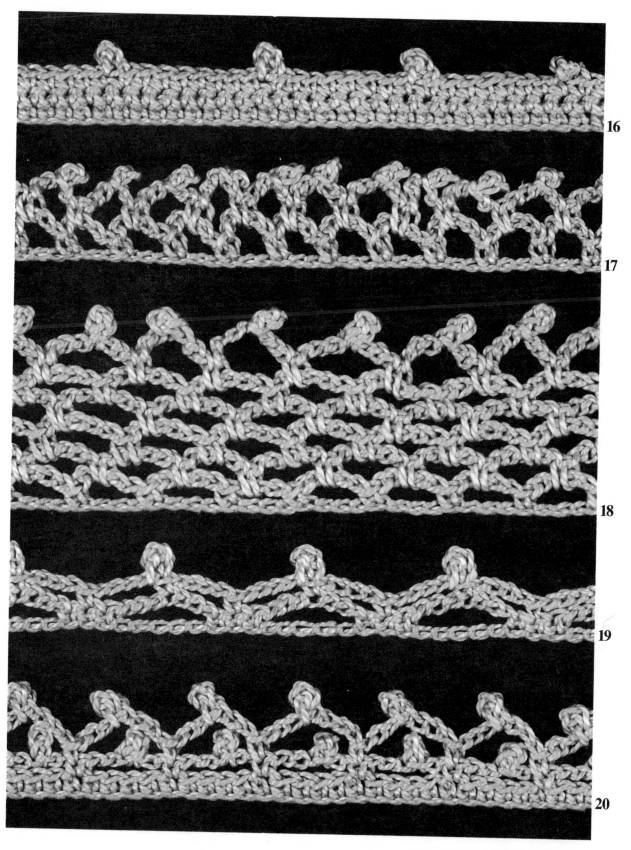

16

17

18

19

20

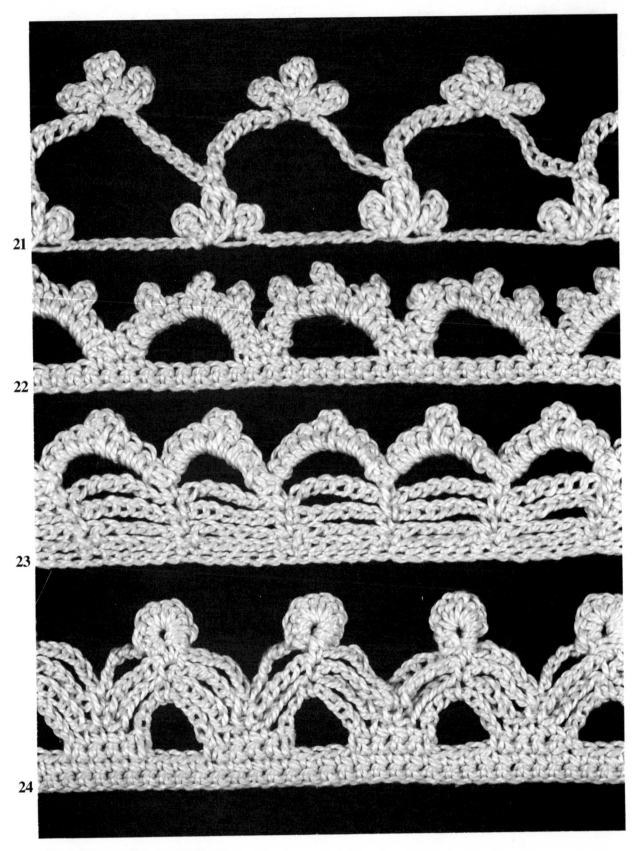

21

22

23

24

34   Single Crochet, Chain and Picot

22. Chain multiples of 8 plus 4.

Row 1: Sc in 2nd ch and in each ch all across the row, ch 1 and turn.

Row 2: Sc in 1st sc and in each of next 2 sc, * ch 8, sc in 6th sc and in each of next 2 sc, rep from *, ending row with sc in each of the last 3 sc, ch 1 and turn.

Row 3: Sc in 1st sc and next sc, * work 3 sc around the beginning of the 8-ch, work 3-ch picot, work 3 sc around the same 8-ch, work another 3-ch picot, work 3 sc around the same 8-ch, work 3-ch picot, work 3 sc around the same 8-ch, work 1 sc in 2nd sc, rep from *, ending row with sc in each of the last 2 sc.

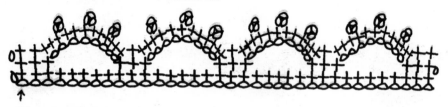

23. Chain multiples of 6 plus 2.

Row 1: Sc in the 2nd ch, * ch 5, sc in the 6th ch, rep from *, ending row with sc in the last ch, ch 1 and turn.

Row 2: *sc in the sc, ch 5 and rep from *, ending row with sc in the last sc, ch 1 and turn.

Row 3: *sc in the sc, ch 7, rep from *, ending row with sc in the last sc, ch 1 and turn.

Row 4: *sc in the sc, ch 8, rep from *, ending row with sc in the last sc, ch 1 and turn.

Row 5: *sc in the sc, ch 9, rep from *, ending row with sc in the last sc, ch 1 and turn.

Row 6: *sc in the sc, 5 sc in the 1st half of the 9-ch, work 3-ch picot, 4 sc around the 2nd part of the 9-ch, rep from *, ending row with sc in the last sc.

24. Chain multiples of 8 plus 4.

Row 1: Sc in the 2nd ch and in each ch all across the row, ch 1 and turn.

Row 2: Sc in each sc all across the row, ch 1 and turn.

Row 3: Sc in the 1st and next 2 sc, *ch 9, sc in the 4th sc and in the 4 sc following, rep from *, ending row with sc in each of the last three sc, ch 1 and turn.

Row 4: Sc in the 1st and next sc, * ch 5, work 1 sc in the middle of the 9-ch, ch 5, sc in the 2nd sc and the next 2 sc, rep from *, ending row with last 2 sc, ch 1 and turn.

Row 5: Sc in 1st sc, *ch 6, sc in the sc, ch 6, sc in the 2nd sc, rep from *, ending row with 1 sc in the last sc, ch 1 and turn.

Row 6: *sc in the sc, ch 6, sc in the sc, work 1 3-ch picot, turn and work 10 sc in the picot, ch 6, rep from *, ending row with sc in last sc.

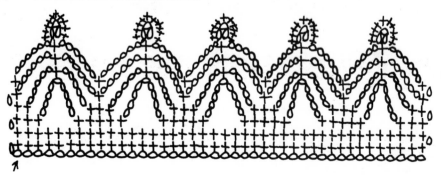

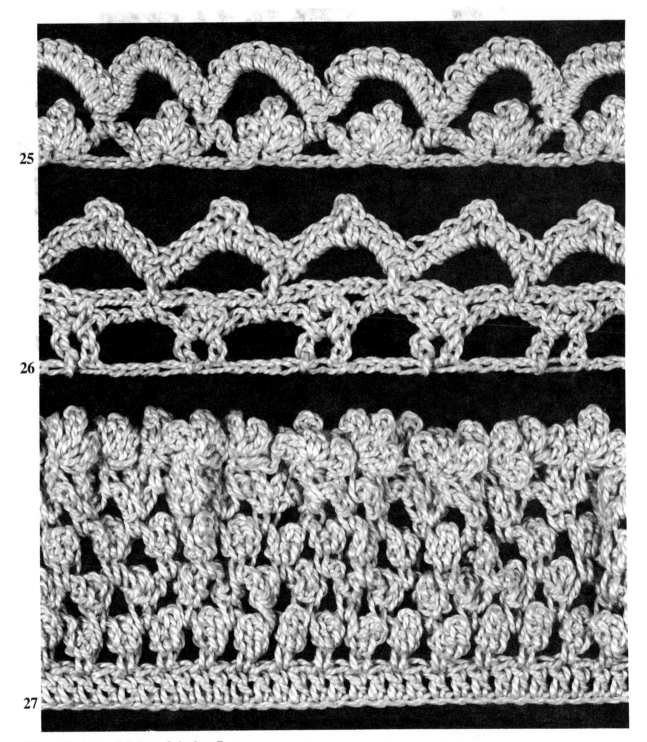

25

26

27

25. Chain multiples of 6 plus 7.

Row 1: Sc in the 8th ch, * work 3-ch picot, sc in the next ch, ch 5, work 3-ch picot and sc in the next ch, ch 5 and sc in the 4th ch, and rep from *, ending row with last set, ch 2 and dc in the 2nd ch, ch 1 and turn.

Row 2: Sc in the dc, *ch 9 and sc around the middle of the 5-ch, rep from *, ending row with sc in the turning ch, ch 1 and turn.

Row 3: *sc in the sc, work 11 sc around the 9-ch, and rep from *, ending row with sc in the last sc.

26. Chain 9.

Row 1: Dc in 2-ch, * ch 8 and sl st last ch to 1st, ch 2, dc, rep from *, ending row with last 8 chs and sl st, cut thread.

Row 2: Sc in top of 7-ch, ch 3 and sc in the same ch, *ch 5 and sc in top of 8-ch, ch 3 and sc in same ch, rep from *, ending row with sc in last 8-ch, ch 3 and turn.

Row 3: *sc in 3-ch, ch 3 and sc in 5-ch, ch 3, rep from *, ending row with sc in last of the 3-chs, ch 8 and turn.

Row 4: Sc in the sc, * ch 8, sc in the 2nd sc, rep from *, ending row with last sc, ch 3 and double trc in the turning ch, ch 1 and turn.

Row 5: Sc in the double trc, work 1 3-ch picot, work 4 sc around the 3-ch, * work 4 sc around the beginning of the 8-ch, work 1 3-ch picot, work another 4 sc around the last part of the 8-ch, rep from *, ending row with 4 sc in the turning ch and 1 3-ch picot.

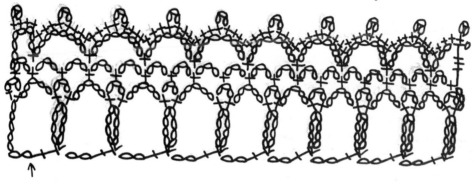

27. Chain multiples of 2 plus 4.

Row 1: Dc in the 4th ch and in each ch all across the row, ch 1 and turn.

Row 2: Sc in the dc, work 5-ch picot, ch 5, *sc in the 2nd dc, ch 1 , work 5-ch picot, ch 4, sc in the 2nd dc, rep from *, ending row with sc in the last set, ch 2 and 1 hdc in the turning ch, ch 5 and turn.

Row 3: Sc in hdc, *sc in the next 5-ch, ch 5 and sc in the same 5-ch, ch 5 and rep from *, ending row with sc in the last 5-ch, ch 5 and turn.

Row 4: *sc in the 5-ch, ch 5 and sc in the same 5-ch, ch

5, sk next 5-ch and rep from *, ending row with sc in the last 5-ch, ch 7 and turn.

Row 5: *sk 1st 5-ch, sc in next 5-ch, ch 5 and rep from *, ending row with sc, ch 3 and dc in the last 5-ch, ch 3 and turn.

Row 6: Dc in the 1st dc, work 5-ch picot, work another 5-ch picot, *ch 3 and sc in the next sc, ch 3, dc in the middle of the 5-ch, work 5-ch picot, work another 5-ch picot and sl st, work another 3-ch picot and sl st, rep from *, ending row with last dc.

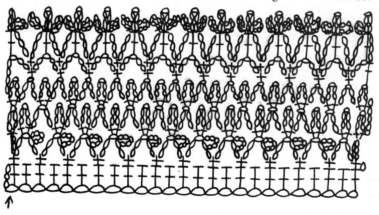

·3·
Double Crochet, Single Crochet, Chain and Picot

28.   Chain multiples of 6 plus 7.

Row 1: Dc in the 5th ch and in each of the next 2 chs, * ch 2 and dc in the 3rd ch, and dc in each of the next 3 chs, rep from *, ending row with 1 dc in each of the last 4 chs, ch 5 and turn.

Row 2: Dc in the 4th dc, *dc in each of the 2 chs, dc in the next dc, ch 2 and dc in the 3rd dc, rep from *, ending row with 2 chs and dc in the turning ch, ch 3 and turn.

Row 3: * 1 dc in each of the 2-chs, dc in the dc, ch 2, dc in the 3rd dc, rep from *, ending row with 3 dc in the turning ch.

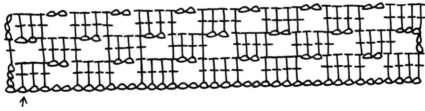

29.   Chain multiples of 3 plus 4.

Row 1: Dc in the 5th ch and in each ch all across the row, ch 5 and turn.

Row 2: Dc in the 4th dc, *ch 2 and dc in the 3rd dc, rep from *, ending row with dc in the turning ch, ch 3 and turn.

Row 3: Dc in each ch and in each dc all across the row.

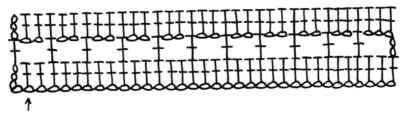

30.   Chain multiples of 9 plus 6.

Row 1: Dc in the 5th ch and the next ch, * ch 2, dc in the 3rd ch, dc in each of the next 6 chs, rep from *, ending row with 1 dc in each of last 5 chs, ch 3 and turn.

Row 2: 1 dc in the 2nd dc, *dc in each of the next 3 dc, dc in each of the next 2-chs, ch 2, dc in the 3rd dc and the next dc, rep from *, ending row with 2 chs and 1 dc in the turning ch, ch 3 and turn.

Row 3: *dc in each of the 2-ch, dc in each of the next 5 dc, ch 2, rep from *, ending row with 1 ch and 1 dc in the turning ch, ch 3 and turn.

Row 4: Dc in the 1-ch, *ch 2, dc in the 3rd dc and dc in each of the next 4 dc, dc in each of the next 2-chs, rep from *, ending row with 6 dc, the last in the turning ch.

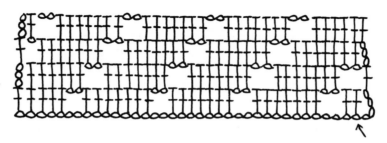

31. Chain multiples of 5 plus 3.

Row 1: Sc in the 2nd ch and the ch after that, *ch 3, sc in the 4th ch and the ch after that, rep from *, ending row with sc in each of the last 2 chs, ch 3 and turn.
Row 2: Dc in the 2nd sc, *ch 3, dc in each sc, rep from *, ending row with dc in each sc, ch 1 and turn.

Row 3: *sc in each dc, ch 3, rep from *, ending row with sc in last dc and in turning ch, ch 3 and turn.
Row 4: Same as row 2, ch 1 and turn.
Row 5: Same as row 3, ch 3 and turn.
Row 6: Same as row 2, ch 1 and turn.
Row 7: Same as row 3, ch 3 and turn.

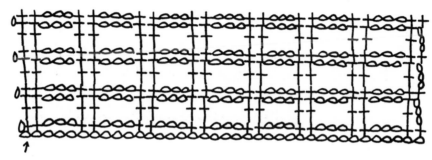

32. Chain multiples of 3 plus 2.

Row 1: Sc in the 2nd ch and in each ch all across the row, ch 4 and turn.
Row 2: Dc in the 3rd sc, dc in the next sc, *ch 1, dc in the

2nd sc and the next sc, rep from *, ending row with dc in the last sc, ch 1 and turn.
Row 3: Sc in the 1st dc, sc in the 1-ch, *ch 5, sc in the 1-ch, rep from *, ending row with 2 sc in the turning ch.

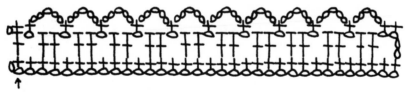

33. Chain multiples of 3 plus 5.

Row 1: Dc in the 5th ch, *ch 1 and dc in the 2nd ch, dc in the next ch, rep from *, ending row with dc in each of the last 2 chs, ch 1 and turn.

Row 2: *sc in each dc, work 3-ch picot, rep from *, ending row with sc in the last dc and sc in the turning ch.

34. Chain multiples of 6 plus 9.

Row 1: Dc in the 7th ch and in the 2 chs following, *ch 5, turn and sl st end of ch into the 1st dc formed, turn again, ch 3, sc in the middle of the 5-ch, ch 3, sl st into the 1st

of the 5-ch formed, ch 3, dc into the 4th ch, dc in each of the next 2 chs, rep from *, ending row after last set with 1 ch and 1 dc in the 2nd and last chs.

Double Crochet, Single Crochet, Chain and Picot 39

35. Chain multiples of 4 plus 5.

Row 1: 1 dc in the 5th ch, *ch 2, dc in the 3rd ch and the ch after that, rep from *, ending row with last 2 dc, ch 3 and turn.

Row 2: Dc in the 2nd dc, *ch 2, sc in the middle of the 2-ch, ch 2, dc in each dc, rep from *, ending row with dc in the last dc and dc in the turning ch.

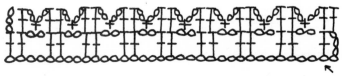

36. Chain multiples of 6 plus 5.

Row 1: Dc in the 5th ch, *ch 3, dc in the 4th ch, dc in each of next 2 chs, rep from *, ending row with dc in each of the last 2 chs, ch 3 and turn.

Row 2: Dc in the 2nd dc, *ch 3, sc around the middle of the next 3-ch, ch 3, dc in each of the next 3 dc, rep from *, ending row with dc in the turning ch.

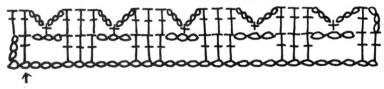

37. Chain multiples of 12 plus 6.

Row 1: Dc in the 5th ch, dc in the next ch, *ch 1 and dc in the 2nd ch, dc in each of the next 2 chs, rep from *, ending row with dc in each of the last 3 chs, ch 3 and turn.

Row 2: Sk 1st dc, dc in each of the next 2 dc, *ch 1 and dc in each of the 3 dc, rep from *, ending row with dc in each of the last 2 dc, and dc in the turning ch, ch 3 and turn.

Row 3: Sk 1st dc, dc in each of the next 2 dc, *ch 1 and dc in each of the next 3 dc, and rep from *, ending row with dc in each of the last 2 dc and dc in the turning ch, ch 1 and turn.

Row 4: *sc in the dc, ch 3, work 3-ch picot, ch 3 and sc in the 2nd dc, ch 3, work 3-ch picot, ch 3 and sc in the next dc, ch 3, work 3-ch picot, ch 3 and sc in the 2nd dc, sc in the 1-ch, sc in each of the next 3 dc, sc in the 1-ch, and rep from *, ending row with sc in the turning ch.

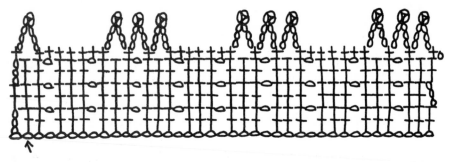

38. Chain multiples of 11 plus 7.

Row 1: Dc in the 5th ch and in the 2 chs following, *ch 3, dc in the 4th ch and dc in the 7 chs following, rep from *, ending row with 1 dc in each of the last 4 chs, ch 3 and turn.

Row 2: Dc in the 2nd dc, * ch 4, sc in the beginning of the 3-ch, ch 7, sc in the last of the 3-chs, ch 4, dc in the 3rd dc, dc in each of the next 3 dc, rep from *, ending row with dc in the last dc and dc in the turning ch.

40   Double Crochet, Single Crochet, Chain and Picot

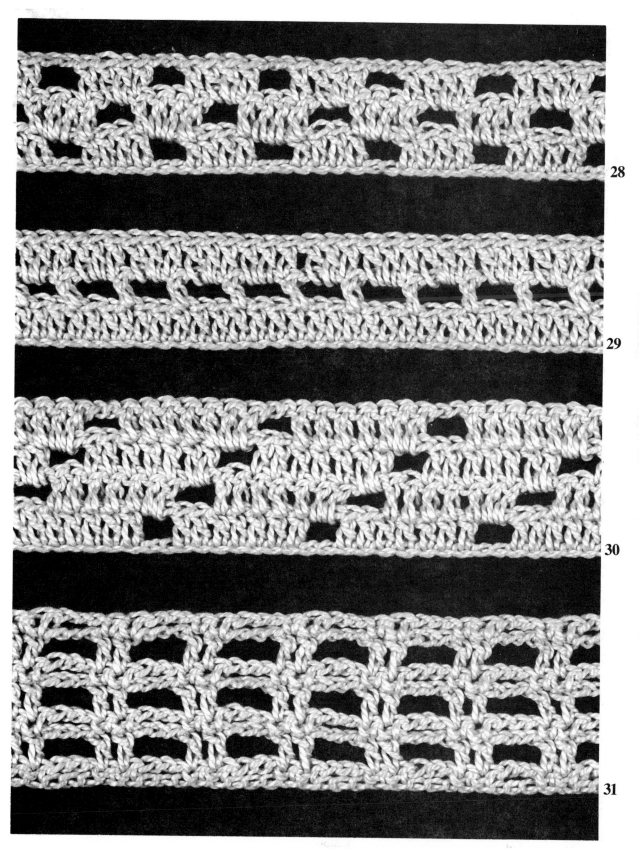

28

29

30

31

Double Crochet, Single Crochet, Chain and Picot 41

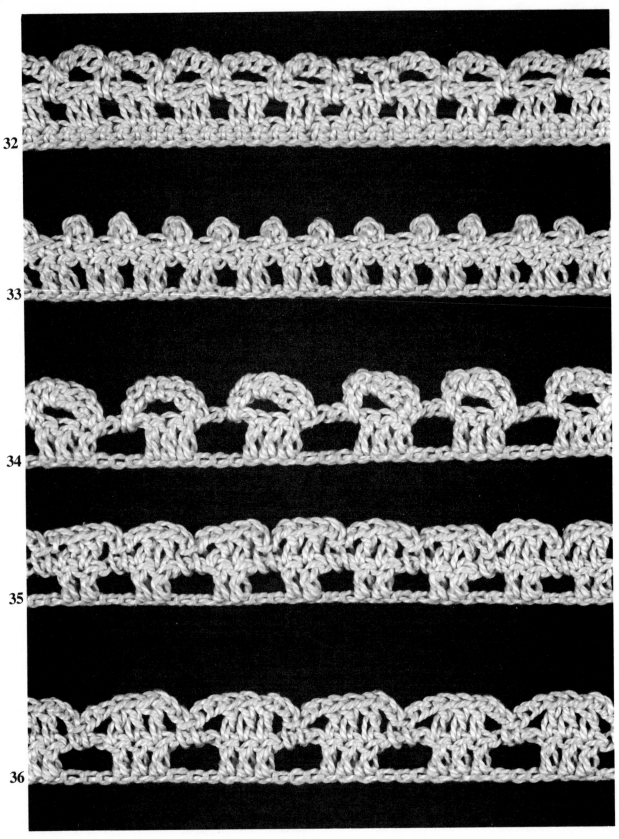

42   **Double Crochet, Single Crochet, Chain and Picot**

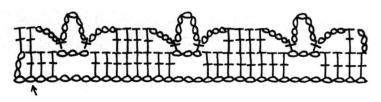

39. Chain multiples of 12 plus 8.

Row 1: Sc in the 2nd ch, * ch 5, and sc in the 6th ch, rep from *, ending row with last sc, ch 3 and turn.

Row 2: *5 dc around the 5-ch, ch 3, sc around the middle of the next 5-ch, ch 3, rep from *, ending row with 5 dc and 1 extra dc in the last sc, ch 3 and turn.

Row 3: Sk 1st dc, *dc in each of the next 5 dc, ch 3, sc in the next sc, ch 3, and rep from *, ending row with last 5 dc and 1 extra dc in the turning ch, ch 3 and turn.

Row 4: Sk 1st dc, *dc in each of the next 5 dc, ch 3, sc in the next sc, work 3-ch picot, ch 3, rep from *, ending row with 5 dc and 1 extra dc in the turning ch.

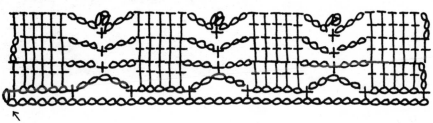

40. Chain multiples of 10 plus 9.

Row 1: Sc in the 10th ch, *sc in each of the next 4 chs, ch 3, dc in the 3rd ch, ch 3, sc in the 3rd ch, rep from *, ending row with last dc, ch 1 and turn.

Row 2: *sc in the dc, sc in the 1st of the 3-chs, ch 3, sc in the 2nd of the sc, sc in each of the next 2 sc, ch 3, sc in the last of the 3-chs, rep from *, ending row with 2 sc in the turning ch, ch 1 and turn.

Row 3: Sc in the 1st sc, * ch 5, sc in the 2nd sc of the next set, rep from *, ending row with sc in the 2nd sc.

41. Chain multiples of 9 plus 9.

Row 1: Dc in the 9th ch, *ch 2 and dc in the 3rd ch, rep from *, ending row with last dc, ch 1 and turn.

Row 2: Sc in each dc and in each ch all across the row, ch 1 and turn.

Row 3: *sc in each of the next 7 sc, ch 5 and sc in the 3rd sc, rep from *, ending row with last 7 sc, ch 1 and turn.

Row 4: Sc in each of the next 5 sc, * ch 5 and sc in the middle of the 5-ch, ch 5 and sc in the 3rd sc and sc in each of the next 2 sc, rep from *, ending row with sc in each of the last 5 sc, ch 1 and turn.

Row 5: Sc in each of the next 4 sc, *work 3 sc in the beginning of the 5-ch, ch 7 and work 3 sc towards the end of the next 5-ch, sc in the 2nd sc, rep from *, ending row with sc in each of the last 4 sc.

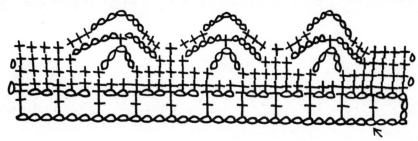

Double Crochet, Single Crochet, Chain and Picot 43

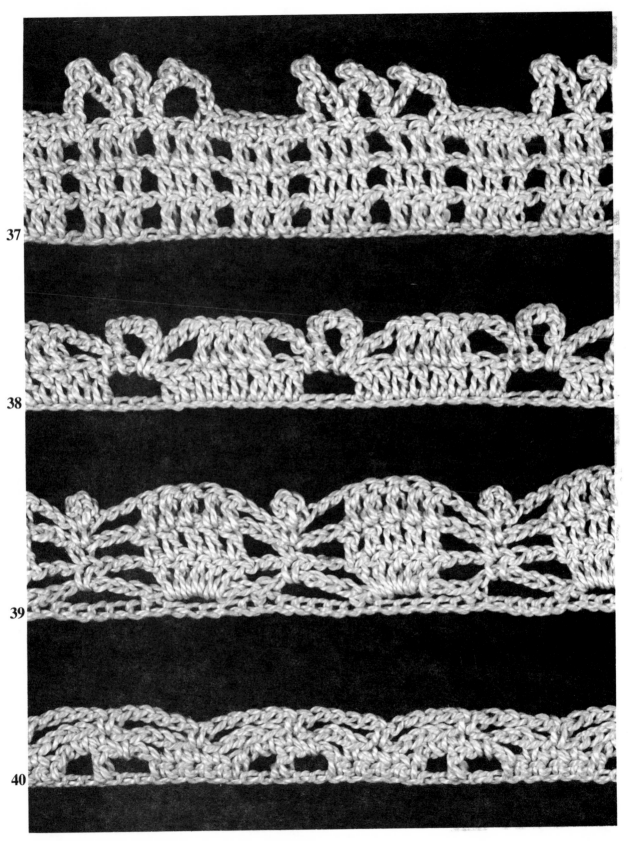

37

38

39

40

44   Double Crochet, Single Crochet, Chain and Picot

42.   Chain multiples of 12 plus 6.

Row 1: Sc in the 2nd ch and in each of the next 4 chs, *ch 5, dc in the 4th ch, ch 5, sc in the 4th ch and in each of the next 4 chs, rep from *, ending row with sc in each of the last 5 chs, ch 1 and turn.

Row 2: *sc in each of the 1st 4 sc, work 5 sc in the next 5-ch, work sc in the dc, work 4-ch picot, work another 5 sc in the next 5-ch, rep from *, ending row with sc in each of the last 5 sc.

43.   Chain multiples of 6 plus 4.

Row 1: Dc in the 5th ch and in each ch all across the row, ch 8 and turn.
Row 2: Dc in the 7th dc, *ch 5, dc in the 6th dc, rep from *, ending row with dc in the turning ch, ch 6 and turn.

Row 3: *sc around the middle of the 5-ch, ch 3, dc in the dc, ch 3, and rep from *, ending row with dc in the turning ch.

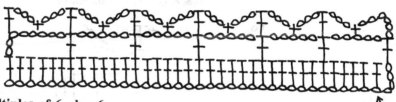

44.   Chain multiples of 6 plus 6.

Row 1: Dc in the 5th ch and in the next ch, *ch 1, dc in the 2nd ch and each of the next 4, rep from *, ending row with dc in each of the last 3 chs, ch 3 and turn.
Row 2: Dc in the 2nd dc and the next dc, *dc in the 1-ch, dc in the next dc and the dc after that, ch 1, dc in the 2nd dc and the dc after that, rep from *, ending row with 5 dc and 1 extra dc in the turning ch, ch 3 and turn.

Row 3: Dc in the 2nd dc, *ch 3, dc in the 4th dc, dc in the 1-ch, dc in the next dc, rep from *, ending row with dc in the turning ch, ch 1 and turn.
Row 4: Sc in the 1st dc, *ch 3, dc in the middle of the 3-ch, ch 3, sc in the 2nd dc, rep from *, ending row with sc in the turning ch.

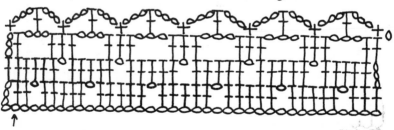

45.   Chain multiples of 12 plus 8.

Row 1: Dc in the 5th ch and in the 3 chs following, *ch 3, dc in the 3rd ch and dc in each of the following 9 chs, rep from *, ending row with 5 dc, ch 3 and turn.
Row 2: Dc in the 2nd dc and the dc after that, *ch 3, sc in the middle of the 3-ch, ch 3, dc in the 3rd dc and the 5 dc following, rep from *, ending row with 2 dc and 1 dc in the turning ch, ch 6 and turn.
Row 3: * sc around the 3-ch, ch 3, sc around the middle of the next 3-ch, ch 3, dc in the 3rd dc and the dc after that, ch 3, rep from *, ending row with dc in the turning ch.

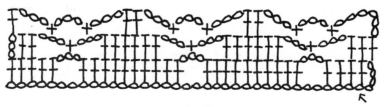

46. Chain multiples of 10 plus 4.

Row 1: Sc in the 2nd ch, *ch 3, dc in the 3rd ch and dc in each of the next 4 chs, ch 3, sc in 3rd ch, rep from *, ending row with sc in the last ch, ch 5 and turn.
Row 2: *sc in the top of each dc, ch 2, dc in the next sc, ch 2, rep from *, ending row with dc in the last sc, ch 1 and turn.
Row 3: * sc in the dc, ch 3, dc in each of the 5 sc, ch 3, rep from *, ending row with sc in the turning ch.

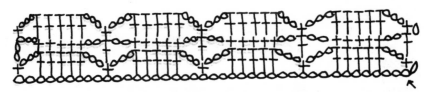

47. Chain multiples of 7 plus 3.

Row 1: Sc in the 2nd ch and in each ch all across the row, ch 3 and turn.
Row 2: 1 dc in the 2nd sc, *ch 5, 1 dc in the 6th sc and 1 dc in the next sc, rep from *, ending row with dc in each of the last 2 sc, ch 3 and turn.
Row 3: Dc in the 2nd dc, *ch 2, sc around the middle of the 5-ch, ch 2, 1 dc in each of the next 2 dc, rep from *, ending row with dc in the turning ch.
Row 4: Dc in the 2nd dc, *ch 5, dc in each of the next 2 dc, rep from *, ending row with dc in the turning ch, ch 3 and turn.
Row 5: Work like row 3, ch 3 and turn.
Row 6: Work like row 4, ch 3 and turn.
Row 7: Dc in the 2nd dc, ch 1, *dc in the 2nd of the 5-ch, ch 2, dc around the 4th of the 5-ch, ch 2, 1 dc between the 2 dc, ch 2, rep from *, ending row with 1 ch, 1 dc in the last dc and 1 dc in the turning ch.

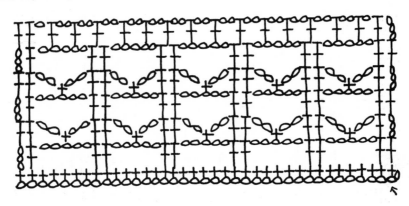

48. Chain multiples of 3 plus 4.

Row 1: Dc in the 5th ch and in each ch all across the row, ch 1 and turn.
Row 2: Sc in the 1st dc, *ch 3, sc in the 3rd dc, rep from *, ending row with sc in the last ch, ch 3 and turn.
Row 3: * sc in the middle of the 3-ch, ch 3, rep from *, ending row with sc in the last 3-ch, ch 1 and 1 hdc in the last sc, ch 1 and turn.
Row 4: Sc in the hdc, *ch 3, sc in the middle of the 3-ch, rep from *, ending row with sc in the turning ch.

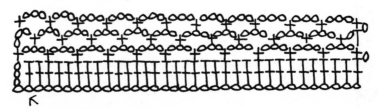

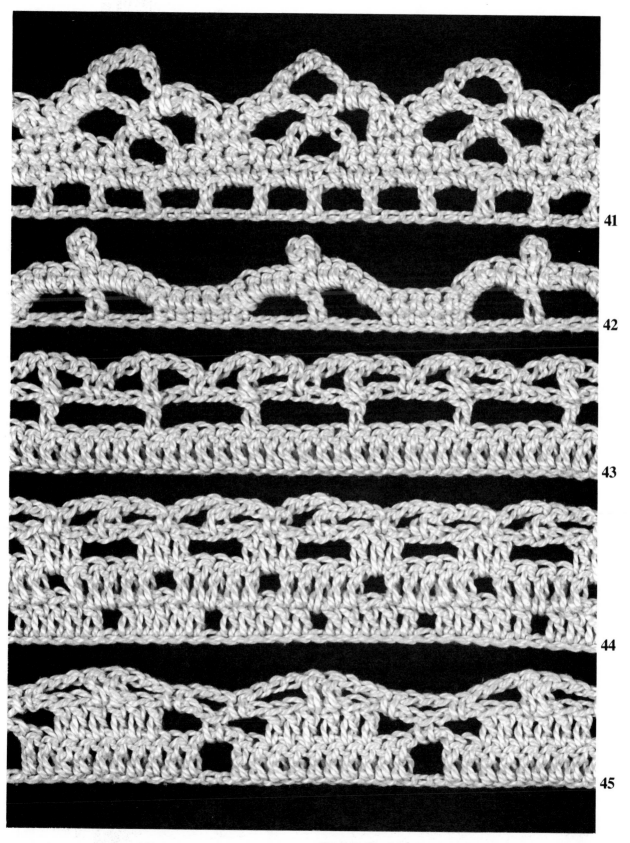

41

42

43

44

45

Double Crochet, Single Crochet, Chain and Picot 47

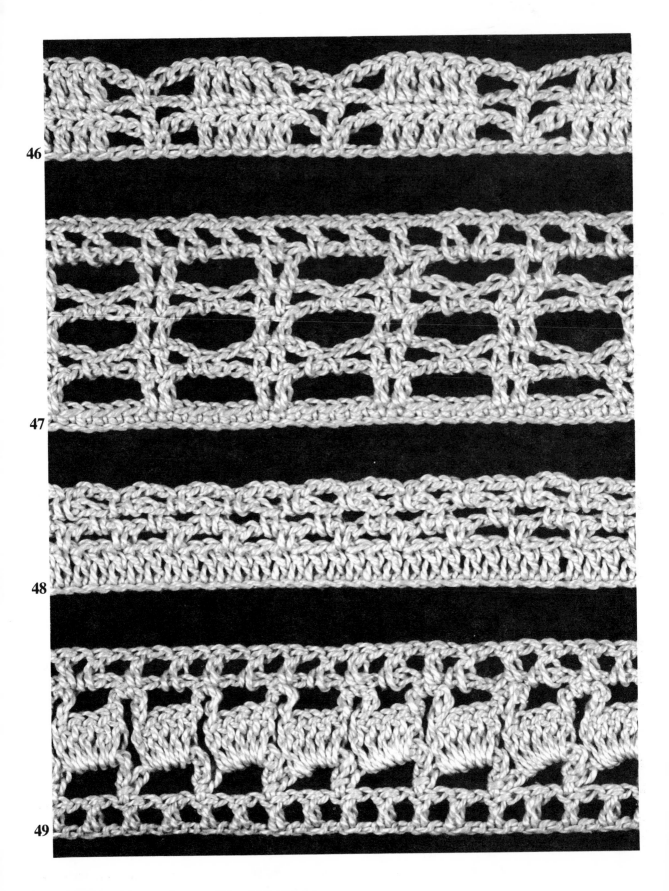

48 Double Crochet, Single Crochet, Chain and Picot

49. Chain multiples of 6 plus 5.

Row 1: Dc in the 7th ch, *ch 1 and dc in the 2nd ch, rep from *, ending row with last dc, ch 1 and turn.

Row 2: Sc in the 1st dc, *ch 9, sc in the 3rd dc, rep from *, ending row with last sc, ch 9 and turn.

Row 3: *work 5 dc around the 9-ch, ch 5, rep from *, ending row with last 5 dc, ch 2 and work 1 double trc in the last sc, ch 1 and turn.

Row 4: Sc in the 1st double trc, * ch 5, sc around the middle of the 5-ch, rep from *, ending row with last sc in the turning ch, ch 5 and turn.

Row 5: *dc in the 2nd ch of the 5-ch, ch 1, dc in the 4th ch of the 5-ch, ch 1, dc in the sc, ch 1 and rep from *, ending row with dc in the last sc.

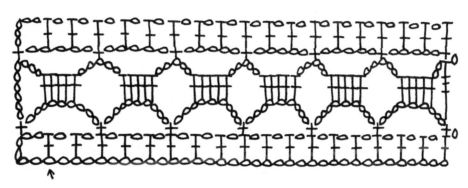

50. Chain multiples of 3 plus 2.

Row 1: Sc in the 2nd ch and in each ch all across the row, ch 5 and turn.

Row 2: Dc in the 4th sc, *ch 2, dc in the 3rd sc, rep from *, ending row with last dc, ch 1 and turn.

Row 3: *sc in the dc, sc in the 1-ch, work 1 3-ch picot, sc in the next ch, rep from *, ending row with last sc in the turning ch, ch 5 and turn.

Row 4: Dc in the 4th sc, *ch 2, dc in the 3rd sc, rep from *, ending row with sc in the last dc, ch 1 and turn.

Row 5: *sc in the dc, sc in the 1st 1-ch, work 1 3-ch picot, sc in the next 1-ch, rep from *, ending row with 1 extra sc in the turning ch, ch 1 and turn.

Row 6: Sc in the sc, *ch 6, sc in 3rd sc, rep from *, ending row with sc in the last sc, ch 1 and turn.

Row 7: Sl st in the 1st sc, *3 sc around the 1st 3 of the 6-ch, work 3-ch picot, work 3 sc around the last 3 of the 6-ch, sl st in the next sc, rep from *, ending row with sl st in the last sc.

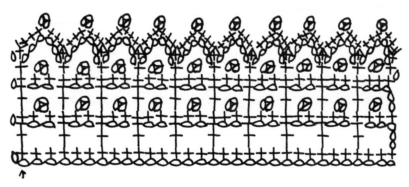

51. Chain multiples of 4 plus 5.

Row 1: Dc in the 7th ch, * ch 1 and dc in the 2nd ch, rep from *, ending row with dc in the last ch, ch 1 and turn.

Row 2: Sc in the 1st dc, *ch 5 and sc in the 2nd dc, rep from *, ending row with 1 sc in the turning ch, ch 5 and turn.

Row 3: *sc around the middle of the 5-ch and ch 5, rep from *, ending row with last sc, ch 3 and dc in the last sc, ch 1 and turn.

Row 4: Sc in the 1st dc, work 2 sc around the 3-ch, sl st in the sc, * work 5 sc around the 5-ch, sl st in the sc and rep from *, ending row with 3 sc in the turning ch.

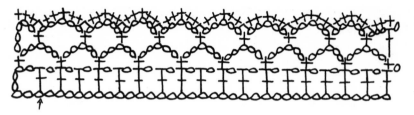

52. Chain multiples of 4 plus 2

Row 1: Sc in the 2nd ch and sc in each ch all across the row, ch 5 and turn.
Row 2: Dc in the 3rd sc, *ch 1 and dc in the 2nd sc, rep from *, ending row with dc in the last sc, ch 1 and turn.
Row 3: Sc in the dc, *ch 5 and sc in the 2nd dc, rep from *, ending row with sc in the turning ch, ch 6 and turn.

Row 4: *sc around the 5-ch, ch 5 and rep from *, ending row with last sc, ch 2 and dc in the last sc, ch 1 and turn.
Row 5: Sc in the dc, *ch 5 and sc around the middle of the next 5-ch, rep from *, ending row with sc in the turning ch, ch 1 and turn.
Row 6: *sc in the sc, work 1 hdc, 3 dc, 1 hdc in the 5-ch and rep from *, ending row with sc in the last sc.

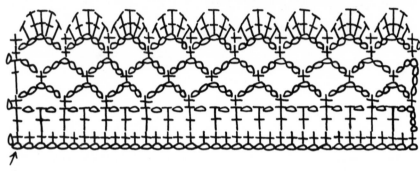

53. Chain multiples of 8 plus 2.

Row 1: Sc in the 2nd ch, ch 5, sc in the 4th ch, rep from *, ending row with sc in the last ch, ch 5 and turn.
Row 2: *sc around the middle of the 5-ch, ch 5, rep from *, ending row with sc around the middle of the last 5-ch, ch 2, dc in the last sc, ch 3 and turn.

Row 3: Dc in the dc, *ch 2, 4 dc around the middle of the 5-ch, ch 2, dc around the middle of the 5-ch, rep from *, ending row with last 2 chs and 1 dc in the turning ch.

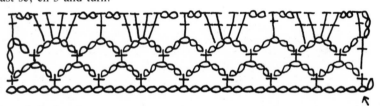

54. Chain multiples of 4 plus 2.

Row 1: Sc in the 2nd ch and in each ch all across the row, ch 6 and turn.
Row 2: Dc in the 4th sc, *ch 3, dc in the 4th sc, rep from *, ending row with last dc, ch 3 and turn.
Row 3: *sc in the middle of the 3-ch, ch 3, rep from *, ending row with sc, 1 ch and 1 hdc in the turning ch, ch 1 and turn.
Row 4: Sc in the hdc, *ch 3, sc around the middle of the 3-ch, rep from *, ending row with sc in the turning ch, ch 3 and turn.
Row 5: *sc around the middle of the 3-ch, ch 3, and rep

from *, ending row with sc around the last 3-ch, 1 ch and 1 hdc in the sc, ch 1 and turn.
Row 6: Sc in 1st hdc, 1 sc in each ch and in each sc all across the row, ch 1 and turn.
Row 7: Sc in the 1st sc, *ch 3, sc in the 4th sc, rep from *, ending row with last sc, ch 1 and turn.
Row 8: Sc in each ch and each sc all across the row, ch 1 and turn.
Row 9: Sl st in each of 1st 2 sc, *ch 4, sk 1 sc, 1 sl st in each of the next 3 sc, rep from *, ending row with last sl st.

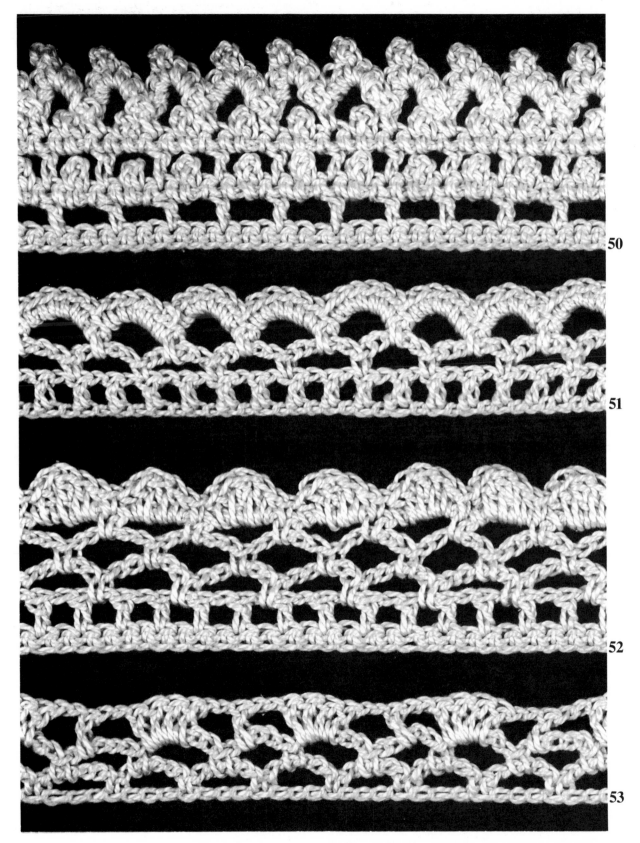

50

51

52

53

Double Crochet, Single Crochet, Chain and Picot   51

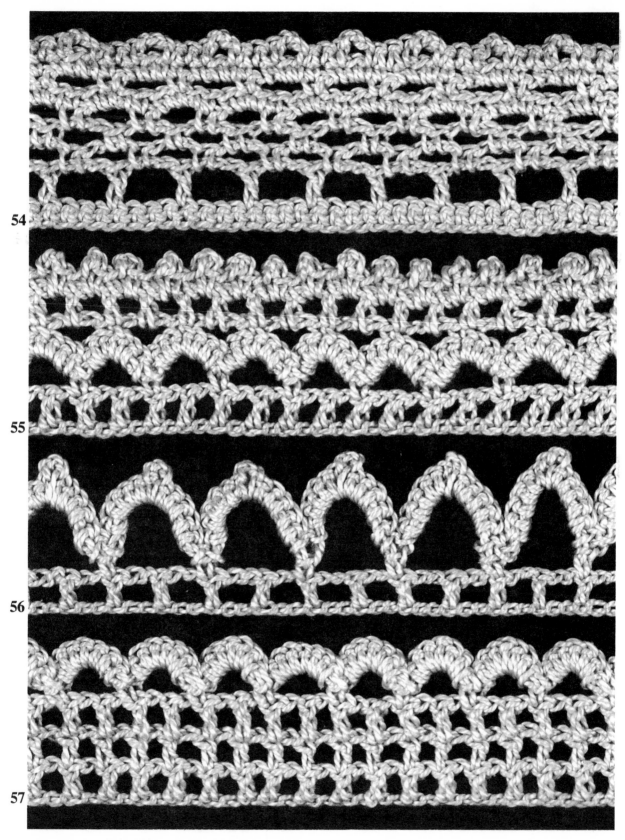

52   Double Crochet, Single Crochet, Chain and Picot

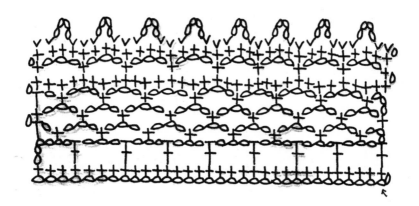

55. Chain multiples of 4 plus 5.

Row 1: Dc in the 7th ch, * ch 1 and dc in the 2nd ch, rep from *, ending row with dc in the last ch, ch 1 and turn.
Row 2: Sc in the dc, *ch 5, sc in the 2nd dc, rep from *, ending row with sc in the turning ch, ch 1 and turn.
Row 3: Sc in the sc, * work 7 sc around the 5-ch, rep from *, ending row with sc in the last sc, ch 4 and turn.
Row 4: * sc in the middle of the 7 sc in each set, ch 3 and rep from *, ending row with last sc, ch 2 and 1 hdc in the last sc, ch 5.
Row 5: *dc in the sc, ch 1 and dc in the middle of the 3-ch, ch 1 and rep from *, ending row with dc in the turning ch, ch 1 and turn.
Row 6: Sc in the dc, *sc in the 1-ch, work 3-ch picot and sc in the same 1-ch, rep from *, ending row with last set and 1 extra sc in the turning ch.

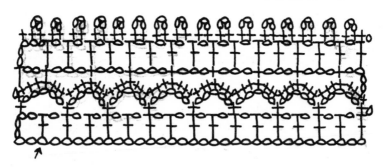

56. Chain multiples of 6 plus 5.

Row 1: 1 dc in the 8th ch, * ch 2, dc in the 3rd ch, rep from *, ending row with dc in the 3rd and last chs, ch 1 and turn.
Row 2: Sc in 1st dc, * ch 13, sc in the 2nd dc, rep from *, ending row with last sc in the turning ch, ch 1 and turn.
Row 3: * Work 6 sc in the 1st half of the 13-ch, work 1 4-ch picot, work another 6 sc into the 2nd half of the 13-ch, rep from *, ending row with last set.

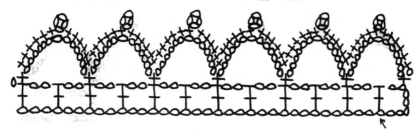

Double Crochet, Single Crochet, Chain and Picot 53

57. Chain multiples of 4 plus 5.

Row 1: Dc in the 7th ch, *ch 1 and dc in the 2nd ch, rep from *, ending row with dc in the last ch, ch 4 and turn.
Row 2: Sk 1st dc, * dc in the next dc, and ch 1, rep from *, ending row with dc in the turning ch, ch 4 and turn.
Row 3: Sk 1st dc, *ch 1 and dc in the next dc, rep from *, ending row with dc in the turning ch, ch 1 and turn.

Row 4: Sc in the 1st dc, *ch 5 and sc in the 2nd dc, rep from *, ending row with sc in the turning ch, ch 1 and turn.
Row 5: Sl st in the 1st sc, * work 7 sc around the 5-ch, rep from *, ending row with last set and sl st in the last sc.

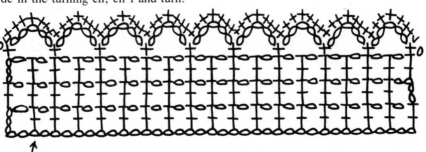

58. Chain multiples of 4 plus 5.

Row 1: Dc in the 7th ch, * ch 1 and dc in the 2nd ch, rep from *, ending row with last dc, ch 1 and turn.
Row 2: Sc in the 1st dc, *ch 5 and sc in the 2nd dc, and rep from *, ending row with sc in the turning ch, ch 5 and turn.
Row 3: *sc around the middle of the 5-ch, ch 5 and rep from *, ending row with last sc, ch 2 and dc in the sc, ch 1 and turn.
Row 4: Sc in the dc, *ch 5 and sc around the middle of the 5-ch, rep from *, ending row with sc in the turning ch, ch 1 and turn.

Row 5: Sc in the 1st sc, *work 5 sc around the 5-ch, sl st over the sc, and rep from *, ending row with sc in the last sc, ch 6 and turn.
Row 6: Sk 1st sc, * sc in the middle of the 5 sc, ch 5 and rep from *, ending row with last sc, ch 2 and dc in the last sc, ch 1 and turn.
Row 7: Sc in the dc and 3-ch picot, work another 2 sc around the same 2-ch, * work 3 sc around the beginning of the 5-ch, work 3-ch picot, work another 3 sc around the same 5-ch, and rep from *, ending row with 4 sc in the turning ch and picot.

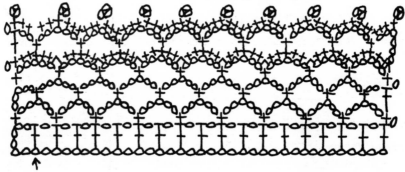

59. Chain multiples of 8 plus 2.

Row 1: Sc in the 2nd ch, * ch 5 and sc in the 4th ch, rep from *, ending row with sc in last ch, ch 5 and turn.
Row 2: *sc around the middle of the 5-ch, ch 5 and rep from *, ending row with sc around the last 5-ch, ch 2 and dc in the last sc, ch 1 and turn.
Row 3: Sc in the dc, * ch 5 and sc around the middle of the 5-ch, rep from *, ending row with sc in the turning ch, ch 5 and turn.
Row 4: *sc around the middle of the 5-ch, ch 5 and rep

from *, ending row with sc in the middle of the last 5-ch, ch 2 and dc in the last sc, ch 1 and turn.
Row 5: Sc in 1st dc, * ch 2 and dc in the 5-ch 10 times, ch 2, sc in the middle of the next 5-ch, rep from *, ending row with sc in the turning ch, ch 1 and turn.
Row 6: Sc in the sc, *ch 4 and sc in the next 2-ch 11 times, rep from *, ending row with sc in the last sc.
Bottom Row: Sc in the 2nd ch and in each ch all across the row.

54   Double Crochet, Single Crochet, Chain and Picot

58

59

60

Double Crochet, Single Crochet, Chain and Picot 55

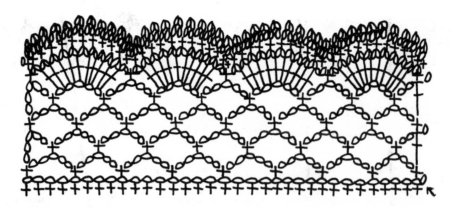

60. Chain multiples of 5 plus 5.

Row 1: Dc in the 5th ch, dc in the next ch, * ch 2, 1 dc in the 3rd ch, and 1 dc in each of the next 2 chs, rep from *, ending row after last set of 3, ch 5 and turn.

Row 2: * work 2 dc in 2-ch, work 1 3-ch picot and 1 more dc in same 2-ch, ch 2, rep from *, ending row with last set, 1 ch and 1 dc in the turning ch, ch 1 and turn.

Row 3: 1 sc in the dc, 1 sc in the 1-ch, * ch 5, 1 sc in the middle of the 2-ch, rep from *, ending row with 2 sc in the turning ch, ch 1 and turn.

Row 4: 1 sc in the 1st sc, *1 sc in the next sc, work 1 3-ch picot, work 1 sc and 1 3-ch picot in the 5-ch 4 times, rep from *, ending row with sc in the last sc.

61. Chain multiples of 8 plus 5.

Row 1: Dc in the 5th ch, *ch 2, dc in the 3rd ch, ch 2 dc in the 3rd ch, dc in each of the next 2 chs, rep from *, ending row with dc in each of the last 2 chs, ch 5 and turn.

Row 2: *sc in the 2-ch, ch 3, sc in the next 2-ch, ch 5, rep from *, ending row with sc in the last 2-ch, ch 2 and dc in the turning ch, ch 3 and turn.

Row 3: 3 dc around the 2-ch, *sc in the 3-ch, work 7 dc around the 5-ch, rep from *, ending row with 4 dc in the turning ch.

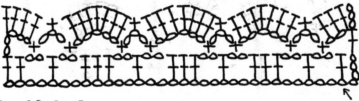

62. Chain multiples of 8 plus 5.

Row 1: Dc in the 7th ch, *ch 1 and dc in the 2nd ch, rep from *, ending row with dc in the last ch, ch 1 and turn.

Row 2: Sc in the dc, *ch 5 and sc in the 2nd dc, rep from *, ending row with sc in the turning ch, ch 5 and turn.

Row 3: *sc around the middle of the 5-ch, ch 5 and rep from *, ending row with sc in the last 5-ch, ch 2 and dc in the last sc, ch 1 and turn.

Row 4: Sc in the dc, * ch 5 and sc in the next 5-ch, rep from *, ending row with sc in the turning ch, ch 3 and turn.

Row 5: Work 2 dc in the 1st sc, *sc around the 5-ch, ch 5 and sc in the middle of the next 5-ch, work 3 dc in the next sc, rep from *, ending row with 2 dc in the last sc, ch 1 and turn.

Row 6: Sc in the dc, * work 10 dc around the 5-ch, sc in the 2nd dc and rep from *, ending row with sc in the turning ch.

56 Double Crochet, Single Crochet, Chain and Picot

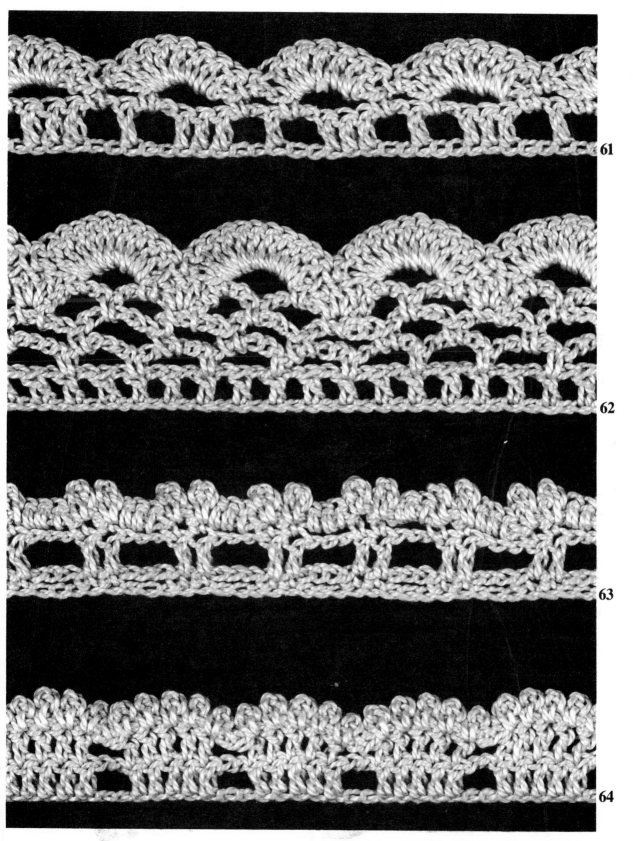

61

62

63

64

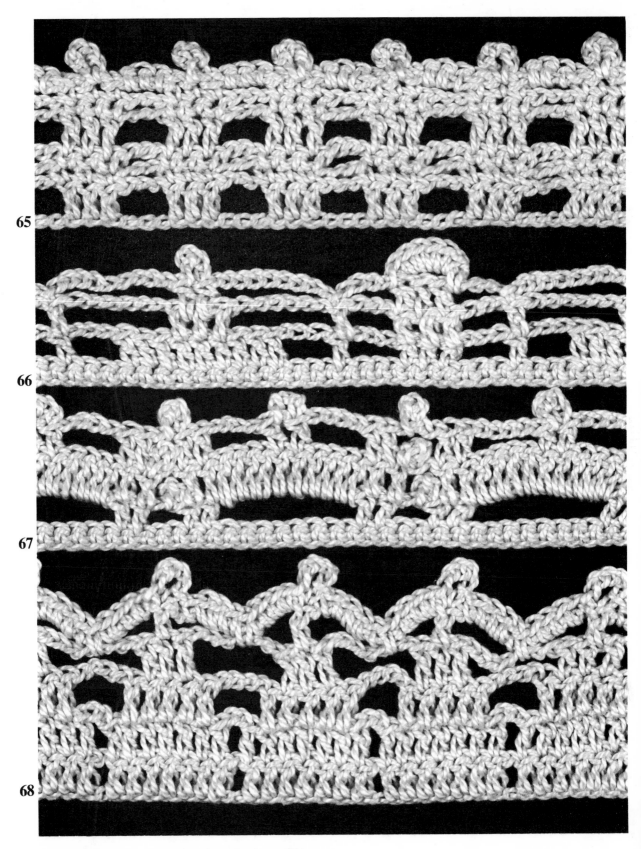

65

66

67

68

Double Crochet, Single Crochet, Chain and Picot

63. Chain multiples of 5 plus 3.

Row 1: Sc in the 2nd ch and the ch after that, *ch 3, sc in the 4th ch and the ch after that, rep from *, ending row with sc in each of the last 2 chs, ch 3 and turn.
Row 2: Dc in the 2nd sc, *ch 3, dc in each sc, rep from *, ending row with dc in each of the last 2 sc, ch 1 and turn.
Row 3: * sc in each dc, ch 3, rep from *, ending row with sc in the last dc and in the turning ch, ch 1 and turn.
Row 4: *work 3-ch picot, sl st in the sc, work another 3-ch picot and sl st in the sc, work 1 sc in each of the next 3 chs, rep from *, ending row with picot in each of the last 2 sc.

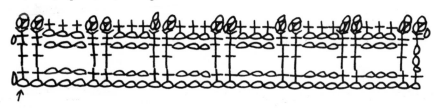

64. Chain multiples of 7 plus 6.

Row 1: Dc in the 5th ch and the ch after that, *ch 2, dc in the 3rd ch and the 4 chs following that, rep from *, ending row with dc in each of the last 3 chs, ch 3 and turn.
Row 2: Dc in the 2nd dc and the dc after that, *ch 2, dc in each of the 5 dc, repeat from *, ending row with dc in the turning ch, ch 1 and turn.
Row 3: Sl st in 1st dc and 3-ch picot, sl st in next dc and 3-ch picot, sl st in next dc and 3-ch picot, *sl st in each of the 2 chs, sl st in each of the next dc and 1 3-ch picot over the dc, rep from *, ending row with sl st in the turning ch.

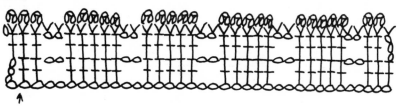

65. Chain multiples of 6 plus 6.

Row 1: Dc in the 5th ch, dc in the next ch, *ch 3, dc in the 4th ch and in each of the next 2 chs, rep from *, ending row with dc in each of the last 3 chs, ch 1 and turn.
Row 2: *sc in each dc, ch 3, rep from *, ending row with sc in the turning ch, ch 1 and turn.
Row 3: *sc in each sc, ch 3, rep from *, ending row with sc, ch 3 and turn.
Row 4: Dc in the 2nd sc and the next sc, *ch 3, dc in each sc, rep from *, ending row with 3 dc, ch 1 and turn.
Row 5: *sc in each dc, ch 3, rep from *, ending row with sc, ch 1 and turn.
Row 6: *sc in each sc, ch 3, rep from *, ending row with sc in the dc, ch 1 and turn.
Row 7: *sl st in 1st 2 sc, work 5-ch picot, sl st in next sc, sc in each of the next 3 chs, rep from *, ending row with sl st in the last sc.

Double Crochet, Single Crochet, Chain and Picot 59

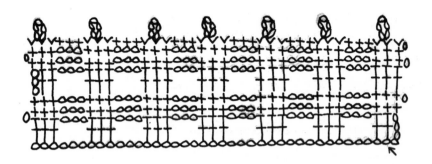

66.   Chain multiples of 27 plus 2.

Row 1: Sc in the 2nd ch and in each ch all across the row, ch 6 and turn.

Row 2: Dc in the 5th sc, * dc in each of the next 8 sc, ch 3 and dc in the 4th sc, ch 3 and dc in the 4th sc and dc in each of the next 2 sc, ch 3 and dc in the 4th sc, ch 3 and dc in the 4th sc, rep from *, ending row with 3 chs and dc in the last sc, ch 9 and turn.

Row 3: Sk 1st dc, * dc in the 4th dc and dc in each of the next 2 dc, ch 6 and dc in the 4th dc, ch 3 and dc in each of the next 3 dc, ch 3 and dc in the next dc, ch 6 and rep from *, ending row with dc in the turning ch, ch 1 and turn.

Row 4: *sc in 1st dc, ch 9, work dc between the next dc and the dc after that, work 4-ch picot, dc between next 2 dc, ch 9 and sc in the 2nd dc, ch 4 and dc in each of the next 3 dc, ch 4 and turn, sl st just before 1st of 3 dc, turn and work 6 sc around the 4-ch, sl st into last dc, ch 4 and rep from *, ending row with sc in the turning ch.

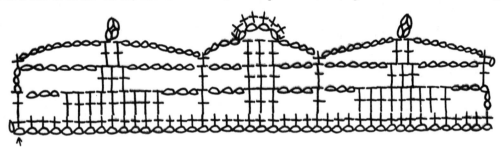

67.   Chain multiples of 13 plus 9.

Row 1: Sc in the 2nd ch and in each ch all across the row, ch 3 and turn.

Row 2: Dc in the 2nd sc, *ch 1, work 3-ch picot, ch 1, dc in the 2nd sc and dc in the next sc, ch 8, dc in 9th sc and next sc, rep from *, ending row with last dc in the turning ch, ch 3 and turn.

Row 3: Dc in 2nd dc, *ch 1, 3-ch picot, ch 1, dc in next dc and dc after that, work 10 dc around the 8-ch, dc in each of next 2 dc, rep from *, ending row with last dc in turning ch, ch 3 and turn.

Row 4: Dc in the 2nd dc, *ch 1, work 3-ch picot, ch 1, dc in each of the next 2 dc, ch 4, dc in the 5th dc, work 4-ch picot, dc in next dc, ch 4, dc in 5th dc and dc in the next dc, rep from *, ending row with dc in the turning ch.

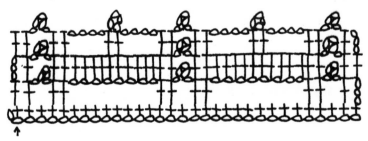

68. Chain multiples of 8 plus 10.

Row 1: Dc in the 5th ch and dc in each of the next 5 chs, * ch 1 and dc in the 2nd ch, dc in each of the next 6 chs, rep from *, ending row with last 7 dc, ch 3 and turn.

Row 2: Sk 1st dc, and dc in each of the next 6 dc, *ch 2 and dc in each of the next 7 dc, rep from *, ending row with last 6 dc and dc in the turning ch, ch 3 and turn.

Row 3: Sk 1st dc, dc in each of the next 5 dc, *ch 4 and dc in the 3rd dc, dc in each of the next 4 dc, rep from *, ending row with last 5 dc and dc in the turning ch, ch 5 and turn.

Row 4: Sk 1st dc, * dc in the 2nd dc, dc in each of the next 2 dc, ch 7, rep from *, ending row with last 3 dc, ch 2 and dc in the turning ch, ch 6 and turn.

Row 5: *dc in the middle of the 3 dc, ch 4 and sl st in the middle of the 7-ch, ch 4 and rep from *, ending row with last dc, ch 2 and dc in the turning ch, ch 1 and turn.

Row 6: Sc in the dc and 2 sc in the 2-ch, *work 4 ch picot, work 4 sc in the 4-ch, sl st in middle of 7-ch, work 4 sc in the next 4 sc, rep from *, ending row with last picot and 3 sc in the turning ch.

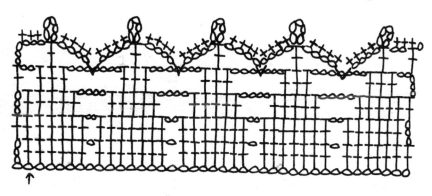

69. Chain multiples of 12 plus 15.

Row 1: Dc in the 9th ch, *ch 2 and dc in the 3rd ch, rep from *, ending row with dc in the last ch, ch 3 and turn.

Row 2: 1 dc in each of the 2-chs, dc in the next dc, *ch 2 and dc in the next dc, dc in each of the 2-chs, dc in the next dc, rep from *, ending row with last dc and 3 dc in the turning ch, ch 3 and turn.

Row 3: Sk 1st dc, dc in each of the next 3 dc, *ch 2 and dc in each of the next 4 dc, rep from *, ending row with 4 dc, ch 3 and turn.

Row 4: Complete as row 3, ch 1 and turn.

Row 5: *sl st in each of the 4 dc, sc in each of the 2-chs, sl st in next dc, ch 5 and turn, attach to dc before the 2-ch, ch 3 and work 3 dc in the 5-ch, work 3-ch picot, work another 2 dc in the 5-ch, work another 3-ch picot, work another 2 dc and 3-ch picot, work 4 dc, sc in each of next 2-chs, rep from *, ending row with last set.

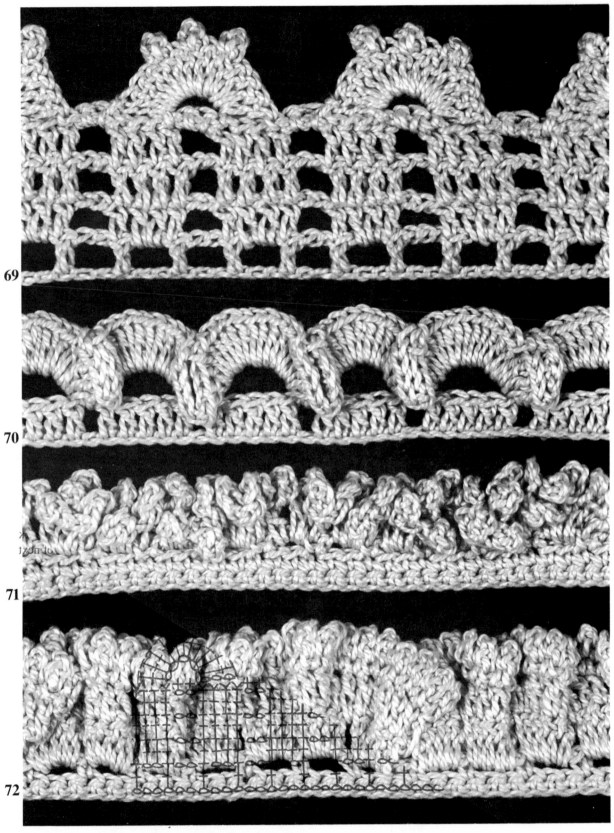

69

70

71

72

Double Crochet, Single Crochet, Chain and Picot

70. Chain multiples of 6 plus 9.

Row 1: Dc in the 5th ch and dc in each of the next 4 chs, *ch 1 and dc in the 2nd ch, dc in each of the next 4 chs, rep from *, ending row with dc in each of the last 6 chs, ch 1 and turn.
Row 2: Sc in the 1st dc, *ch 6 and sc in the 1-ch, rep from *, ending row with sc in the turning ch, ch 3.
Row 3: *work 20 dc in the 6-ch, rep from *, ending row with last set of 20.
Finishing: Attach 16th dc of one set to 5th dc of the next set.

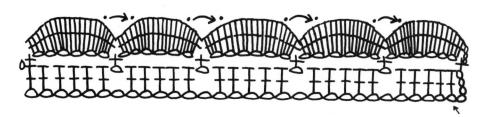

71. Chain multiples of 3 plus 2.

Row 1: Sc in the 2nd ch and in each ch all across the row, ch 1 and turn.
Row 2: Sc in the 1st sc and in each sc all across the row, ch 1 and turn.
Row 3: Sc in the 1st sc, *ch 2 and sc in the 3rd sc, rep from *, ending row with sc in the last sc, ch 4 and turn.
Row 4: *work 3-ch picot and dc in the 2-ch 3 times, 3-ch picot, dc in sc, rep from *, ending row with last dc.

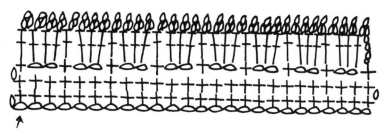

72. Chain multiples of 3 plus 2.

Row 1: Sc in the 2nd ch and in each ch all across the row, ch 1 and turn.
Row 2: Sc in the 1st sc, * ch 3 and sc in the 3rd sc, rep from *, ending row with sc in the last sc, ch 3 and turn.
Row 3: *work 5 dc in the next 3-ch, and ch 1, rep from *, ending row with 5 dc and 1 dc in the last sc, ch 3 and turn.
Row 4: Dc in each dc and in each ch all across the row, ending row with 1 dc in the turning ch, ch 1 and turn.
Row 5: Work 1 sc in each dc and 1 4-ch picot, ending row with last set.

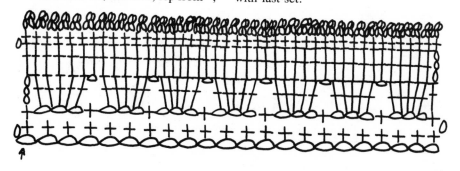

•4•
Half Double Crochet

73. Chain multiples of 2 plus 2

Row 1: Sc in 2nd ch and in each ch all across the row.
Row 2: Work 3-ch picot, hdc in the 3rd sc, *work 3-ch picot, hdc in the 2nd sc, rep from *, ending row with hdc.

74. Chain multiples of 3 plus 3.

Row 1: Hdc in the 4th ch, *ch 1 and hdc in the 2nd ch, hdc in the next ch and rep from *, ending row with 2 hdc, ch 3 and turn.
Row 2: Ch 2, dc in the 1st hdc, ch 2, dc in the next hdc, ch 2, hdc in the same hdc, *ch 2, sc in the 1-ch, ch 2, dc in the next hdc, ch 2, dc in the same hdc, ch 2, dc in the next hdc, ch 2, dc in the same hdc, rep from *, ending row with last set in the turning ch.

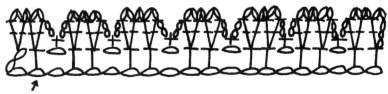

75. Chain multiples of 9 plus 2.

Row 1: Sc in the 2nd ch, and sc in each of the next 5 chs, *ch 2 and dc in the sc just formed, work another dc, ch 2 and sc in each of the next 9 chs, rep from *, ending row with 4 sc in the last 4 chs, ch 1 and turn.
Row 2: Sc in the 1st sc, *ch 11, and sc in the 9th sc, rep from *, ending row with last sc, ch 1 and turn.
Row 3: Sc in the 1st sc, * work 14 hdc around the 11-ch, and rep from *, ending row with last set and sc in last sc.

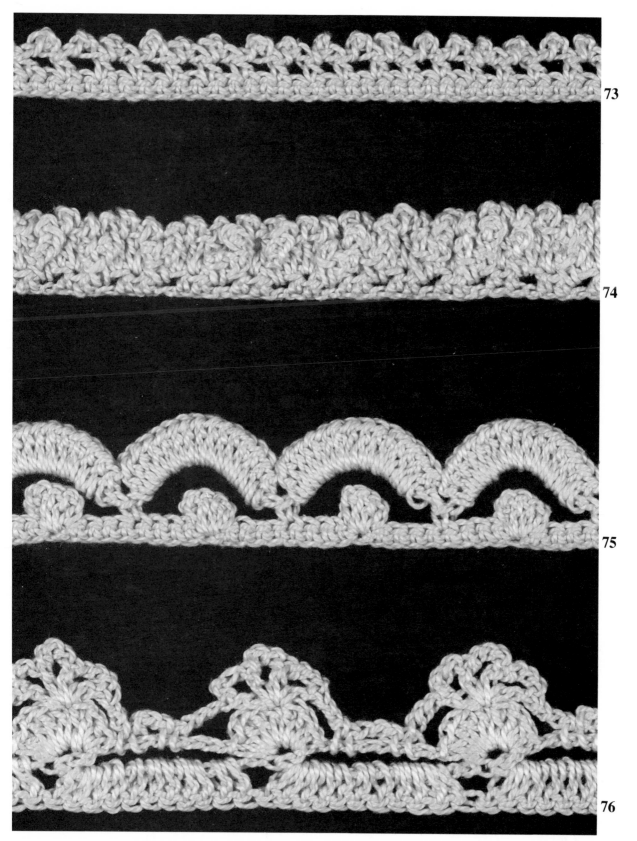

73

74

75

76

76. Chain 4.

Row 1: * ch 8 and sl st into previous ch, ch 11 and rep from *, ending row with 4 ch, ch 6 and turn.

Row 2: * sc in the 6-ch, hdc in the same 6-ch, work 5 dc in the same 6-ch, 1 hdc, and 1 sc in the same 6-ch, ch 7 and rep from *, ending row with last set, ch 3 and dc in the last ch, ch 1 and turn.

Row 3: Sc in the dc, * ch 3 and dc in the 3rd dc, ch 3 and dc in the same dc, ch 3 and dc in the same dc, ch 3 and dc in the same dc, ch 3 and sc around the 1st part of the 7-ch, ch 3 and sc around the last part of the 7-ch, rep from *, ending row with sc in the turning ch, break thread.

Bottom Row: Attach thread and ch 3, work dc in each ch all across the row.

·5·
Triple Stitch Variations

77. Chain multiples of 6 plus 6.

Row 1: Dc in the 9th ch, *ch 2, dc in the 3rd ch, rep from *, ending row with last dc, ch 3 and turn.
Row 2: *work 3 trc in the 2-ch, ch 3, work 3 sc in the next 2-ch, ch 3, rep from *, ending row with 3 sc in the turning ch.

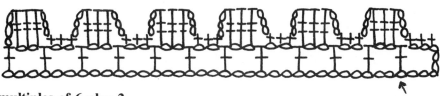

78. Chain multiples of 6 plus 2.

Row 1: Sc in the 2nd ch, * ch 7 and sc in the 6th ch, rep from *, ending row with sc in the last ch, ch 5 and turn.
Row 2: * work 4 trc around the 7-ch, ch 1 and rep from *, ending row with an extra trc in the last sc, ch 1 and turn.

Row 3: Sc in the trc, *ch 3 and work 3-ch picot, ch 3 and sc in the 1-ch, rep from *, ending row with sc in the turning ch.

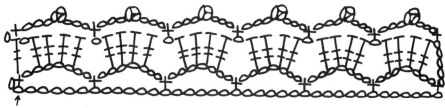

79. Chain multiples of 14 plus 4.

Row 1: Sc in the 2nd ch, *ch 3, sc in 2nd ch, ch 7, work trc in the 4th ch and trc in each of the next 4 chs, ch 7, sc in the 4th sc, rep from *, ending row with last sc, ch 6 and turn.

Row 2: * sc in the 3-ch, ch 7, sc around the last of the 7-ch, ch 5, sc around the 1st of the next 7-ch, ch 7 and rep from *, ending row with last sc, ch 2 and dc in the last sc.

80. Chain multiples of 8 plus 9.

Row 1: Work trc in the 6th ch and trc in each of the next 3 chs, * ch 3 and trc in the 4th ch and in each of the next 4 chs, rep from *, ending row with 1 trc in each of the last 5 chs, ch 1 and turn.

Row 2: Sl st in the 1st trc and sl st in the next trc, sc in the next trc, *ch 2, work 2 dc in the beginning of the 3-ch, work 3 4-ch picot and sl st together, work 2 dc into last part of 3-ch, ch 2 and sc in the 3rd trc, rep from *, ending row with sc and sl st in the last trc and sl st in the turning ch.

81. Chain multiples of 8 plus 6.

Row 1: Dc in the 8th ch, *ch 1 and dc in the 2nd ch, rep from *, ending row with dc in the last ch, ch 1 and turn.

Row 2: Sl st in the 1st dc, sk 1st 1-ch, *ch 4, work 5 trc in the 2nd 1-ch, ch 8 and sl st in the end of the 4-ch, ch 1, work 3 sc around the beginning of the 8-ch, work 3-ch picot, work 3 more sc around the end of the 8-ch, sl st in the top of the last trc, ch 4, sl st in the 2nd 1-ch, rep from *, ending row with sl st in the turning ch.

82. Chain multiples of 9 plus 6.

Row 1: Trc in the 6th ch, *work 5 ch picot, ch 2 and trc in the 3rd ch, trc in each of the next 3 chs, ch 7 and turn, sl st into last ch before the trc, turn and work 6 sc around the beginning of the 7-ch, ch 5 and work 6 sc around the last part of the 7-ch, sl st into last of the trc, ch 2 and trc in the 3rd ch, and rep from *, ending row with last trc.

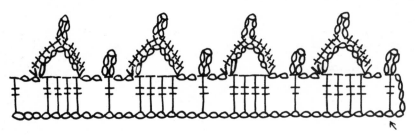

83. Chain multiples of 10 plus 6.

Row 1: Trc in the 6th ch, trc in the next ch, *ch 2, trc in the 3rd ch and in each of next 2 chs, rep from *, ending row with trc in each of the last 3 chs, ch 1 and turn.

Row 2: *sc in each of the next 3 trc, ch 4, trc in the next trc, ch 2, trc in the 2nd trc, ch 4, rep from *, ending row with sc in each of the last trc, and 1 sc in the turning ch, ch 1 and turn.

Row 3: Sl st in the 1st sc, * work 2 sc around the beginning of the 4-ch, work 3 dc in the same 4-ch, work 5 dc in the 2-ch, work 3 dc in the beginning of the 4-ch, work 2 sc in the end of the 4-ch, sl st in the 2nd sc, rep from *, ending row with last sl st.

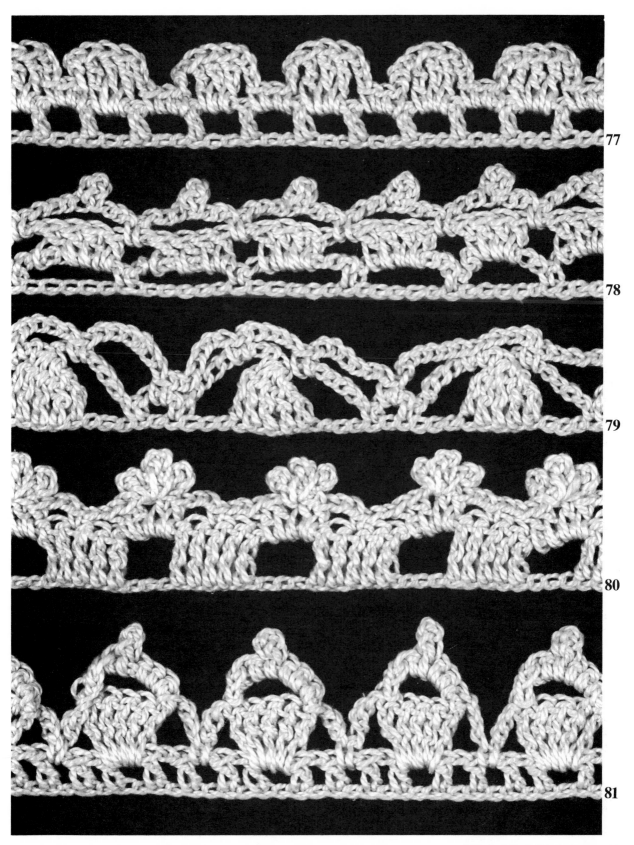

77

78

79

80

81

Triple Stitch Variations 69

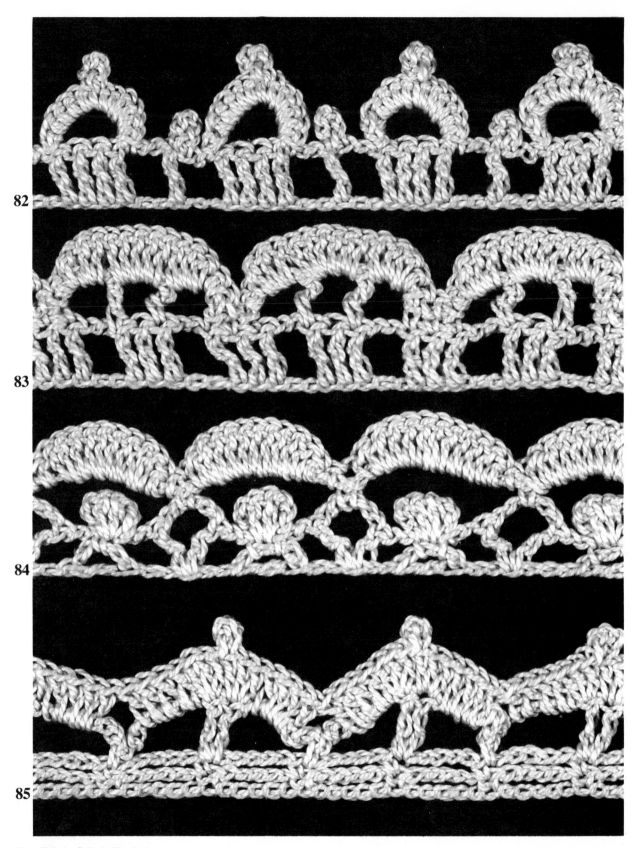

82

83

84

85

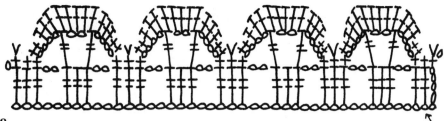

84. Chain 8.

Row 1: Dc back 6 ch, *ch 10 and dc back in the 6th ch, rep from *, ending row with last dc, ch 10 and turn.

Row 2: Trc back in the 8th ch, *ch 2, sc in the middle of the 5-ch, ch 3, work 2 dc in the sc, ch 3 and sl st in the sc, ch 2 and trc in the middle of the 2nd set of 5-chs, ch 5 and trc in the same ch, rep from *, ending row with trc, 3 ch and trc in the last ch, ch 3 and turn.

Row 3: Sc in the 1st 3-ch, *ch 9 and sc in the next 5-ch, rep from *, ending row with sc in the turning ch, ch 1 and turn.

Row 4: Sl st in the sc, *sc around the 9-ch, 1 hdc, work 9 dc in the same 9-ch, 1 hdc and 1 sc in the 9-ch, and rep from *, ending row with sl st in the last sc.

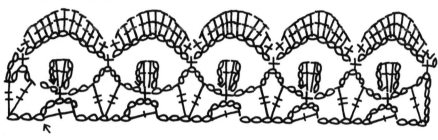

85. Chain multiples of 6 plus 2.

Row 1: Sc in the 2nd ch, *ch 5 and sc in the 6th ch, rep from *, ending row with sc in the last ch, ch 1 and turn.

Row 2: *sc in the sc, ch 5 and rep from *, ending row with last sc, ch 1 and turn.

Row 3: *ch 7 and work double trc in the 3rd ch, work another double trc in the same ch, ch 7 and sc in the next sc, rep from *, ending row with last sc, ch 4 and turn.

Row 4: * work 4 dc in the last part of the 7-ch, work 3 dc in the double trc, work 4-ch picot, work 3 dc in the next double trc, work 4 dc in the beginning of the next 7-ch, rep from *, ending row with last set and dc in the turning ch.

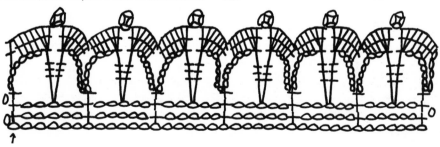

86. Chain multiples of 12 plus 2.

Row 1: Sc in the 2nd ch, *ch 5 and sc in the 4th ch, rep from *, ending row with sc, ch 3 and dc in the 3rd and last ch, ch 1 and turn.

Row 2: Sc in the dc, *ch 3 and sc around the middle of the 3-ch, rep from *, ending row with sc in the last 5-ch, ch 1 and hdc in the sc, ch 5 and turn.

Row 3: *sc in the sc, ch 5 and sc in the next sc, sc in each of the 3 chs, sc in the next sc, ch 5 and rep from *, ending row with 5 chs and last sc, ch 3 and turn.

Row 4: 2 dc in the 1st sc, * sc in the 5-ch, ch 4 and trc in the 3rd sc, ch 2 and trc in the same ch, ch 4 and sc in the 5-ch, work 5 dc in the sc, rep from *, ending row with 5 dc and sc in the turning ch, ch 1 and turn.

Row 5: Sl st in each of the 1st 2 dc, sc in the next dc, * work 5 dc around the 4-ch, dc in the trc, work 3 dc in the 2-ch, dc in the next trc, work 5 dc around the 4-ch, sc in the 3rd dc, rep from *, ending row with sc in the turning ch.

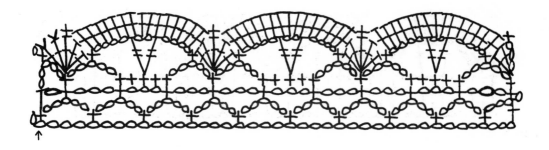

87. Chain multiples of 16 plus 9.

Row 1: Dc in the 5th ch, *ch 3, dc in the 3rd ch, dc in the next ch, rep from *, ending row with dc in each of the last 2 chs, ch 3 and turn.

Row 2: Dc in the 2nd dc, *ch 3, dc in each of the next 2 dc, rep from *, ending row with last dc and dc in the turning ch, ch 1 and turn.

Row 3: Sc in the dc, *sc in the next dc, 2 sc in the beginning of the 3-ch, ch 3, work 2 sc in the end of the same 3-ch, sc in each of the next 2 dc, ch 4, work 8 trc in the 2nd 3-ch, turn and ch 7, sl st last ch into the ch just before the 1st trc, turn and work 3 sc around the beginning of the 7-ch, work 1 3-ch picot, 2 sc around the middle of the same 7-ch, work another 3-ch picot, work another 2 sc around the middle of the same 7-ch, work another 3-ch picot, work 3 more sc around the end of the 7-ch, sl st into the last trc, ch 4 and sc in the 3rd dc, rep from *, ending row with sc in the turning ch.

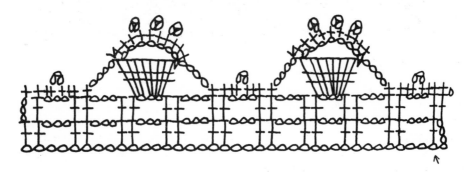

88. Chain multiples of 9 plus 7.

Row 1: Trc in the 10th ch, *ch 2 and trc in the 3rd ch, rep from *, ending row with trc in the last ch, ch 5 and turn.

Row 2: Sk 1st trc, * work 5-ch picot, trc in the next trc, ch 2, trc in the next trc and trc in each of the next 2 chs, trc in the next trc, ch 7 and turn, sl st end of 7-ch into the last 2-ch before the trc, ch 3 and turn, work 3 dc around the beginning of the 7-ch, ch 5 and work another 3 dc around the same 7-ch, ch 5 and work another 3 dc around the same 7-ch, ch 5 and 3 dc around the same 7-ch, ch 2 and sl st into the last trc, ch 1 and rep from *, ending row with 2 chs and dc in the turning ch.

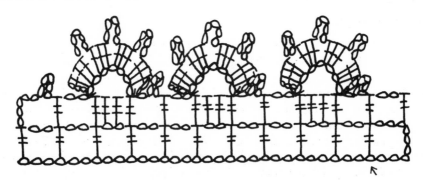

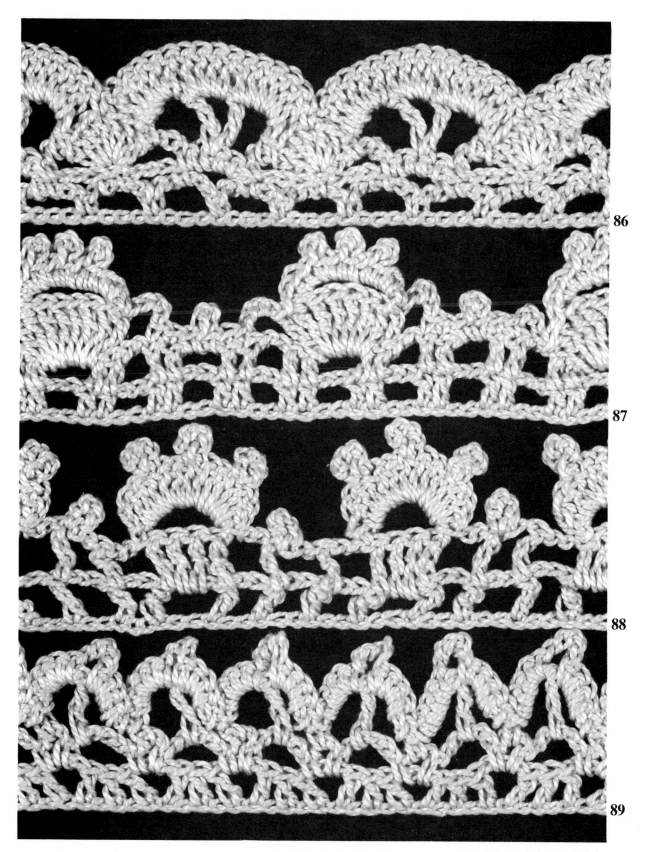

86

87

88

89

90

91

92

74   Triple Stitch Variations

89. Chain multiples of 5 plus 5.

Row 1: Dc in the 5th ch, *dc in the 2nd ch, dc in the 2nd dc, ch 3, dc in the next ch, rep from *, ending row with last set, 1 ch and 1 dc in the same ch as the last dc of the previous set, ch 1 and turn.

Row 2: Sc in the dc, sc in the 1-ch, * ch 5, sc in the beginning of the 3-ch, ch 3, sc in the end of the 3-ch, rep from *, ending row with sc in the turning ch, ch 3 and

another sc in the turning ch, ch 1 and turn.

Row 3: *sc in the 3-ch, ch 4, work trc in the middle of the 5-ch, ch 4, rep from *, ending row with sc in the last sc, ch 1 and turn.

Row 4: *work 5 sc around the 4-ch, ch 5, work 5 sc around the next 4-ch, rep from *, ending row with last sc.

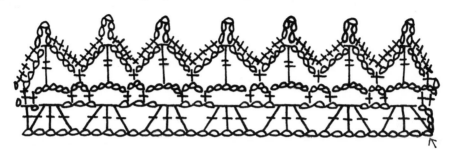

90. Chain multiples of 8 plus 8.

Row 1: Sc in the 12th ch, *ch 3 and dc in the 4th ch, ch 3 and sc in the 4th ch, rep from *, ending row with dc in the last ch, ch 1 and turn.

Row 2: *sc in the dc, ch 2, and work 3 trc in the sc, ch 3 and work another 3 trc in the same sc, ch 2 and rep from *, ending row with sc in the turning ch, ch 1 and turn.

Row 3: *sc in the sc, ch 4 and sc in the 3-ch, ch 4 and rep from *, ending row with sc in the last sc, ch 6 and turn.

Row 4: *sc in the sc, ch 3 and dc in the sc, ch 3 and rep from *, ending row with dc in the last sc, ch 1 and turn.

Row 5: *sc in the dc, ch 2, work 3 trc in the sc, ch 3, work another 3 trc in the same sc, ch 2 and rep from *, ending row with sc in the turning ch.

91. Chain multiples of 12 plus 4.

Row 1: Dc in the 5th ch, *ch 2 and dc in the ch just used, dc in the 3rd ch, rep from *, ending row with last set, ch 5 and turn.

Row 2: Sc in the 2nd dc, * ch 5 and sc after the 2nd set of V-stitches and the next set, rep from *, ending row with sc, 2 chs and dc in the turning ch, ch 3 and turn.

Row 3: Work 6 dc in the 2-ch, *sc in the middle of the next 5-ch, ch 5 and sc in the same 5-ch, work 13 dc around the next 5-ch, rep from *, ending row with sc, 5 chs and sc in the turning ch, ch 9 and turn.

Row 4: Work 1 trc in the 5-ch, ch 2 and work another trc in the same 5-ch, *ch 2 and sc in the 7th dc, ch 2 and trc in the next 5-ch, ch 2 and trc in same 5-ch, ch 2 and trc in same 5-ch, rep from *, ending row with last set, ch 2 and sc in the turning ch, ch 1 and turn.

Row 5: Sc in sc, sc in the 1st 2-ch, sc in each trc and each ch all across the row, ending row with 2 sc in the turning ch.

92.   Chain multiples of 12 plus 11.

Row 1: Trc in the 6th ch, trc in each of the next 5 chs, * ch 5 and trc in the 6th ch, and trc in each of the next 6 chs, rep from *, ending row with 1 trc in each of the last 7 chs, ch 4 and turn.

Row 2: Sk 1st trc, trc in each of the next 6 trc, * ch 5 and trc in each of the next 7 trc, rep from *, ending row with trc in each of the last 6 trc and trc in the turning ch, ch 4 and turn.

Row 3: Sk 1st trc, trc in each of the next 5 trc, * ch 5 and trc in the middle of the next 5-ch, ch 5 and trc in the 2nd trc, trc in each of the next 4 trc, rep from *, ending row with last 5 trc and trc in the turning ch, ch 5 and turn.

Row 4: Trc in the 3rd trc, and trc in each of the next 2 trc, *ch 6 and work 2 trc in the 2nd trc, ch 6 and work 1 trc in the 2nd trc, and trc in each of the next 2 trc, rep from *, ending row with last 3 trc, ch 1 and trc in the turning ch, ch 6 and turn.

Row 5: Sk 1st trc, *sc in the middle of the 3 trc, ch 5 and skip next trc, and work 1 dc in between the 2 sides of the next 2 trc, work 3-ch picot, work another dc and 3-ch picot 3 times, another dc in the same space, ch 5 and rep from *, ending row with last sc, ch 3 and dc in the turning ch.

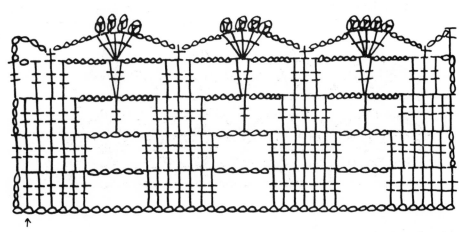

93.   Chain multiples of 10 plus 2.

Row 1: Sc in the 2nd ch, * ch 2 and trc in the 5th ch, ch 2 and trc in the same ch 6 more times, ch 2 and sc in the 5th ch, rep from *, ending row with sc in the last ch, ch 4 and turn.

Row 2: Sk 1st 2-ch, *sc in the next 2-ch and 4 chs 5 times, sc in the next 2-ch, ch 4 and rep from *, ending row with last set, 1 ch and 1 dc in the last sc, ch 1 and turn.

Row 3: Sc in the dc, ch 4, * sc in the 4-ch, ch 4 and work another sc in the same 4-ch, 4 chs 4 times, sc in the next 4-ch, ch 4 and sc in the same 4-ch, ch 4 and sc in the middle of the next 4-ch, ch 4 and rep from *, ending row after the last set with 4 chs and 1 sc in the turning ch.

Bottom Row: Sc in the 2nd ch and in each ch all across the row.

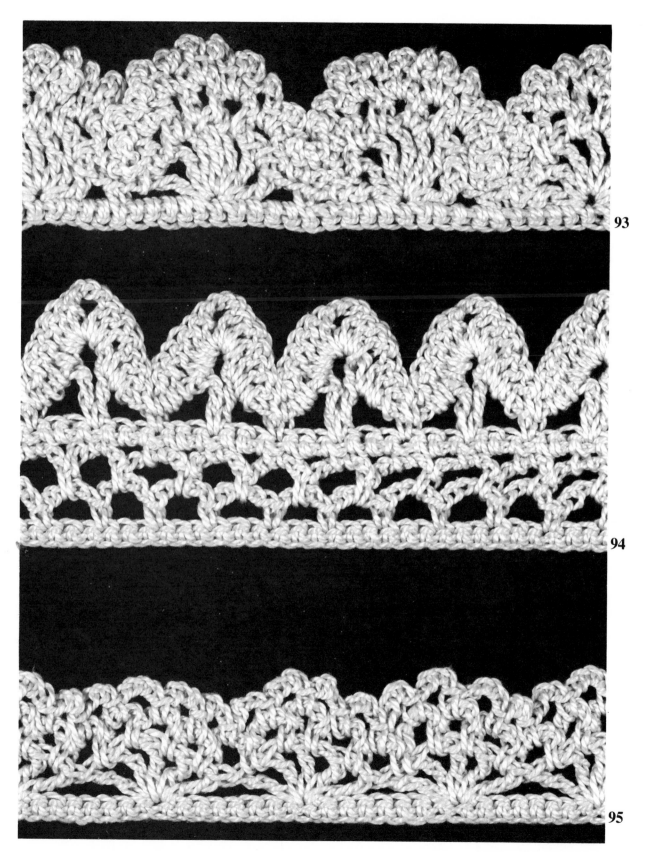

93

94

95

94. Chain multiples of 6 plus 2.

Row 1: Sc in the 2nd ch and in each ch all across the row, ch 1 and turn.

Row 2: Sc in the 1st sc, *ch 5 and sc in the 3rd sc, rep from *, ending row with sc in the last sc, ch 6 and turn.

Row 3: *sc in the middle of the 5-ch, ch 5 and rep from *, ending row with sc in the last 5-ch, ch 2 and dc in the last sc, ch 1 and turn.

Row 4: Sc in the dc, *ch 2 and sc in the middle of the 5-ch, rep from *, ending row with sc in the turning ch, ch 1 and turn.

Row 5: Sc in each ch and each sc all across the row, ch 1 and turn.

Row 6: Sc in the 1st sc, *ch 3 and trc in the 3rd sc, ch 5 and trc in the same sc just used, ch 3 and sc in the 3rd sc, rep from *, ending row with sc in the last sc, ch 1 and turn.

Row 7: Sc in sc, * work 1 dc in last of 3-ch, dc around the beginning of the 5-ch, work 3-ch picot, work another 6 dc around the last part of the 5-ch, 1 dc at beginning of 3-ch, sc in the next sc, rep from *, ending row with sc in the last sc.

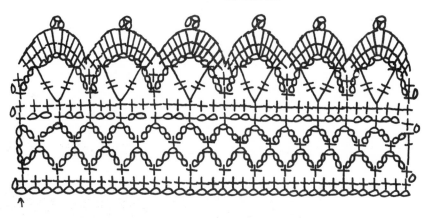

95. Chain multiples of 8 plus 2.

Row 1: Sc in the 2nd ch and in each ch all across the row, ch 3 and turn.

Row 2: Work trc in the 5th sc, *ch 1 and trc in the same sc 4 more times, trc in the 8th sc, and rep from *, ending row with last set and dc in the last sc, ch 5 and turn.

Row 3: Sc in the 1-ch and ch 4 all across the row, ending row with last sc, ch 2 and dc in the turning ch, ch 1 and turn.

Row 4: Sc in the dc, ch 4 and sc in the middle of the 4-ch all across the row, ending row with sc in the turning ch.

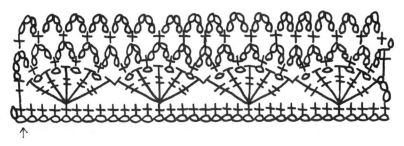

• 6 •
Mixed Stitch

96. Chain multiples of 12 plus 2.

Row 1: Sc in the 2nd ch, *ch 2, dc in the 2nd ch, ch 2, trc in the 2nd ch, ch 2, double trc in the 2nd ch, ch 2, trc in the 2nd ch, ch 2 and dc in the 2nd ch, ch 2 and sc in the 2nd ch, rep from *, ending row with sc in the last ch.

97. Chain multiples of 6 plus 2.

Row 1: Sc in the 2nd ch, *dc in the next ch, trc in the next ch, ch 5, sc in the 4th ch, rep from *, ending row with trc.

98. Chain multiples of 6 plus 2.

Row 1: 1 sc in the 2nd ch, *dc in the next ch, trc in the next ch, work 5-ch picot on top of trc, work 2 more 5-ch picot in the top of the same trc and sl st together, ch 5 and sc in 4th ch, rep from *, ending row with last trc.

99. Chain multiples of 3 plus 20.

Row 1: Sc in the 2nd ch and in each ch all across the row, ch 4 and turn.
Row 2: Work 1 double trc in the 2nd sc, and in each sc all across the row, ch 1 and turn.

Row 3: Sc in each double trc all across the row. After you finish, *ch stitch next 3 double trc together, ch 2, rep from *, ending row after chaining last 3 stitches together, leave 1 double trc freestanding.

100. Chain multiples of 10 plus 2.

Row 1: Sc in the 2nd ch and in each ch all across the row, ch 1 and turn.

Row 2: *sl st in 1st sc, sc in next sc, hdc in the next sc, dc in the next sc, trc in the next sc, work 5 double trc in the next ch, trc in the next sc, dc in the next sc, hdc in the next sc, sc in the next sc, and rep from *, ending row with sl st in the last sc.

101. Chain multiples of 3 plus 2.

Row 1: Sc in the 2nd ch and in each ch all across the row, ch 1 and turn.

Row 2: Sc in each of the next 2 sc, * ch 8 and dc back between the 3rd ch and the next ch, ch 3 and sc in the next sc, sc in each of the next 2 sc, rep from *, ending row with last ch, and sc in each of the last 3 sc.

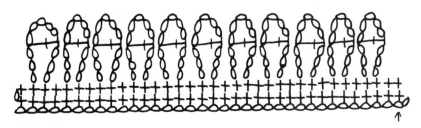

102. Chain multiples of 10 plus 2.

Row 1: Sc in the 2nd ch and in each ch all across the row, ch 4 and turn.

Row 2: Dc in the 3rd sc, ch 1 and dc in the 2nd sc, twice, *ch 4, dc in the 4th sc, ch 1, dc in the 2nd sc, ch 1, dc in the 2nd sc, ch 1, dc in the 2nd sc, rep from *, ending row with last dc, ch 4 and turn.

Row 3: Dc in 2nd dc, ch 1 and dc in dc twice, *ch 4, dc in the next dc, ch 1 and dc in the next dc 3 times, rep from *, ending row with dc in the turning ch, ch 4 and turn.

Row 4: Dc in the 2nd dc, ch 1 and dc in the next dc, twice, * ch 7, dc in next dc, ch 1 and turn, work 11 sc around the 7-ch, ch 1 and turn, sl st before the first sc, ch 3, sl st in 3rd sc, ch 3, sl st in 3rd sc, ch 3, sl st in 3rd sc and ch 3, sl st after the last sc, ch 1, dc in the next dc, ch 1 and dc in the next dc, ch 1 and dc in the next dc, rep from *, ending row with last dc in the turning ch.

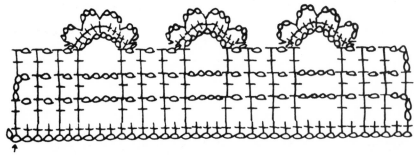

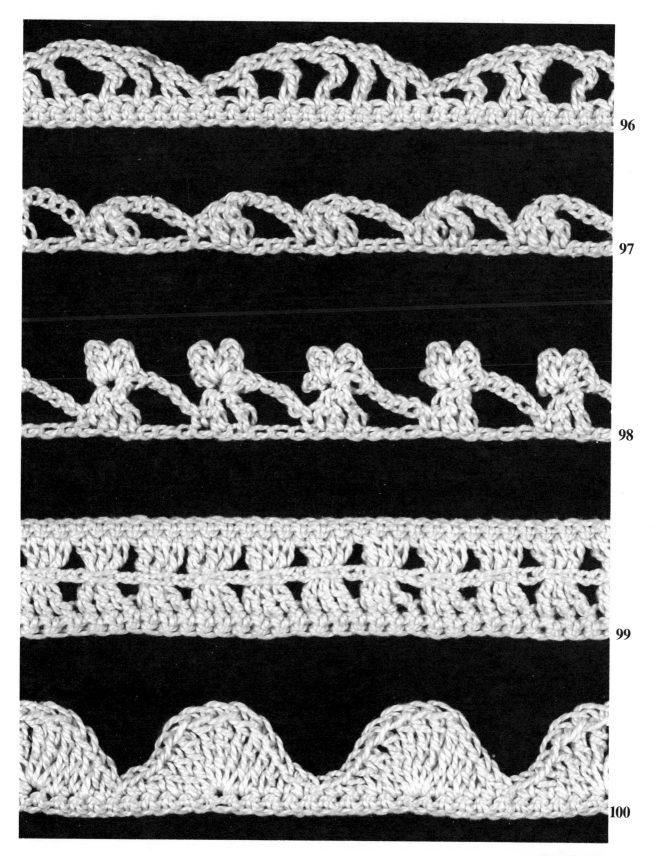

96

97

98

99

100

101

102

103

103.   Chain multiples of 5 plus 2.

Row 1: Sc in the 2nd ch and sc in each ch all across the row, ch 1 and turn.

Row 2: Sc in the 1st sc and in each sc all across the row, ch 1 and turn.

Row 3: Sc in the 1st and next sc, *ch 5, sc in the 3rd sc and sc in each of the next 2 sc, rep from *, ending row with sc in each of the last 2 sc, ch 1 and turn.

Row 4: Sc in the 1st sc, *ch 1 and dc in the 5-ch 5 times, ch 1 and sc in the 2nd sc, rep from *, ending row with sc in the last sc, ch 1 and turn.

Row 5: Ch 2 and sc in the 2nd dc, *ch 2, work 3-ch picot, ch 2 and sc in the next dc, ch 2, work 3-ch picot, ch 2 and sc in the next dc, ch 2 and sc in the 3rd dc, rep from *, ending row with last set, ch 1 and dc in the last sc.

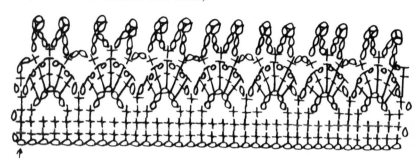

104.   Chain multiples of 3 plus 6.

Row 1: Dc in the 8th ch, *ch 2 and dc in the 3rd ch, rep from *, ending row with dc in the last ch, ch 1 and turn.

Row 2: *sc in the dc, ch 3, work 1 dc in the next ch, ch 3, work 7 dc back around the dc just formed at a perpendicular angle, rep from *, ending row with sc in the turning ch, break thread.

Bottom Row: Attach thread and sc in 2nd ch and sc in each ch all across the row.

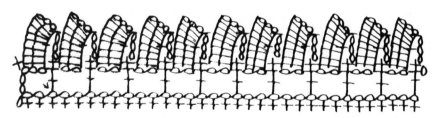

105.   Chain multiples of 9 plus 6.

Row 1: Dc in the 9th ch, *ch 2 and dc in the 3rd ch, rep from *, ending row with last dc, ch 1 and turn.

Row 2: Sc in each dc and in each ch all across the row, ch 7 and turn.

Row 3: Sc in the 5th sc, *ch 3, sc in the next sc, ch 9, and sc in the 8th sc, rep from *, ending row with 5 chs and 1 dc in the last sc, ch 1 and turn.

Row 4: Sc in the 1st dc, ch 2, work 5 dc around the 5-ch, * sc in the middle of the 3-ch, work 5 dc around the first half of the 9-ch, ch 2, sc in the middle of the 9-ch, ch 2, work 5 dc around the last half of the 9-ch, rep from *, ending row with 5 dc, 2 chs and 1 sc in the turning ch, ch 6 and turn.

Row 5: *sc in the top of the 2-ch, ch 9, sc in the top of the next 2-ch, ch 3 and rep from *, ending row with 3-ch and 1 dc in the last sc, ch 2 and turn.

Row 6: *sc in the 3-ch, work 5 dc around the first half of the 9-ch, ch 2, sc in the middle of the 9-ch, ch 2, work 5 dc around the last half of the 9-ch, rep from *, ending row with sc in the turning ch.

Bottom Row: Sc in the 2nd ch and in each ch all across the row.

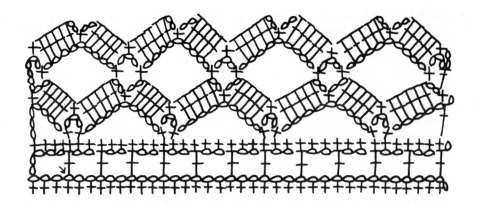

106. Chain multiples of 4 plus 4.

Row 1: Dc in the 5th ch and in each ch all across the row, ch 1 and turn.

Row 2: Sc in the 1st dc, *ch 5, sc in the 4th dc, rep from *, ending row with sc in the turning ch, ch 4 and turn.

Row 3: *dc in the 5-ch, ch 1, dc in the same 5-ch, ch 1, rep from *, ending row with trc in the last sc, ch 5 and turn.

Row 4: Sc in the 1st 1-ch, *ch 5, sc in the 2nd 1-ch, rep from *, ending row with last sc in the 1-ch, ch 2 and 1 dc in the turning ch, ch 1 and turn.

Row 5: Sc in the dc, *3 dc in the 1st sc, sc in the middle of the 5-ch, rep from *, ending row with sc in the turning ch.

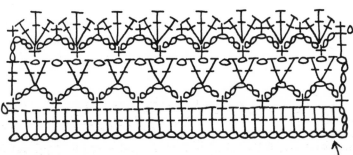

107. Chain multiples of 8 plus 4.

Row 1: Dc in the 4th ch and in each ch all across the row, ch 4 and turn.

Row 2: 2 dc in the 5th dc, *ch 3, 2 dc in the same dc, dc in the 4th dc, ch 3, dc in the same dc, 2 dc in the 4th dc, rep from *, ending row with last set, ch 1 and 1 dc in the turning ch, ch 1 and turn.

Row 3: Sc in the 1st dc, *ch 7, sc in the middle of the 3-ch, rep from *, ending row with sc in the turning ch, ch 1 and turn.

Row 4: Sc in the 1st sc, ch 3, sc in the 7-ch, ch 3 and sc in the same 7-ch 3 times, *sc in the next 7-ch, ch 3 and sc in the 7-ch 3 times, rep from *, ending row with last set, ch 3 and sc in the last sc.

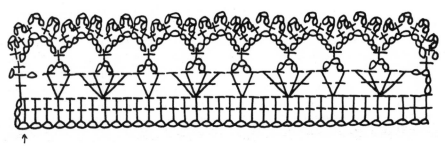

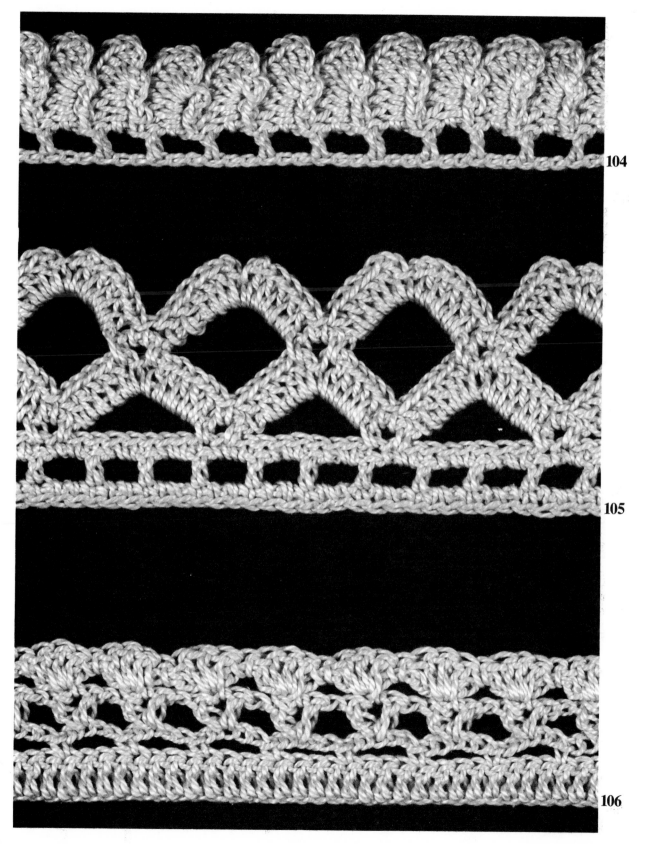

104

105

106

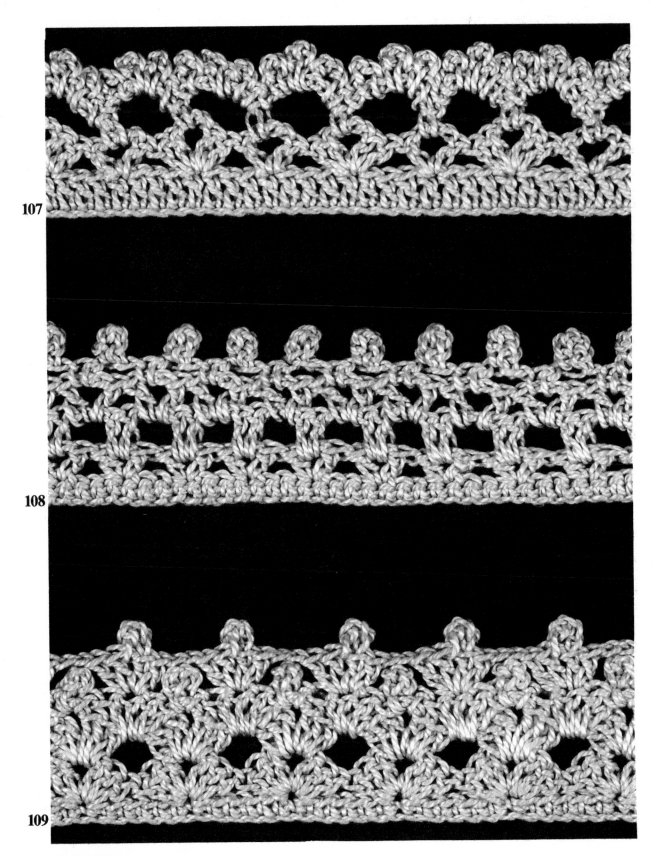

107

108

109

86 Mixed Stitch

108. Chain multiples of 4 plus 2.

Row 1: Sc in the 2nd ch and in each ch all across the row, ch 4 and turn.

Row 2: Dc in the 4th sc, *ch 2 and dc in the same dc just used, dc in the 4th sc, rep from *, ending row with last set and 1 dc in the 2nd sc, ch 5 and turn.

Row 3: *work 1 dc in each of the 2-ch, and ch 2, rep from *, ending row with last set, ch 2 and dc in the turning ch, ch 4 and turn.

Row 4: *dc in the 2-ch, ch 2 and dc in the same 2-ch, rep from *, ending row with the last set, the 2nd dc finished together with 1 dc in the turning ch, ch 1 and turn.

Row 5: Sc in the top of the 2 dc, * sc in the 2-ch, ch 1, work 5-ch picot, ch 1, and rep from *, ending row with last sc, ch 1 and sc in the turning ch.

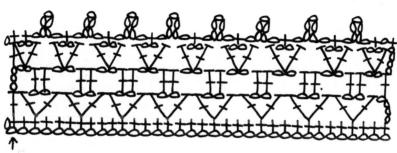

109. Chain multiples of 6 plus 2.

Row 1: Sc in the 2nd ch and each ch all across the row, ch 2 and turn.

Row 2: Work 3 dc in the 1st sc, * work 3 dc in the 6th sc, ch 2, work 3 dc in the same sc, rep from *, ending row with last set, work 3 dc in the last sc, ch 2 and dc in the same sc, ch 3 and turn.

Row 3: Work 3 dc in the 1st dc, * ch 1, work 3 dc in the 2-ch, ch 2 and work 3 dc in the same 2-ch, rep from *, ending row with 3 dc in the turning ch, ch 5 and turn.

Row 4: Sc in the 1st dc, * work 3 dc in the 1-ch, sc in the 2-ch, ch 4, work another sc in the same 2-ch, rep from *, ending row with sc, ch 4 and sc in the turning ch, ch 5 and turn.

Row 5: * work 2 dc in the 2nd dc, ch 1, work 4-ch picot, work another 2 dc in the same dc, ch 2 and rep from *, ending row with 1 ch and hdc in the turning ch.

110. Chain multiples of 4 plus 4.

Row 1: Dc in the 4th ch, *ch 2 and dc in the 3rd ch, dc in the next ch, rep from *, ending row with dc in each of the last 2 chs, ch 4 and turn.

Row 2: *work 3 dc in the 2-ch, ch 1 and rep from *, ending row with last 1-ch and dc in the turning ch, ch 1 and turn.

Row 3: Sc in the 1st dc, *ch 1, work 3 sc in the 2nd dc, rep from *, ending row with sc in the turning ch, ch 3 and turn.

Row 4: * sc in the 1st sc, dc in the next sc, ch 4 and dc in the same sc, sc in the next sc, rep from *, ending row with last set, sc in the 1-ch and dc in the last sc.

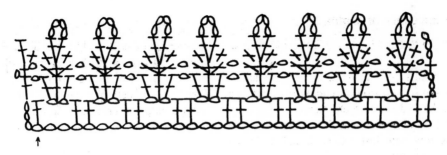

111.   Chain multiples of 8 plus 4.

Row 1: Dc in the 4th ch and in each ch across the row, ch 3 and turn.

Row 2: Work 3 dc in the 3rd dc, *sc in the 4th dc, ch 3 and work 3 dc in the same dc, work 3 dc in the 4th dc, rep from *, ending row with last set and 1 dc in the turning ch, ch 2 and turn.

Row 3: Sk 1st dc, *sc just after the next dc, dc in the next dc, ch 3 and dc in the same dc, sc in the space after the next dc, rep from *, ending row with sc, ch 6 and turn.

Row 4: *dc in the 3-ch, ch 3 and dc in the same 3-ch, rep from *, ending row with last dc, ch 1 and turn.

Row 5: Sc before 1st dc, *sc in 3-ch, ch 3, sc in the same 3-ch, sc in the space between the 2 sets, ch 3 and sc in the same space, rep from *, ending row with sc in the turning ch.

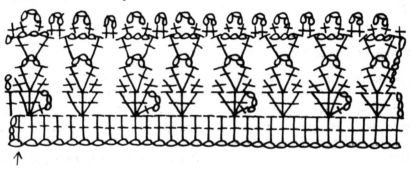

112.   Chain multiples of 5 plus 2.

Row 1: Sc in the 2nd ch, *ch 5 and sc in the 5th ch, rep from *, ending row with sc in the last ch, ch 5 and turn.

Row 2: *work trc around the beginning of the 5-ch, dc in the same 5-ch, work 4-ch picot, dc in the same 5-ch and trc in the same 5-ch, ch 2 and rep from *, ending row with last set, ch 1 and trc in the last sc, ch 1 and turn.

Row 3: Sc in 1st trc, *ch 6 and sc in 2-ch, rep from *, ending row with sc in the turning ch, ch 4 and turn.

Row 4: *work 1 trc and 1 dc in the 5-ch, work 4-ch picot, 1 dc and 1 trc in the same 5-ch, ch 3 and rep from *, ending row with last set and trc in the last sc, ch 1 and turn.

Row 5: Sc in the 1st trc, *ch 4 and work 5-ch picot, work another 5-ch picot and sl st, work another 5-ch picot and sl st, ch 4 and sc in the 3-ch, rep from *, ending row with sc in the turning ch.

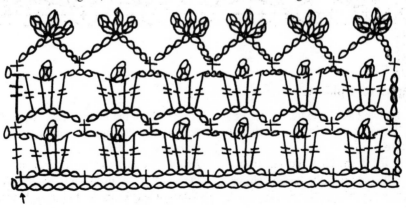

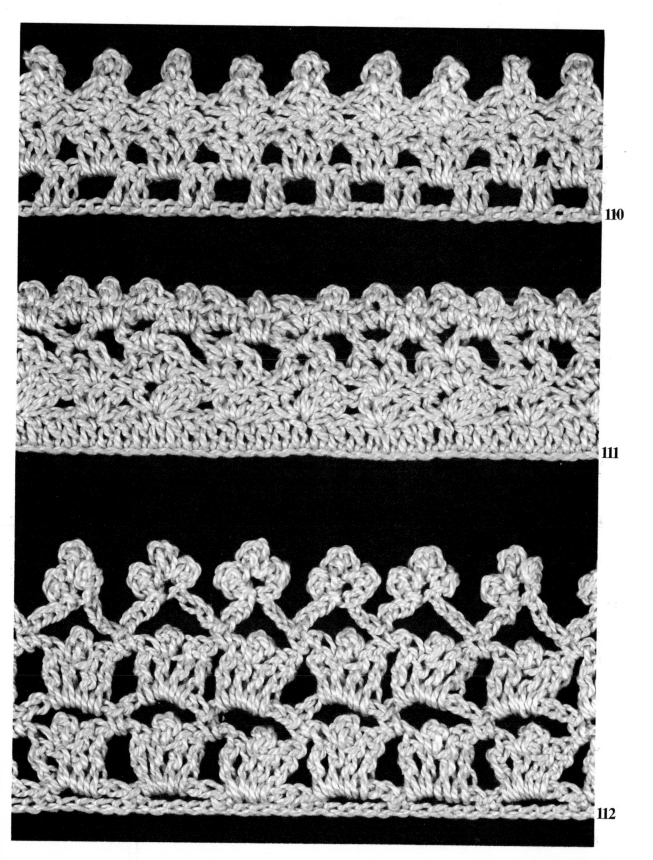

110

111

112

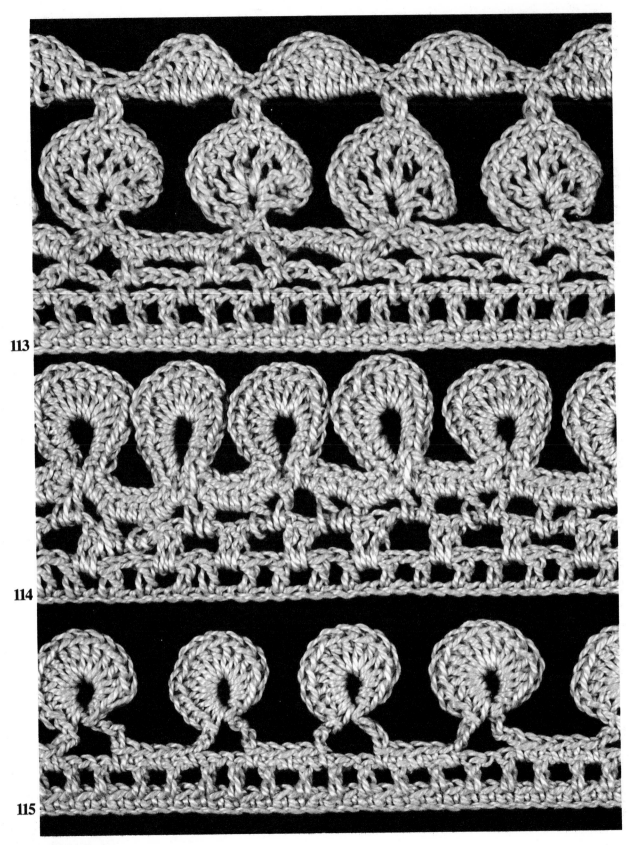

113

114

115

90 Mixed Stitch

113.   Chain multiples of 8 plus 2.

Row 1: Sc in the 2nd ch and sc in each ch all across the row, ch 5 and turn.

Row 2: Dc in the 3rd sc, *ch 1 and dc in the 2nd sc, rep from *, ending row with last dc, ch 1 and turn.

Row 3: Sc in the 1st dc, ch 3 and sc in the 1-ch, *ch 5 and sc in the 2nd 1-ch, rep from *, ending row with sc in the turning ch, ch 6 and turn.

Row 4: *sc around the 5-ch, ch 5 and rep from *, ending row with sc in the last 3-ch, ch 1 and turn.

Row 5: *work 5 sc around the next 5-ch, ch 2 and sc in the middle of the next 5-ch, ch 5 and attach last ch to 1st, forming a circle, ch 4 and turn, work 1 dc back in the 5-ch circle, ch 1 and dc in the same circle 5 more times, ch 1 and turn, sc in the dc and sc in the ch, 3 times, work 3-ch picot, sc in the dc and sc in the ch 3 more times, sl st in each of the 4-chs, sl st in the next sc, ch 2 and rep from *, ending row with 3 sc in the turning ch, ch 12 and turn.

Row 6: *sc in the 3-ch picot, ch 7 and rep from *, ending row with sc in the last picot, ch 4 and sc in the double trc, ch 1 and turn.

Row 7: Sc in the triple trc, hdc in the beginning of the 4-ch, work 2 dc in the middle of the same 4-ch and hdc towards the end of the 4-ch, sc in the last ch, *sc in the beginning of the 7-ch, work 1 hdc, 1 dc, 3 trc, 1 dc, 1 hdc and 1 sc in the same 7-ch, rep from *, ending row with sc, hdc, 2 dc, hdc and sc in the turning ch.

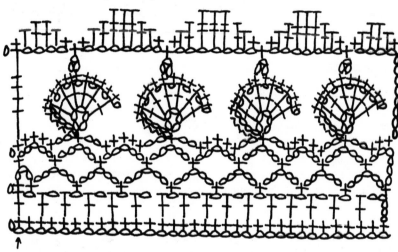

114.   Chain multiples of 10 plus 5.

Row 1: Dc in the 7th ch, *ch 1 and dc in the 2nd ch, rep from *, ending row with last dc, ch 3 and turn.

Row 2: Dc in 1st 1-ch, *ch 3, work 2 dc in the 2nd 1-ch, rep from *, ending row with 2 dc in the turning ch, ch 4 and turn.

Row 3: *1 dc in the 1st of the 3-ch, ch 1, 1 dc in the last of the same 3-ch, ch 1, sk 2 dc, rep from *, ending row with dc in the turning ch, ch 1 and turn.

Row 4: Sc in the next dc, 2 sc in the 1-ch, 3 times, *ch 8, 3 sc in the 2nd 1-ch, and 3 sc in the 1-ch 3 more times, rep from *, ending row with 3 sc in the turning ch, ch 1 and turn.

Row 5: Sl st in the next 8 sc, *2 sc around the beginning of the 8-ch, work 2 hdc, 9 dc, 2 hdc and 2 sc in the same 8-ch, sk 1st sc and work sl st in next 10 sc, rep from *, ending row with 1 sc in the last dc.

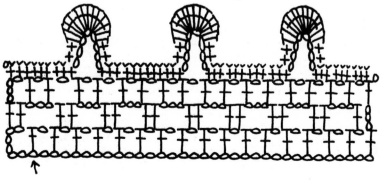

115. Chain multiples of 8 plus 2.

Row 1: Sc in 2nd ch and in each ch all across the row, ch 5 and turn.

Row 2: 1 dc in the 3rd sc, *ch 1, dc in the 2nd sc, rep from *, ending row with last dc, ch 1 and turn.

Row 3: Sc in the 1st dc, sc in the 1-ch, *ch 3, ch 7 and sl st back into the 1st of the 7-ch, turn and work 1 sc, 1 hdc, 12 dc, 1 hdc and 1 sc into the middle of the 7-ch, ch 3, sc in the 2nd 1-ch, sc in the next dc, sc into the next ch, the next dc and the next ch, rep from *, ending row with 2 sc in the turning ch.

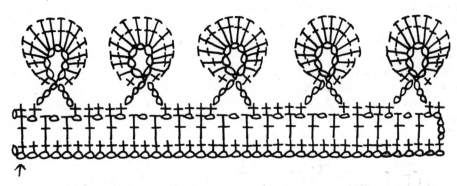

116. Chain multiples of 6 plus 2.

Row 1: Sc in the 2nd ch and in each ch all across the row, ch 4 and turn.

Row 2: Dc in the 3rd sc, *ch 1, and dc in the 2nd sc, rep from *, ending row with dc in the last sc, ch 1 and turn.

Row 3: Sc in the 1st dc, the 1-ch and the dc, *ch 14, sc in the next dc, the ch, the next dc, the ch and the next dc, rep from *, ending row with last ch and sc in the turning ch, ch 1 and turn.

Row 4: *work 17 sc around the 14-ch, sl st into each of next 2 sc, and rep from *, ending row with last sc, ch 1 and turn.

Row 5: Sl st into 1st 4 sc, * work sc into each of the next 4 sc, work 4-ch picot, sc into next 4 sc, sk to next 14-ch, sk 1st 5 sc and rep from *, ending row with last sc and sl st into the last 5 sc of the last set.

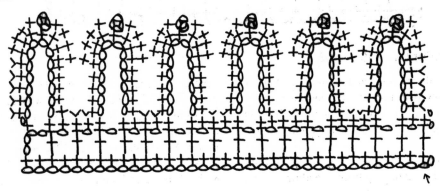

117. Chain multiples of 8 plus 2.

Row 1: Sc in the 2nd ch and in each ch all across the row, ch 1 and turn.

Row 2: Sc in each of the next 4 sc, work 1 sc in the next sc, * ch 7 and sc in the same sc, sc in each of the next 8 sc, and rep from *, ending row with last sc, ch 4 and turn.

Row 3: Sc in the 2nd sc, *sl st in the next sc, work 9 sc around the 7-ch, sl st in the next sc, sc in the next sc, dc in the next sc, sc in the next sc, and rep from *, ending row with last dc, ch 1 and turn.

Row 4: *sc in the dc, ch 4, sc in the middle of the 9 sc, ch 5 and sc in the same sc, ch 4 and rep from *, ending row with sc in the turning ch, ch 1 and turn.

Row 5: Sc in the sc, *work 3 sc in the 4-ch, work 5 sc in the 5-ch, work 3 sc in the next 4-ch, sc in the sc, rep from *, ending row with sc in the last sc.

116

117

118

118.   Chain multiples of 13 plus 4.

Row 1: Dc in the 5th ch and dc in each ch all across the row, ch 1 and turn.

Row 2: Sc in the 1st dc, *ch 11, sc in the next dc, ch 5 and sc in the 3rd dc, ch 5 and sc in the 3rd dc, ch 5 and sc in the 3rd dc, ch 5 and sc in the 3rd dc, rep from *, ending row with sc, ch 6 and double trc in the last sc, ch 1 and turn.

Row 3: Sc in double trc, work 5 sc around the 6-ch, *sc in the middle of the 5-ch, ch 3 and sc in the next 5-ch, ch 3 and sc in the middle of the next 5-ch, ch 3 and sc in the middle of the next 5-ch, work 11 sc around the middle of the 11-ch, rep from *, ending row with 6 sc around the 1st half of the 11-ch, ch 5 and turn.

Row 4: Work 3-ch picot, ch 1 and trc in the sc, work 3-ch picot, ch 1 and trc in the next sc 3 more times, *ch 2 and sc in the 2nd 3-ch, ch 2 and trc in the 2nd sc of the 11 sc worked around the 11-ch, 3-ch picot, ch 1 and trc in the next sc 8 times, rep from *, ending with trc, ch 1 and turn.

Row 5: Sc in the trc, *ch 5 and sc in the next trc, ch 10, and sc in the 4th trc of the next set, ch 5 and sc in the next trc, rep from *, ending row with sc in the turning ch, ch 6 and turn.

Row 6: *sc around the 5-ch, ch 5 and sc around the 1st part of the 10-ch, ch 5 and sc towards the end of the 10-ch, ch 5 and sc in the 5-ch, ch 5 and rep from *, ending row with sc in the last 5-ch, ch 2 and dc in the last sc, ch 1 and turn.

Row 7: Sc in the dc, *ch 5 and sc in the next 5-ch, rep from *, ending row with sc in the turning ch, ch 1 and turn.

Row 8: Work 6 sc in each 5-ch, all across the row.

·7·
V-Stitches and Small Shells

119. Chain multiples of 8 plus 5.

Row 1: Dc in the 7th ch, *ch 1, and dc in the 2nd ch, rep from *, ending row with last dc, ch 6 and turn.
Row 2: Dc in the 1st dc, *ch 5, dc in the 4th dc, ch 5, dc in the dc just used, rep from *, ending row with dc in the turning ch, ch 3, dc in the ch just used.

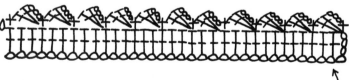

120. Chain multiples of 3 plus 4.

Row 1: 1 dc in the 4th ch and in each ch all across the row, ch 1 and turn.
Row 2: Sc in the 1st dc, *work 2 dc in the 3rd dc, ch 3, sc in the dc just used, rep from *, ending row with sc in the turning ch.

121. Chain multiples of 10 plus 6.

Row 1: Sc in the 2nd ch and in each of the next 4 chs, *ch 2, dc in the 3rd ch, ch 2, dc in the same ch, ch 2 and dc in the same ch, ch 2 and sc in the 3rd ch, sc in each of the next 4 chs, rep from *, ending row with sc in each of the last 5 chs.

122. Chain multiples of 6 plus 2.

Row 1: Sc in the 2nd ch and in each ch all across the row, ch 3 and turn.
Row 2: Ch 4, work 3 dc back in the 1st sc, * work 3 dc in the 6th sc, ch 5, work another 3 dc in the same sc, rep from *, ending row with 3 dc in the last sc, ch 4, sl st in last ch.

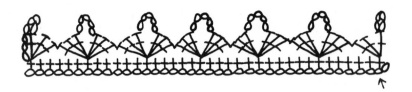

123. Chain multiples of 16 plus 2.

Row 1: Sc in the 2nd ch and in each ch all across the row, ch 1 and turn.

Row 2: Sc in the 1st sc, *ch 7 and work 2 dc in the 8th sc, ch 2, work 2 dc in the same sc, ch 7 and sc in the 8th ch, rep from *, ending row with sc in the last sc, ch 1 and turn.

Row 3: *sc in the sc, ch 3, sc in the same sc, ch 7, work 2 dc in the 2-ch, ch 2 and work 2 dc in the same 2-ch, ch 7, rep from *, ending row with last sc.

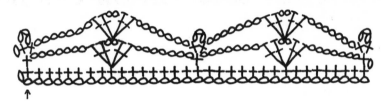

124. Chain multiples of 5 plus 4.

Row 1: Work 2 dc in the 6th ch, *ch 1, work 2 dc in the ch just used, ch 2, work 2 dc in the 5th ch, rep from *, ending row with last set and dc in the 2nd and last ch, ch 3 and turn.

Row 2: *work 2 dc in the 1-ch, ch 1 and work 2 dc in the same 1-ch, ch 2, rep from *, ending row with last set and 1 extra dc in the turning ch, ch 3 and turn.

Row 3: *work 2 dc in the 1-ch, work 3-ch picot, work 2 dc in the same 1-ch, ch 2, rep from *, ending row with last set and 1 extra dc in the turning ch.

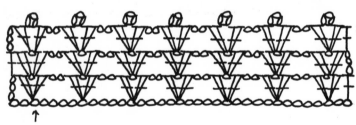

125. Chain multiples of 10 plus 7.

Row 1: Work 3 dc in the 12th ch, *ch 3, dc in the 5th ch, ch 3, 3 dc in the 5th ch, rep from *, ending row with dc in the last ch, ch 3 and turn.

Row 2: Dc in the 1st dc, *ch 3, dc in the 2nd dc, ch 3, work 3 dc in the next dc, rep from *, ending row with 2 dc in the turning ch, ch 3 and turn.

Row 3: 2 dc in the 2nd dc, *ch 2, dc in the next dc, ch 2, 2 dc in the next dc, dc in the next dc, 2 dc in the next dc, rep from *, ending row with 2 dc in the last dc and 1 dc in the turning ch, ch 3 and turn.

Row 4: 3 dc in the 3rd dc, *ch 1, 3 dc in the 2nd dc, ch 1, 3 dc in the 4th dc, rep from *, ending row with last set and 1 dc in the turning ch.

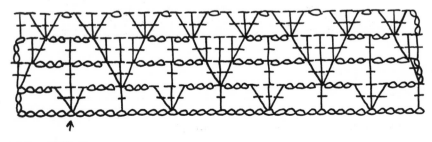

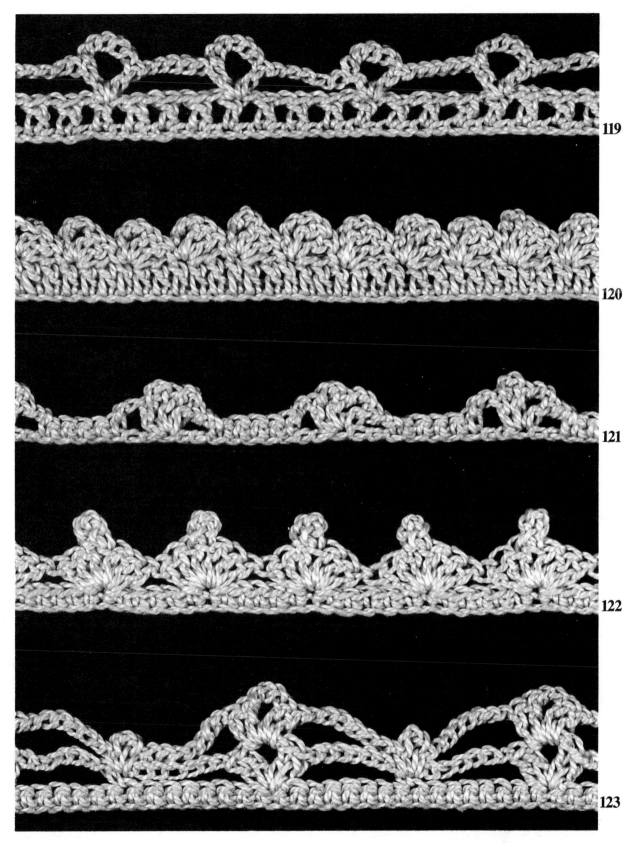

119

120

121

122

123

V-Stitches and Small Shells   97

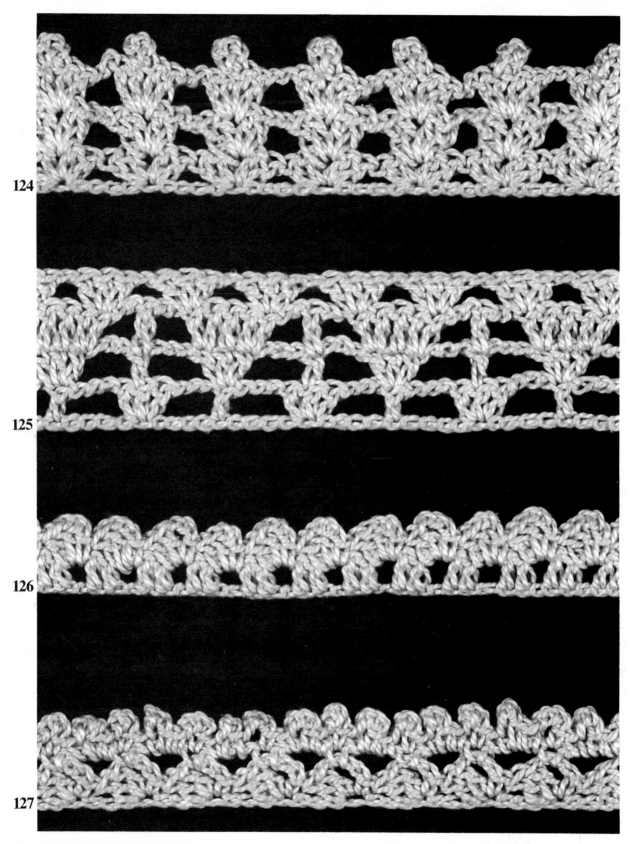

124

125

126

127

98   V-Stitches and Small Shells

126. Chain multiples of 3 plus 2.

Row 1: Sc in the 2nd ch and in each ch all across the row, ch 4 and turn.
Row 2: Dc in the 3rd sc and dc in the next sc, *ch 1, dc in the 2nd sc and the sc after that, rep from *, ending row with a single dc, ch 1 and turn.

Row 3: Sc in the 1st dc, ch 3, *work 2 dc in the 1-ch, ch 3, sc in the same 1-ch, rep from *, ending row with sc in the turning ch.

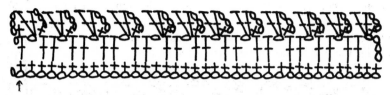

127. Chain multiples of 5 plus 2.

Row 1: 1 sc in the 2nd ch, *ch 3, work 2 dc in the same ch used for the sc, sc in the 5th ch, rep from *, ending row with sc in the 5th and last chs, ch 4 and turn.
Row 2: *sc in the top of the 3-ch, ch 3, rep from *, ending row with sc in the last 3-ch, ch 1, dc in the last sc, ch 1 and turn.

Row 3: Sc in the dc, work 3-ch picot, 1 sc in the 1-ch, *1 sc in the sc, work a 3-ch picot, sc in each of the next 2 chs, 3-ch picot, 1 sc in the 3rd ch, rep from *, ending row with 2 sc in the turning ch.

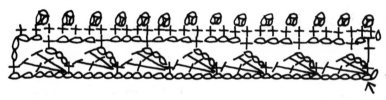

128. Chain multiples of 4 plus 2.

Row 1: Sc in the 2nd ch, *ch 5 and sc in the 4th ch, rep from *, ending row with sc in the last ch, ch 4 and turn.
Row 2: *sc around the 5-ch, ch 3, rep from *, ending row with last sc, ch 1 and dc in the sc, ch 3 and turn.
Row 3: 2 dc in the 1st dc, *sc in the next sc, ch 2, work 2 dc back in the sc just formed, rep from *, ending row with sc in the last sc, ch 2 and finish 2 dc together in the last sc and in the turning ch, ch 1 and turn.
Row 4: Sc in the top of the 2 dc finished together, *ch 2,

work 2 dc around the 2-ch at a perpendicular angle, sc in the top of the 2-ch, rep from *, ending row with last 2-ch and 1 sc in the top of the turning ch, ch 5 and turn.
Row 5: *sc in the top of the 2-ch, ch 5 and rep from *, ending row with sc and 2 chs, dc in the last sc, ch 1 and turn.
Row 6: Sc in the dc, *ch 5 and sc around the middle of the 5-ch, rep from *, ending row with sc in the turning ch.

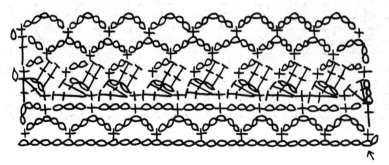

129.   Chain multiples of 8 plus 2.

Row 1: Sc in the 2nd ch, *ch 4, sc in the 4th ch, ch 3, work 2 dc back in the sc just formed, rep from *, ending row with sc in the last ch, ch 5 and turn.

Row 2: * sc around the middle of the 4-ch, ch 4, sc around the top of the 3-ch, ch 3, work 2 dc in the base of the sc just formed, rep from *, ending row with dc in the last sc, ch 1 and turn.

Row 3: Sc in the top of the dc, * ch 4, sc in the top of the 3-ch, ch 3, 2 dc worked back in the sc just formed, sc around the middle of the 4-ch, rep from *, ending row with sc in the turning ch, ch 5 and turn.

Row 4: *sc around the 4-ch, ch 4, sc in the top of the 3-ch, ch 3, work 2 dc back in the base of the sc, rep from *, ending row with dc in the last sc, ch 1 and turn.

Row 5: Sc in the dc, * ch 4, sc in the top of the 3-ch, ch 3, work 2 dc back in the sc just formed, sc around the middle of the 4-ch, rep from *, ending row with sc in the turning ch.

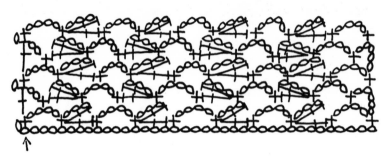

130.   Chain multiples of 3 plus 2.

Row 1: Sc in the 2nd ch and in each ch all across the row, ch 1 and turn.

Row 2: Sc in the 1st sc and in each sc all across the row, ch 1 and turn.

Row 3: Sc in the 1st sc and in each sc all across the row, ch 1 and turn.

Row 4: Sc in the 1st sc and in each sc all across the row, ch 4 and turn.

Row 5: Dc in the 4th sc, ch 2 and dc in the same sc, * dc in the 3rd sc, ch 2 and dc in the same sc, rep from *, ending row with last set, ch 1 and dc in the last sc, ch 4 and turn.

Row 6: Sk 1st dc, * dc in the 2-ch, ch 2 and dc in the same 2-ch, rep from *, ending row with last set, 1 ch and dc in the turning ch, ch 4 and turn.

Row 7–8: Same as row 6, ch 1 and turn.

Row 9: Sc in dc, sc in 1-ch, * sc in dc, 1 sc in the middle of the 2-ch, sc in the dc, rep from *, ending row with 2 sc in the turning ch, ch 1 and turn.

Rows 10–12: Sc in each sc all across the row, ch 1 and turn.

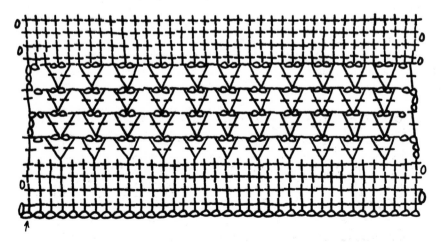

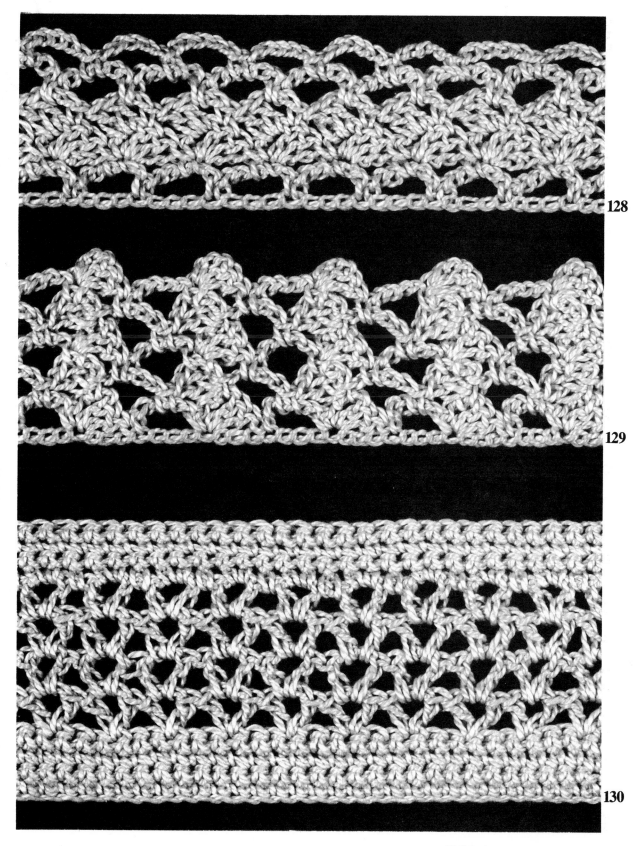

128

129

130

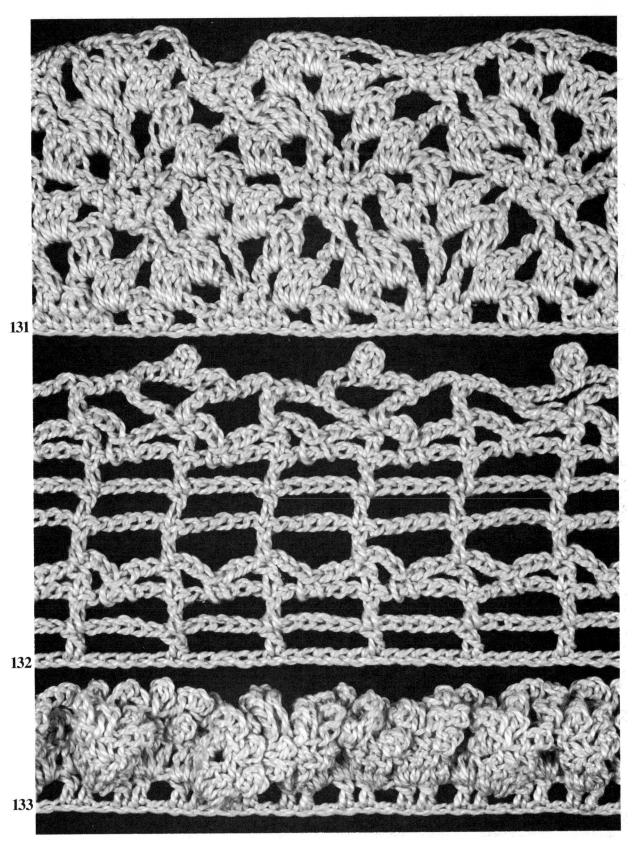

131

132

133

131. Chain multiples of 10 plus 2.

Row 1: Sc in the 2nd ch, sc in each of the next 2 chs, *ch 3 and work 3 dc in the 3rd ch, ch 3 and sc in the 3rd ch, sc in each of the next 4 chs, and rep from *, ending row with sc in each of the last 3 chs, ch 1 and turn.

Row 2: Sc in the 1st and next sc, *ch 3 and work 3 dc in the last of the 3-ch, ch 3 and work another 3 dc in the next 3-ch, ch 3 and sc in the 2nd sc, sc in each of the next 2 sc, rep from *, ending row with sc in each of the last 2 sc, ch 6 and turn.

Row 3: *work 3 dc in the last of the 3-ch, ch 3 and dc in the 3-ch, ch 3 and work 3 dc in the beginning of the next 3-ch, ch 3 and dc in the 2nd sc, ch 3 and rep from *, ending row with dc in the last sc, ch 6 and turn.

Row 4: *work 3 dc in the end of the 3-ch, ch 3 and sc in the last of the 3-ch, sc in the next dc, sc in the beginning of the 3-ch, ch 3 and work 3 dc in the beginning of the 3-ch, ch 1 and rep from *, ending row with 3 dc, ch 1 and trc in the turning ch, ch 3 and turn.

Row 5: Dc in the trc, *ch 3 and sc in the last of the 3-ch, sc in each of the next 3 sc, sc in the beginning of the next 3-ch, ch 3 and work 3 dc in the 1-ch, rep from *, ending row with 2 dc in the turning ch, ch 4 and turn.

Row 6: Work 3 dc in the beginning of the 3-ch, *ch 3 and sc in the 2nd sc, sc in each of the next 2 sc, ch 3 and work 3 dc towards the end of the 3-ch, ch 3 and work 3 dc in the beginning of the next 3-ch, rep from *, ending row with dc in the turning ch, ch 5 and turn.

Row 7: *work 3 dc in the beginning of the next 3-ch, ch 3 and dc in the 2nd sc, ch 3 and work 3 dc towards the end of the next 3-ch, ch 3 and dc in the 3-ch, ch 3 and rep from *, ending row with 2 ch and dc in the turning ch, ch 1 and turn.

Row 8: Sc in the dc and sc in the beginning of the 2-ch, *ch 3 and work 3 dc in the beginning of the 3-ch, ch 1 and work another 3 dc towards the end of the next 3-ch, ch 3 and sc in the 3-ch, sc in the dc and sc in the next 3-ch, rep from *, ending row with 2 sc in the turning ch, ch 1 and turn.

Row 9: Sc in each of the 1st 2 sc, sc in the beginning of the 3-ch, *ch 3 and work 3 dc in the 1-ch, ch 3 and work sc towards the end of the next 3-ch, sc in each of the next 3 sc, sc in the beginning of the next 3-ch, rep from *, ending row with last sc.

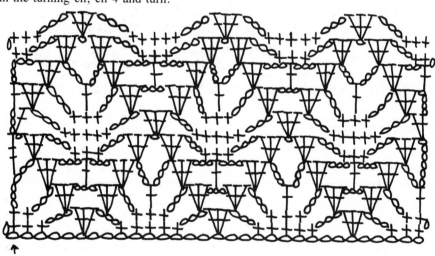

132. Chain multiples of 12 plus 9.

Row 1: Dc in the 15th ch, * ch 5 and dc in the 6th ch, rep from *, ending row with dc in the last set, ch 8 and turn.

Row 2: Sk 1st dc, * dc in the next dc and ch 5, rep from *, ending row with dc in the turning ch, ch 6 and turn.

Row 3: *sc around the middle of the 5-ch, ch 3 and dc in the next dc, ch 3 and rep from *, ending row with dc in the turning ch, ch 8 and turn.

Row 4: Sk 1st dc, * dc in the next dc, ch 5, rep from *, ending row with dc in the turning ch, ch 8 and turn.

Row 5: Sk 1st dc, * dc in the next dc and ch 5, rep from *, ending row with dc in the turning ch, ch 8 and turn.

Row 6: Sk 1st dc, * dc in the next dc and ch 5, rep from *, ending row with dc in the turning ch, ch 6 and turn.

Row 7: *sc around the 5-ch, ch 3 and dc in the next dc, ch 3 and rep from *, ending row with dc in the turning ch, ch 6 and turn.

Row 8: Sk 1st dc, *dc in the next dc, ch 3, work 5-ch picot, ch 3 and dc in the same dc, ch 3 and dc in the next dc, ch 3 and rep from *, ending row with dc in the turning ch.

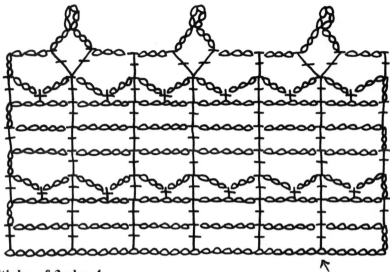

133.   Chain multiples of 3 plus 4.

Row 1: Dc in the 5th ch, *ch 1 and dc in the 2nd ch, dc in the next ch, rep from *, ch 3 and turn.

Row 2: Work 2 dc in the 1st dc, *work 3 dc in the next ch, ch 3 and work 3 dc in the next dc, rep from *, ending row with 2 dc in the turning ch, ch 1 and turn.

Row 3: Sc in the 1st dc, ch 3 and sc in the next dc, *sc in the next dc, ch 3 and sc in the 2nd dc, ch 5 and sc in the next dc, ch 3 and sc in the 2nd dc, rep from *, ending row with sc in the turning ch.

134.   Chain multiples of 16 plus 4.

Row 1: Sc in the 2nd ch and in each of the next 2 chs, * ch 7 and trc in the 6th ch, ch 7 and sc in the 6th ch, sc in each of the next 4 chs, rep from *, ending row with sc in each of the last 3 chs, ch 1 and turn.

Row 2: Sc in the 1st and the next sc, *ch 7 and sc in the last of the next 7-ch, sc in the trc, sc in the beginning of the next 7-ch, ch 7 and sc in the 2nd sc, and sc in each of the next 2 sc, rep from *, ending row with sc in each of the last 2 sc, ch 11 and turn.

Row 3: * sc in the last of the next 7-ch, sc in each of the next 3 sc, sc in the beginning of the next 7-ch, ch 7 and trc in the 2nd sc, ch 7 and rep from *, ending row with trc in the last sc, ch 1 and turn.

Row 4: Sc in the trc, *sc in the beginning of the next 7-ch, ch 7 and sc in the 2nd sc, sc in each of the next 2 sc, ch 7 and sc in the last of the next 7-ch, sc in the trc, and rep from *, ending row with 2 sc in the turning ch, ch 1 and turn.

Row 5: Sc in each of the next 2 sc, *sc in the beginning of the 7-ch, ch 7 and trc in the 2nd sc, ch 7 and sc in the end of the 7-ch, sc in each of the next 3 sc, rep from *, ending row with sc in the end of the 7-ch, and sc in each of the last 2 sc, ch 1 and turn.

Row 6: Sc in each of the 1st 2 sc, *ch 7 and sc in the end of the 7-ch, sc in the trc, sc in the beginning of the next 7-ch, ch 7 and sc in the 2nd sc, sc in each of the next 2 sc, rep from *, ending row with sc in each of the last 2 sc, ch 3 and turn.

Row 7: Work 2 dc in the 2nd sc, * ch 7 and sc in the 2nd sc, ch 7 and work 2 dc in the next sc, work 2 dc in the next sc and 2 dc in the next sc, rep from *, ending row with 2 dc in the next to the last sc and 1 dc in the last sc, ch 3 and turn.

Row 8: * work 4-ch picot, dc in the next dc and work another 4-ch picot, dc in the next dc, ch 6 and sc in the next sc, ch 6 and dc in the next dc, work 4-ch picot, and dc in the next dc, work another 4-ch picot and dc in the next dc, work another 4-ch picot, dc in the next dc, rep from *, ending row with dc, picot, dc, picot, dc in the turning ch.

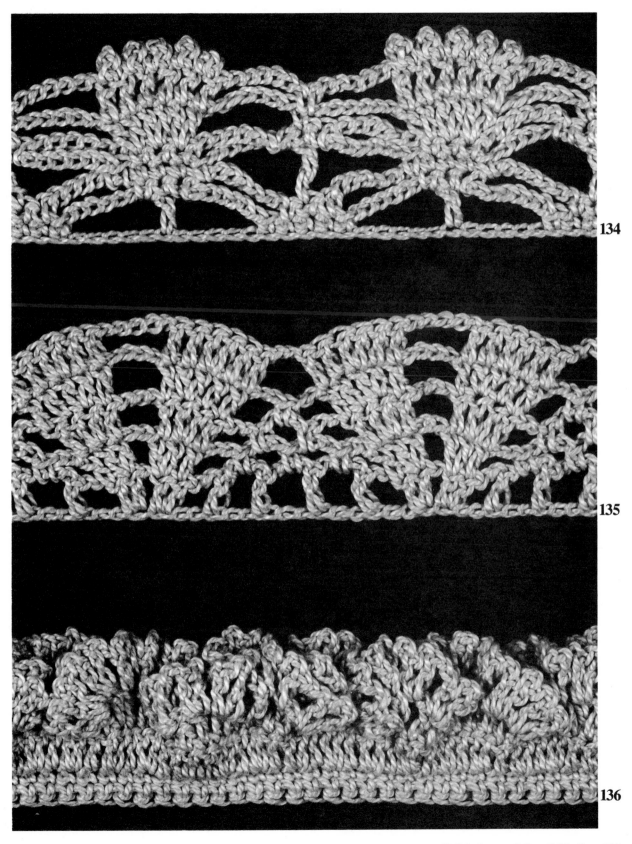

134

135

136

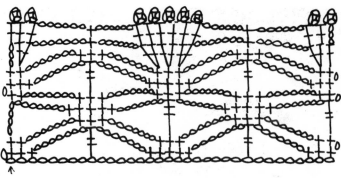

135. Chain multiples of 16 plus 6.

Row 1: Dc in the 8th ch, *ch 3 and dc in the 3rd ch, ch 2, work 2 dc in the 3rd ch, ch 1 and 2 dc in the next ch, ch 2 and dc in the 3rd ch, ch 3 and dc in the 3rd ch, ch 3 and dc in the 3rd ch, rep from *, ending row with dc in the last ch, ch 1 and turn.

Row 2: Sc in the 1st dc, ch 3, sc in the 2nd 3-ch, *ch 2, dc in the 2nd dc, work 2 dc in the next dc, ch 2, work 2 dc in the next dc, dc in the next dc, ch 2 and sc in the next 3-ch, ch 3 and sc in the next 3-ch, ch 3 and sc in the next 3-ch, rep from *, ending row with sc in the turning ch, ch 6 and turn.

Row 3: *sc around the 3-ch, ch 2, and 1 dc in the next dc, 2 dc in the next dc, 1 dc in the next dc, ch 3 and dc in the next dc, work 2 dc in the next dc, dc in the next dc, ch 2 and sc around the 3-ch, ch 3 and rep from *, ending row with sc, ch 3 and dc in the last sc, ch 1 and turn.

Row 4: Sc in the dc, ch 3, *dc in each of the next 2 dc, work 2 dc in the next dc, dc in the next dc, ch 4, dc in the next dc, work 2 dc in the next dc and dc in each of the next 2 dc, ch 2 and sc in the middle of the 3-ch, ch 2 and rep from *, ending row with 3 chs and 1 sc in the turning ch, ch 6 and turn.

Row 5: *dc in each of the next 2 dc, 2 dc in the next dc, dc in each of the next 2 dc, ch 5, dc in each of the next 2 dc, 2 dc in the next dc, 1 dc in each of the next 2 dc, ch 2 and rep from *, ending row with last set, 2 chs and dc in the last sc.

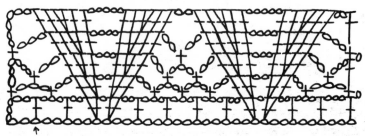

136. Chain multiples of 2 plus 2.

Row 1: Sc in the 2nd ch and in each ch all across the row, ch 3 and turn.

Row 2: 2 dc in the 2nd sc, *dc in the next sc, 2 dc in the next sc, rep from *, ending row with dc in the turning ch, ch 3 and turn.

Row 3: Sk 1st dc, *dc in dc and ch 1, rep from *, ending row with dc in the turning ch, ch 4 and turn.

Row 4: Sk 1st dc, *dc in dc, ch 2, dc in same dc, ch 2, and rep from *, ending row with last set and dc in the turning ch, break thread.

Bottom Row: Attach thread, sc in 2nd ch and in each ch all across the row.

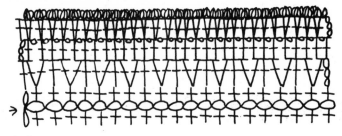

•8•
Staggered Squares

137. Chain multiples of 5 plus 3.

Row 1: 1 hdc in the 3rd ch and in each ch all across the row, ch 6 and turn.
Row 2: *work 3 dc in the 1st 3-ch of the 6-ch just made at a perpendicular angle, work hdc in the 4th hdc and 1 hdc in the next hdc, sl st in next hdc rep from *, ending row with last hdc in the hdc.

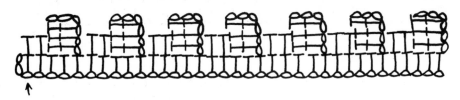

138. Chain multiples of 6 plus 5.

Row 1: Dc in the 6th ch, *ch 1 and dc in the 2nd ch, rep from *, ending row with dc in the last ch, ch 4 and turn.
Row 2: Sk 1st dc, *dc in next dc and ch 1, rep from *, ending row with dc in the turning ch, ch 3 and turn.

Row 3: * dc in the 2nd 1-ch, ch 3, 3 dc worked perpendicular to the dc just formed, dc in 2nd dc, rep from *, ending row with dc in the turning ch.

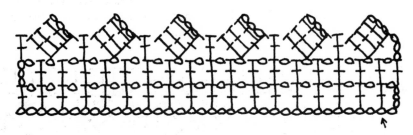

139. Chain multiples of 6 plus 7.

Row 1: Trc in the 10th ch, * ch 2 and trc in the 3rd ch, rep from *, ending row with last trc, ch 6 and turn.
Row 2: Work 3 trc back around the 6-ch, *ch 1, work 1 trc in the beginning of the 3rd 2-ch, ch 4, work 4 trc back around the trc at a perpendicular angle, rep from *, ending row with last set.

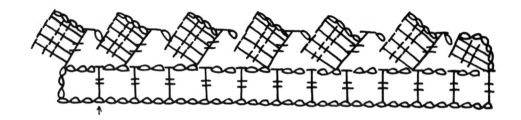

140. Chain multiples of 5 plus 2.

Row 1: Sc in the 2nd ch and in each ch all across the row, ch 1 and turn.

Row 2: Sc in the 1st sc, * ch 5 and work sc in the 5th sc, ch 5, and sc in the same sc, rep from *, ending row with sc in the last sc, ch 3 and turn.

Row 3: *work dc in the middle of the 5-ch, ch 3, work 5 dc back around the 1st dc made at a perpendicular angle,

rep from *, ending row with last set and sc in the last sc, ch 5 and turn.

Row 4: *work 1 sc in the top of the 3-ch, ch 3, work another sc in the same place, ch 3, work another sc in the same place, ch 3 and work another sc in the same place, ch 3, rep from *, ending row with last set, ch 2 and dc in the turning ch.

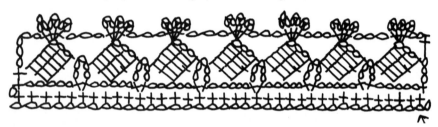

141. Chain multiples of 15 plus 4.

Row 1: Dc in the 5th ch and in each ch all across the row, ch 3 and turn.

Row 2: Dc in the 2nd dc, *trc in the 3rd dc, ch 3, work 3 dc back perpendicular around the trc just formed, dc in the 3rd dc, dc in the next dc, rep from *, ending row with dc in the last dc and 1 dc in the turning ch, ch 3 and turn.

Row 3: Dc in the 2nd dc, *ch 3, sc in the top of the 3-ch, 2 dc in the next dc, 2 dc in the next dc, ch 3, sc in top of 3-ch, dc in each of next 2 dc, rep from *, ending row with last dc, and dc in the turning ch, ch 3 and turn.

Row 4: Dc in the 2nd dc, *work trc in the 1st of the 1-ch, ch 3, work 3 dc perpendicular around the trc, finish 2 dc together worked in the next 2 dc, finish 2 dc together in

the next 2 dc, work trc in the 1st of the 3-ch, ch 3, work 3 dc perpendicular around the trc, dc in each of the next 2 dc, rep from *, ending row with last dc and dc in the turning ch, ch 3 and turn.

Row 5: Dc in 2nd dc, *ch 3, sc in the top of the 3-ch, ch 3, dc in the top of the 2 dc finished together, 1 dc in the top of the next 2 dc finished together, rep from *, ending row with last dc and dc in the turning ch, ch 3 and turn.

Row 6: Dc in 2nd dc, * 2 dc around the 3-ch, dc in the sc, 2 dc around the next 2-ch, dc in each of the next 2 dc, rep from *, ending row with dc in the last dc and 1 dc in the turning ch.

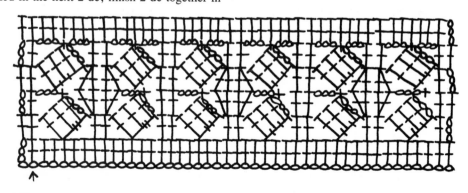

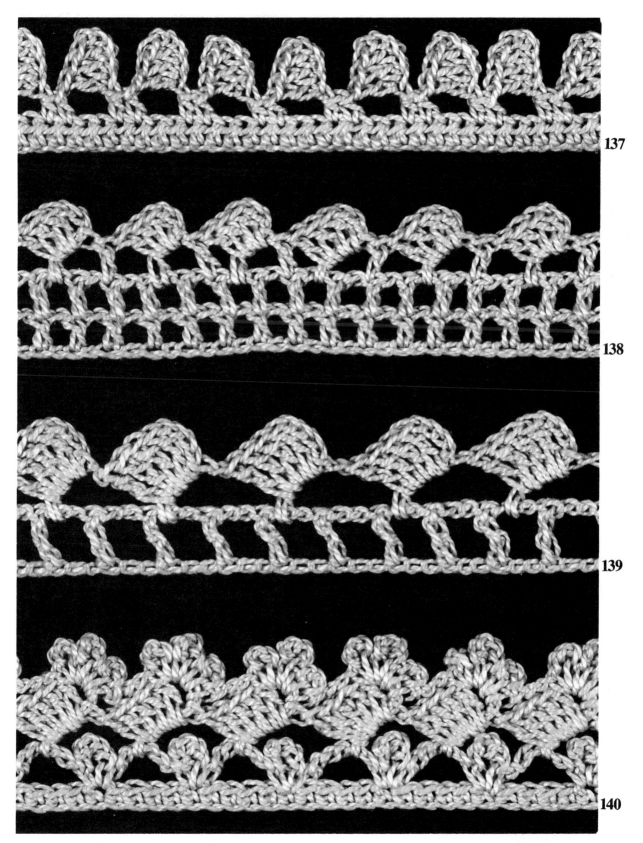

137

138

139

140

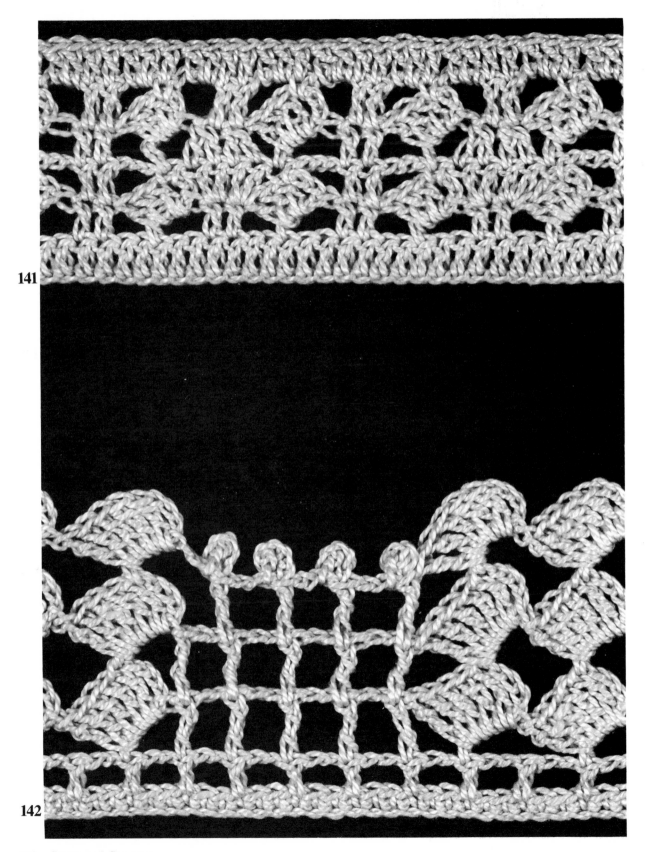

141

142

110   **Staggered Squares**

142.   Chain multiples of 30 plus 15.

Row 1: Sc in the 2nd ch and in each ch all across the row, ch 5 and turn.

Row 2: Dc in the 4th sc, *ch 2 and dc in the 3rd sc, rep from *, ending row with dc in the last sc, break off yarn and go back to the other side.

Row 3: Attach thread, ch 6, trc in the dc, ch 2, trc in next dc, ch 2, trc in next dc, ch 2, trc in next dc, *work another trc in the next dc, ch 4, work 5 trc around the trc just made at a perpendicular angle, work trc in the 2nd dc, ch 4, work 5 trc at a perpendicular angle around the trc just formed, trc in the 2nd dc, ch 4, work 5 trc around the trc just formed, at a perpendicular angle, trc in next dc and ch 2 4 times, trc in last dc, break off thread.

Row 4: Attach thread, ch 6, trc in the trc and ch 2 3 times, trc in the next trc, trc in the top of the 4-ch, ch 4, work 5 trc around the trc at a perpendicular angle, work trc in the top of the next 4-ch, ch 4, work 5 trc at a perpendicular angle around the last trc formed, work trc in the next 4-ch, ch 4, work 5 trc around the last trc at a perpendicular angle, trc in the next trc and 2 chs, 4 times, trc in the last trc, break thread.

Row 5: Attach thread, ch 4, work 5-ch picot, ch 2, trc in next trc, work 5-ch picot with 2 chs 3 times, trc in next trc, * trc in the top of the next 4-ch, ch 4, work 5 trc around the last trc at a perpendicular angle, work trc in the top of the next 4-ch, ch 4, work 5 trc around the last trc at perpendicular angles, work trc in the next 4-ch, ch 4, work 5 trc around the last trc at a perpendicular angle, trc in the next trc, work 5-ch picot, ch 2 4 times in each of the next trc, trc in the last trc.

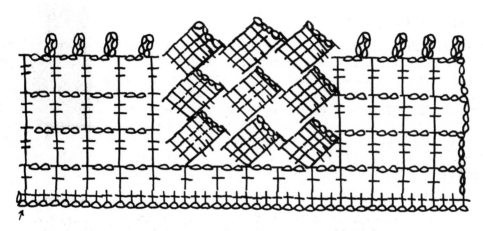

◆9◆
Dropped Stitch and Crossed Stitch

143. Chain multiples of 10 plus 2.

Row 1: Sc in the 2nd ch, ch 2, sc in the 3rd ch, *sc in each of next 4 chs, ch 5, sc in 6th ch, rep from *, ending row with 2 chs and 1 sc in the last ch, ch 1 and turn.

Row 2: Sc in the 1st sc, ch 2, *sc in each of the next 5 sc, ch 5, rep from *, ending row with sc in the last sc, ch 1 and turn.

Row 3: Sc in the 1st sc, sc in each of the next 2-ch, *ch 5, sc in each of the next 2 chs, sl st around the 2 rows of chs below, sc in each of the next 2 chs, rep from *, ending row with sc in the last sc, ch 1 and turn.

Row 4: Sc in each of the 1st 3 sc, *ch 5, sc in each of the 2 sc, the sl st and the 2 sc, rep from *, ending row with sc in the last sc, ch 1 and turn.

Row 5: Sc in the 1st sc, ch 2, sc in each of the 2 chs, sl st around the 2 rows below, sc in each of the next 2 chs, ch 5, rep from *, ending row with sc in the last sc, ch 1 and turn.

Row 6: Sc in the sc, ch 2, *sc in each sc and sc, sl st, ch 5 and rep from *, ending row with last sc.

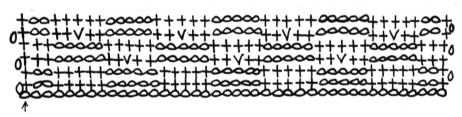

144. Chain multiples of 8 plus 2.

Row 1: Sc in the 2nd ch and each of the next 5 chs, *ch 2, sc in the 3rd ch and each of the next 5 chs, rep from *, ending row with sc in each of the last 6 chs, ch 1 and turn.

Row 2: *sc in each of the 6 sc, and ch 2, rep from *, ending row with 6 sc, ch 1 and turn.

Row 3: *sc in each of the 6 sc, sl st around the 3 rows of chs below, work 4-ch picot and rep from *, ending row with last 6 sc.

145.   Chain multiples of 11 plus 7.

Row 1: Sc in the 10th ch, * 1 sc in each of the next 4 chs, ch 9, sc in the 7th ch, rep from *, ending row with 5 sc, ch 3, 1 dc in the 3rd and final ch, ch 1 and turn.
Row 2: 1 sc in the dc, ch 5, *1 sc in the 2nd sc, and sc in the next 2 sc, ch 10, rep from *, ending row with 3 sc, 5 chs and 1 sc in the turning ch, ch 6 and turn.
Row 3: *1 dc in the middle of the 3 sc, ch 10, rep from *, ending row with 1 sc in the last sc, ch 1 and turn.

Row 4: *ch 15, sl st around 3 rows of chs below, rep from *, ending row with 1 sc in the turning ch, ch 1 and turn.
Row 5: * 3 sc in the 15-ch, work 3-ch picot, 4 sc in the same 15-ch, 3-ch picot, 4 sc in the same 15-ch, work 3-ch picot, 3 sc in the same 15-ch, rep from *, ending row after the last set.

146.   Chain multiples of 6 plus 2.

Row 1: Sc in the 2nd ch, *ch 7, sc in the 6th ch, rep from *, ending row with sc in the last ch, ch 8 and turn.
Row 2: Sk 1st sc, *dc in the next sc, ch 5, rep from *, ending row with dc in the last sc, ch 6 and turn.

Row 3: *sc around the 2 rows of chs below, ch 3, dc in the next dc, ch 3, rep from *, ending row with dc in the turning ch.

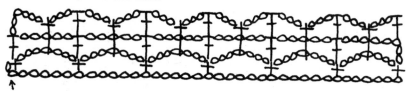

147.   Chain multiples of 9 plus 4.

Row 1: Dc in the 5th ch and dc in each of the next 2 chs, * ch 5, dc in the 6th ch and dc in each of the following 3 chs, rep from *, ending row with 4 dc, ch 3 and turn.
Row 2: Dc in the 2nd dc and the 2 dc following that, *ch 3, sc around the 2 rows of chs below, ch 3, dc in each of

the next 4 dc, rep from *, ending row with dc in the turning ch, ch 6 and turn.
Row 3: Dc in the 3rd and next dc, *dc in the next dc and the dc after that, ch 5, dc in the next dc and the dc after that, rep from *, ending row with 2 dc, ch 4 and dc in the turning ch.

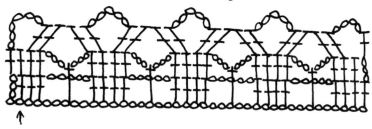

148.   Chain multiples of 14 plus 7.

Row 1: 2 dc in the 4th ch, *dc in the 3rd ch, ch 7, dc in the 8th ch, 5 dc in the 3rd ch, rep from *, ending row with 3 dc in the 3rd and last ch, ch 3 and turn.
Row 2: 2 dc in the 1st dc, dc in the 3rd dc, * ch 7, dc in next dc, work 5 dc in the 3rd dc, dc in 3rd dc, rep from *,

ending row with 3 dc in the turning ch, ch 3 and turn.
Row 3: 2 dc in the 1st dc, *dc in the 3rd dc, ch 3, sc worked around the 3 rows of chs below, ch 3, dc in the next dc, work 5 dc in the 3rd dc, rep from *, ending row with 3 dc in the turning ch.

Dropped Stitch and Crossed Stitch   113

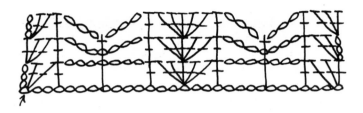

149. Chain multiples of 6 plus 4.

Row 1: Dc in the 4th ch and in each ch all across the row, ch 3 and turn.

Row 2: Dc in the 2nd dc and dc in each dc all across the row, dc in the turning ch, ch 6 and turn.

Row 3: Work 2 dc in the 5th dc, *ch 1, and 2 dc in the dc just used, ch 6 and work 2 dc in the 6th dc, rep from *, ending row with last set, ch 3 and dc in the turning ch, ch 6 and turn.

Row 4: *2 dc in the 1-ch, ch 1 and 2 dc in the same 1-ch, ch 4 and rep from *, ending row with last set, ch 2 and dc in the turning ch, ch 5 and turn.

Row 5: Same as row 4, ch 6.

Row 6: *dc around the 3 rows of chs below, ch 3, work 2 dc in the 1-ch, ch 1 and 2 dc in the same 1-ch, ch 3 and rep from *, ending row with last set, ch 2 and dc in the turning ch, ch 1 and turn.

Row 7: Sc in the dc, ch 3, *sc in the 1-ch, ch 5 and rep from *, ending row with sc in the last 1-ch, ch 3 and sc in the turning ch, ch 3 and turn.

Row 8: Dc in each ch and in each sc all across the row, ending with dc in the last sc, ch 3 and turn.

Row 9: Dc in the 2nd dc and dc in each dc all across the row.

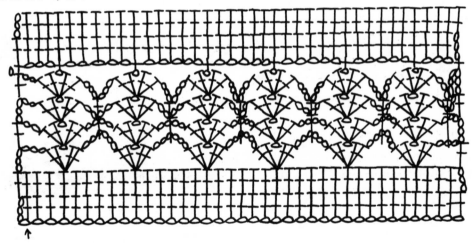

150. Chain multiples of 4 plus 2.

Row 1: Sc in the 2nd ch and in each ch all across the row, ch 3 and turn.

Row 2: Dc in the 2nd sc, *dc in the next sc, dc backwards in the sc before 2nd dc, ch 2, dc in the 3rd sc, rep from *, ending row with last set, 2 ch and dc in the last sc, ch 1 and turn.

Row 3: Sc in each dc and in each ch all across the row.

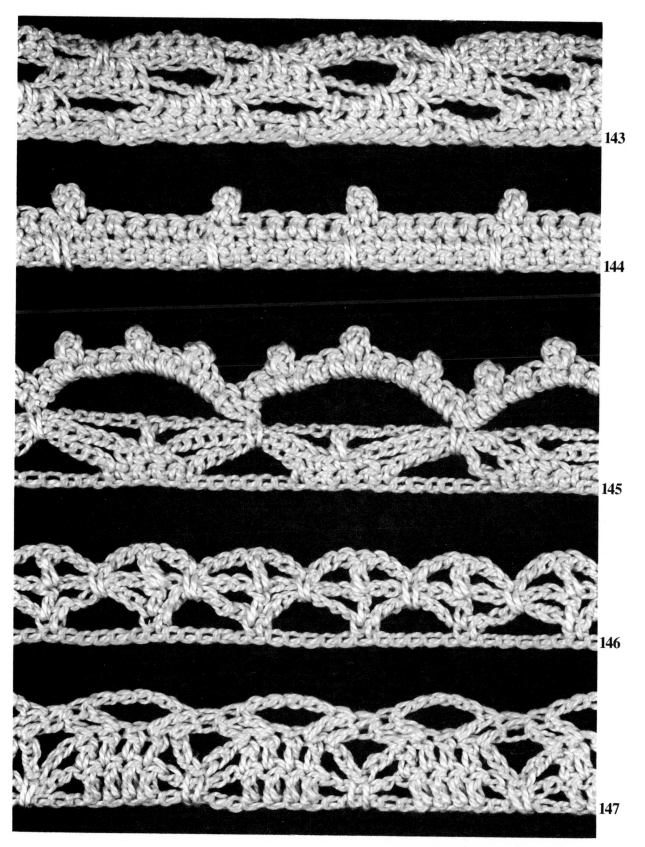

143

144

145

146

147

Dropped Stitch and Crossed Stitch   115

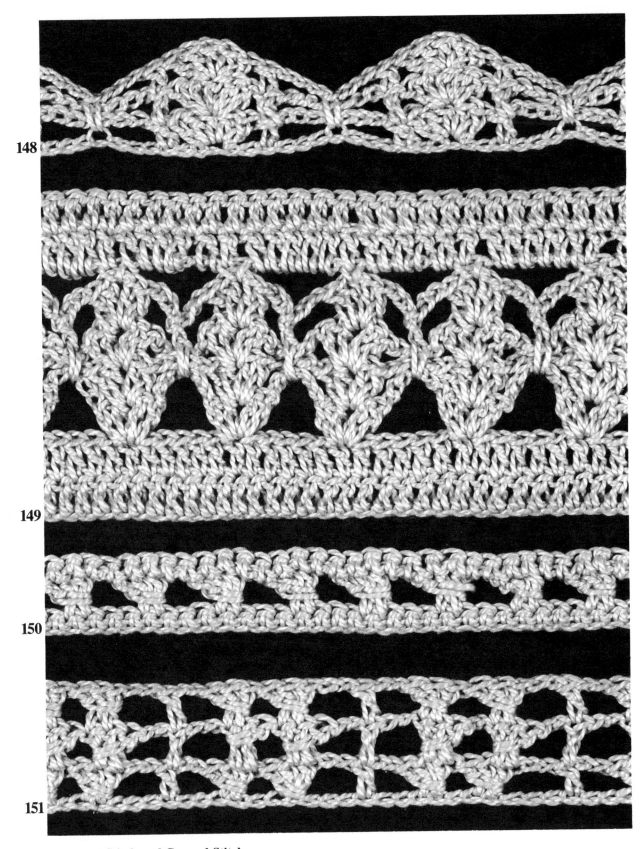

148

149

150

151

116   Dropped Stitch and Crossed Stitch

151. Chain multiples of 11 plus 4.

Row 1: Dc in the 6th ch, *dc in the next ch, dc backwards in the ch before the 1st dc, dc in the 2nd ch, dc in the ch after that, dc backwards in the ch before the dc, ch 2, dc in the 3rd ch, ch 2, dc in the 4th ch, rep from *, ending row with last set, ch 1 and dc in the 2nd ch, ch 4 and turn.

Row 2: 1 dc in the 2nd dc, *ch 2, dc in the 2nd dc, dc in the next dc, dc backwards in the dc before these 2, dc in the 2nd dc, dc in the next dc, dc backwards in the dc before these 2, ch 2, dc in the next dc, rep from *, ending row with dc in the turning ch, ch 3 and turn.

Row 3: Sk 1st dc, *dc in the 2nd dc, dc in the next dc, dc backwards in the dc before the 2 just made, dc in the 2nd dc, dc in the next dc, dc backwards before the 2 dc just made, ch 2, dc in the next dc, ch 2, rep from *, ending row with dc in the turning ch.

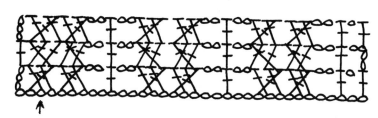

·10·
Simple Filet and Shells in Grid

152. Chain multiples of 8 plus 5.

Row 1: Dc in the 7th ch, *ch 1 and dc in the 2nd ch, rep from *, ending row with last dc, ch 4 and turn.

Row 2: Sk 1st dc, *dc in next dc, ch 1, dc in next dc, dc in next 1-ch, dc in next dc, dc in next 1-ch, dc in next dc, ch 1, rep from *, ending row with dc in the turning ch, ch 4 and turn.

Row 3: Sk 1st dc, *dc in next dc, ch 1, dc in each of next 5 dc, ch 1, rep from *, ending row with dc in turning ch, ch 4 and turn.

Row 4: Sk 1st dc, dc in next dc, ch 1, dc in next dc, ch 1, dc in 2nd dc, ch 1, dc in 2nd dc, ch 1, rep from *, ending row with dc in the turning ch.

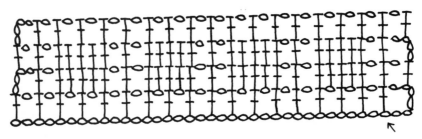

153. Chain multiples of 10 plus 6.

Row 1: Work 2 dc in the 6th ch, * work 2 dc in the 6th ch, ch 2, dc in the ch just used, ch 1 and dc in the 2nd ch, ch 1 and dc in the 2nd ch, ch 2, 2 dc in the same ch, rep from *, ending row with 2 dc, 2 chs and 1 dc in the same ch, ch 5 and turn.

Row 2: Work 2 dc in the 1st dc, * work 2 dc in the 5th dc, ch 2, dc in the dc just used, ch 1, dc in the next dc, ch 1, dc in the next dc, ch 2, 2 dc in the dc just used, rep from *, ending row with 2 dc, 2 chs and 1 dc in the turning ch, ch 5 and turn.

Row 3: 2 dc in the 1st dc, *2 dc in the 5th dc, ch 2, dc in the dc just used, ch 1 and dc in the next dc, ch 1 and dc in the next dc, ch 2, 2 dc in the dc just used, rep from *, ending row with 2 dc, 2 chs and 1 dc in the same turning ch.

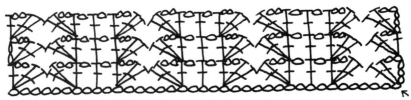

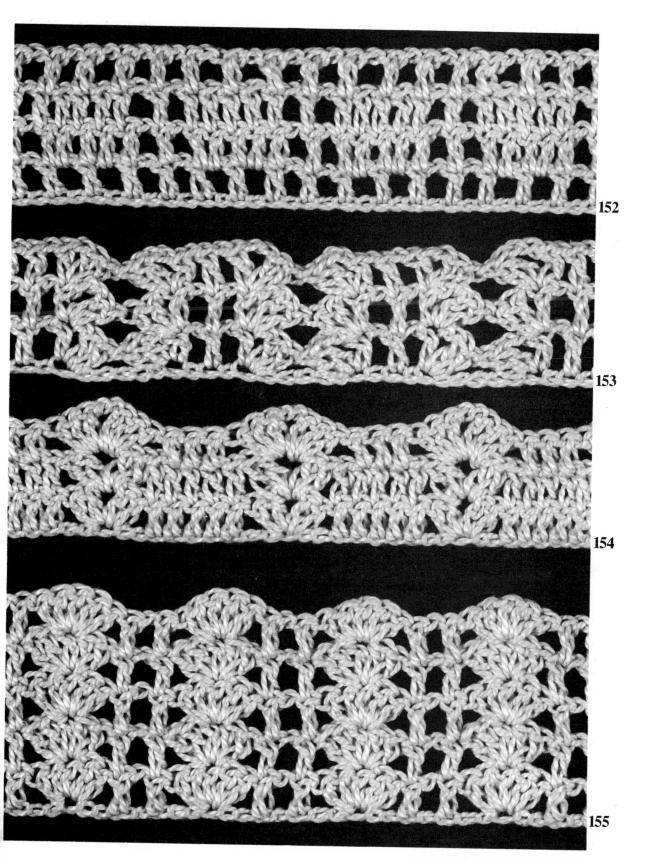

152

153

154

155

Simple Filet and Shells in Grid   119

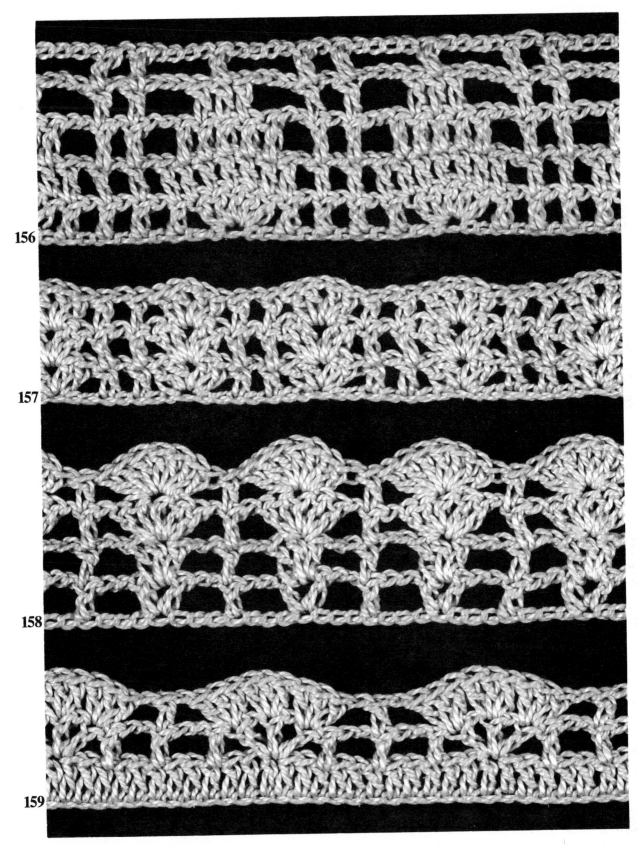

156

157

158

159

120   Simple Filet and Shells in Grid

154. Chain multiples of 10 plus 6.

Row 1: 1 dc in the 5th ch, dc in the next ch, *2 dc in the 3rd ch, ch 2, 2 dc in the same ch, dc in the 3rd ch and dc in each of the next 4 chs, rep from *, ending row with dc in each of the last 3 chs, ch 3 and turn.

Row 2: Dc in the 2nd dc and the next dc, *2 dc in the 2-ch, ch 2, 2 dc in the same 2-ch, dc in each of the next 5 dc, rep from *, ending row with dc in the turning ch, ch 3 and turn.

Row 3: Dc in the 2nd dc, *3 dc in the 2-ch, ch 2, 3 dc in the same 2-ch, sk last 2 dc of the V-stitch below, dc in the 2nd dc and dc in each of the next 2 dc, rep from *, ending row with dc in the turning ch.

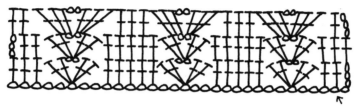

155. Chain multiples of 8 plus 7.

Row 1: Dc in the 7th ch, *work 5 dc in the 3rd ch, dc in the 3rd ch, ch 1 and dc in the 2nd ch, rep from *, ending row with dc, ch, and dc in the last ch, ch 4 and turn.

Row 2: Dc in the 2nd dc, *work 5 dc in the 3rd dc, dc in the 3rd dc, ch 1, dc in the next dc, rep from *, ending row with dc in the last dc, ch 1 and dc in the turning ch, ch 4 and turn.

Rows 3–5: Same as row 2.

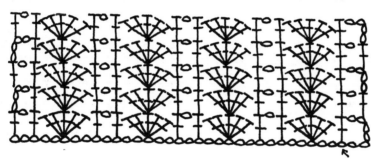

156. Chain multiples of 12 plus 5.

Row 1: Dc in the 7th ch, *work 5 dc in the 3rd ch, dc in the 3rd ch, ch 1 and dc in the 2nd ch, ch 1 and dc in the 2nd ch, ch 1 and dc in the 2nd ch, rep from *, ending row with 1 ch and 1 dc in the last ch, ch 5 and turn.

Row 2: Sk 1st dc, *dc in the next 7 dc, ch 1 and dc in the next dc 2 times, ch 1 and rep from *, ending row with 1 ch and 1 dc in the turning ch, ch 5 and turn.

Row 3: Sk 1st dc, *dc in the 2nd dc and dc in the next 4 dc, ch 2, dc in the 2nd dc, ch 1 and dc in the next dc, ch 2 and rep from *, ending row with 2 chs and 1 dc in the turning ch, ch 6 and turn.

Row 4: Sk 1st dc, *dc in the 2nd dc and the next 2 dc, ch 3 and dc in the 2nd dc, ch 1 and dc in the next dc, ch 3, rep from *, ending row with dc in the turning ch, ch 7 and turn.

Row 5: Sk 1st dc, *dc in the 2nd dc, ch 4, dc in the 2nd dc and ch 1, dc in the next dc and ch 4, rep from *, ending row with dc in the turning ch.

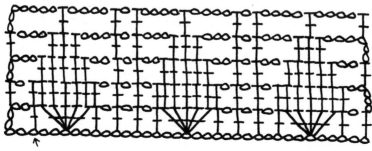

Simple Filet and Shells in Grid 121

157. Chain multiples of 8 plus 5.

Row 1: Dc in the 5th ch, *2 dc in the 3rd ch, ch 1, 2 dc in the same ch, dc in the 3rd ch, ch 1, dc in the 2nd ch, rep from *, ending row with 1 dc in each of the last 2 chs, ch 3 and turn.

Row 2: Sk 1st dc, dc in the next dc, *2 dc in the 1-ch, ch 1, 2 dc in the same 1-ch, dc in the 3rd dc, ch 1, dc in the next dc, rep from *, ending row with dc in the turning ch, ch 3 and turn.

Row 3: Sk 1st dc, dc in the next dc, *2 dc in the 1-ch, ch 1, 2 dc in the same 1-ch, dc in the 3rd dc, ch 1, dc in the next dc, rep from *, ending row with dc in the turning ch.

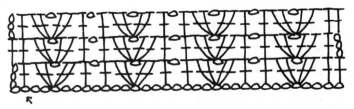

158. Chain multiples of 8 plus 4.

Row 1: Dc in the 4th ch, *ch 2, dc in the 4th ch, ch 2, dc in the 4th ch, ch 1, dc in the same ch, rep from *, ending row with last dc, ch 5 and turn.

Row 2: * work 3 dc in the 1-ch, ch 2, dc in the 2nd dc, ch 2, rep from *, ending row with 2 dc in the turning ch, ch 3 and turn.

Row 3: Work 2 dc in the 1st dc, *ch 1, dc in the 2nd dc, ch 1, work 5 dc in the 2nd dc, rep from *, ending row with dc in the turning ch, ch 3 and turn.

Row 4: Sk 1st dc, * work 7 dc in the 3rd dc, dc in the 3rd dc, rep from *, ending row with 4 dc in the turning ch.

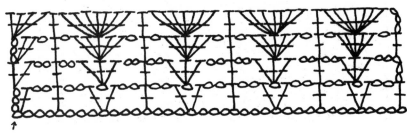

159. Chain multiples of 12 plus 4.

Row 1: Dc in the 5th ch and in each ch all across the row, ch 5 and turn.

Row 2: Dc in the 4th dc, *dc in the 3rd dc, ch 1, dc in the same dc, ch 1, dc in the same dc, dc in the 3rd dc, ch 2, dc in the 3rd dc, ch 2, dc in the 3rd dc, rep from *, ending row with dc in the turning ch, ch 4 and turn.

Row 3: Sk 1st dc, *3 dc in the 2nd dc, 3 dc in the next dc, 3 dc in the next dc, ch 1, dc in the 2nd dc, ch 1 and rep from *, ending row after last set with dc in the turning ch.

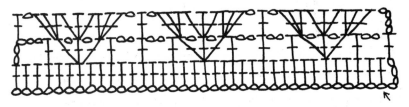

160. Chain multiples of 14 plus 4.

Row 1: 2 dc in the 4th ch, *dc in the 3rd ch, ch 7, dc in the 8th ch, 5 dc in the 3rd ch, rep from *, ending row with 3 dc in the 3rd and last ch, ch 3 and turn.

Row 2: 2 dc in the 1st dc, *dc in the 3rd dc, ch 7, dc in the next dc, 5 dc in the 3rd dc, rep from *, ending row with 3 dc in the turning ch, ch 3 and turn.

Row 3: 2 dc in the 1st dc, *dc in the 3rd dc, ch 7, dc in the next dc, 5 dc in the 3rd dc, rep from *, ending row with 3 dc in the turning ch.

122 Simple Filet and Shells in Grid

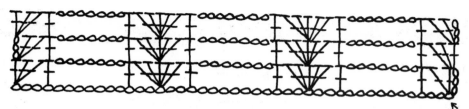

161. Chain multiples of 12 plus 6.

Row 1: Work 1 dc in the 9th ch, * 1 dc in the 3rd ch, ch 1, 1 dc in the ch just used, ch 1, 1 dc in the ch just used, dc in the 3rd ch, ch 2, dc in the 3rd ch, ch 2, dc in the 3rd ch, rep from *, ending row with dc in the last ch, ch 5 and turn.

Row 2: Dc in the 2nd dc, *dc in the 2nd dc, ch 1, dc in the dc just used, ch 1, dc in the dc just used, dc in the 2nd dc, ch 2, dc in the next dc, ch 2, dc in the next dc, rep from *, ending row with dc in the turning ch, ch 5 and turn.

Rows 3–4: Same as row 2, ch 1 and turn.

Row 5: Sc in the 1st dc, *ch 2, dc in the 2nd dc, ch 2, dc in the next 1-ch, ch 2, dc in the next dc, ch 2, dc in the next 1-ch, ch 2, dc in the next dc, ch 2, sc in the 2nd dc, rep from *, ending row with sc in the turning ch.

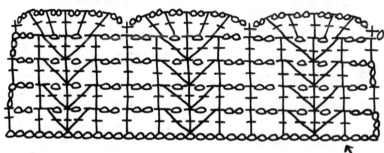

162. Chain multiples of 8 plus 6.

Row 1: Dc in the 8th ch, *ch 1 and dc in the 2nd ch, rep from *, ending row with dc in the last ch, ch 1 and turn.

Row 2: Sc in the 1st dc, *ch 5 and sc in the 2nd dc and rep from *, ending row with sc in the turning ch, ch 5 and turn.

Row 3: *sc around 5-ch, work 3 dc in the next sc, sc around the next 5-ch, ch 5 and rep from *, ending row with sc in the last 5-ch, ch 2 and dc in the last sc, ch 1 and turn.

Row 4: Sc in the dc, *work 3 dc in the next sc, sc around the middle of the 5-ch, work 3 dc in the next sc, sc in the 2nd dc, rep from *, ending row with sc in the turning ch, ch 4 and turn.

Row 5: Dc in the 1st sc, * sc in the 3rd dc, ch 5, and sc in the 2nd dc, work 3 dc in the sc, rep from *, ending row with 2 dc in the last sc, ch 1 and turn.

Row 6: Sc in the 1st dc, *ch 3 and sc in the 2nd dc, ch 3 and sc around the middle of the 5-ch, rep from *, ending row with sc in the turning ch, ch 4 and turn.

Row 7: *dc in the 3-ch, ch 1 and dc in the sc, ch 1, rep from *, ending row with dc in the last sc.

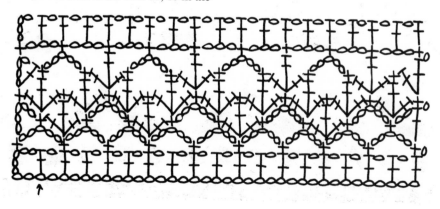

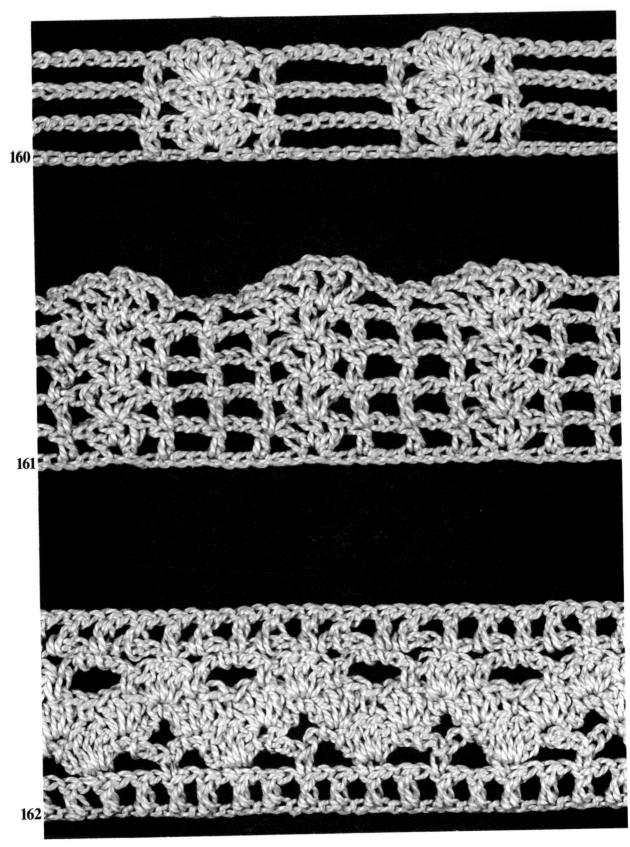

160

161

162

124   Simple Filet and Shells in Grid

163.   Chain multiples of 17 plus 6.

Row 1: Sc in the 2nd ch, *ch 5, sc in the 5th ch, dc in the 3rd ch, ch 1, dc in the ch just used, ch 1, dc in the ch just used, sc in the 3rd ch, dc in the 3rd ch, ch 1, dc in the ch just used, ch 1, dc in the ch just used, sc in the 3rd ch, rep from *, ending row with last sc, ch 5 and turn.

Row 2: *sc around the middle of the 5-ch, ch 5, sc in the 2nd dc, dc in the next sc, ch 1, dc in the sc just used, ch 1, dc in the sc just used, sc in the 2nd dc, ch 5, rep from *, ending row with sc in the last 5-ch, ch 2, dc in the last sc, ch 1 and turn.

Row 3: Sc in the 1st dc, *ch 5, sc around the middle of the 5-ch, dc in the next sc, ch 1, dc in the sc just used, ch 1, dc in the sc just used, sc in the 2nd dc, dc in the sc, ch 1, dc in the sc just used, ch 1, dc in the sc just used, sc around next 5-ch, rep from *, ending row with sc in the turning ch.

164.   Chain multiples of 12 plus 2.

Row 1: Sc in the 2nd ch and sc in each ch all across the row, ch 1 and turn.

Row 2: Sc in the 1st sc, *ch 5 and sc in the 4th sc, and rep from *, ending row with sc in the last sc, ch 4 and turn.

Row 3: Dc in the 1st sc, *sc in the middle of the next 5-ch, ch 5, sc around the middle of the next 5-ch, ch 5 and sc in the middle of the next 5-ch, dc in the next sc, ch 1 and dc in the same sc, ch 1 and dc in the same sc, rep from *, ending row with sc around the last 5-ch, ch 2 and trc in the last sc, ch 1 and turn.

Row 4: Sc in the trc, *dc in the sc, ch 1 and dc in the same sc, ch 1 and dc in the same sc, sc in the 2nd dc, dc in the next sc, ch 1 and dc in the same sc, ch 1 and dc in the same sc, sc in the middle of the next 5-ch, ch 5 and sc in the middle of the next 5-ch, rep from *, ending row with sc in the turning ch, ch 7 and turn.

Row 5: Sc in the 2nd dc, *dc in the next sc, ch 1 and dc in the same sc, ch 1 and dc in the same sc, sc in the middle of the next 5-ch, dc in the next sc, ch 1 and dc in the same sc, ch 1 and dc in the same sc, sc in the 2nd dc, ch 5 and sc in 2nd dc, rep from *, ending row with dc in the last sc, ch 1 and dc in the same sc, ch 1 and turn.

Row 6: Sc in the 1st dc, *ch 5 and sc around the middle of the 5-ch, ch 5 and sc in the 2nd dc, dc in the next sc, ch 1 and dc in the same sc, ch 1 and dc in the same sc, sc in the 2nd dc, rep from *, ending row with sc in the turning ch.

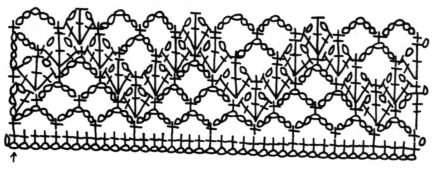

165.   Chain multiples of 10 plus 2.

Row 1: Sc in the 2nd ch, *ch 6 and sc in the 5th ch, rep from *, ending row with last sc, ch 3 and turn.

Row 2: *work 3 dc in the next 6-ch, ch 3 and work another 3 dc in the same 6-ch, ch 2 and sc in the next 6-ch, ch 2, rep from *, ending row with last set and dc in the last sc, ch 3 and turn.

Row 3: *3 dc in the 3-ch, ch 3 and work another 3 dc in the same 3-ch, ch 3, rep from *, ending row with last set and dc in the turning ch, ch 3 and turn.

Rows 4–7: Same as row 3.

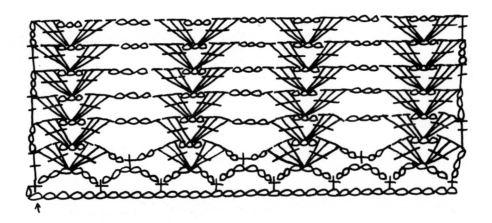

166. Chain multiples of 14 plus 8.

Row 1: Dc in the 7th ch, *ch 1, dc in the 2nd ch, rep from *, ending row with last dc, ch 1 and turn.

Row 2: Sc in the 1st dc, sc in the next 1-ch, * sc in the next dc, sc in the next 1-ch, ch 4, 2 dc in the 3rd 1-ch, ch 3, 2 dc in the 1-ch just used, ch 4, sc in 3rd 1-ch, rep from *, ending row with the 3 sc and 1 extra sc in the turning ch, ch 1 and turn.

Row 3: 1 sc in each of the 4 sc; 1 sc in the 1st of the 4-ch, ch 3, 3 dc in the 3-ch, ch 4, 3 dc in the same 3-ch, ch 3, 1 sc in the last of the 4-ch, sc in each of the next 3 sc, rep from *, ending row with sc in the last of the 4-ch and in each of the 4 sc, ch 1 and turn.

Row 4: Sc in each of the 1st 4 sc, * ch 4, work 1 dc and 1 ch 6 times in the 4-ch, 1 more dc in the same 4-ch, ch 4, sc in the 2nd sc and in each of the next 2 sc, rep from *, ending row with 4 sc, ch 1 and turn.

Row 5: Sc in each of the 1st 3 sc, *ch 4, sc in the next 1-ch, and 3 chs 5 times, 1 more sc in the next 1-ch, ch 4, sc in the 2nd sc, rep from *, ending row with 3 sc.

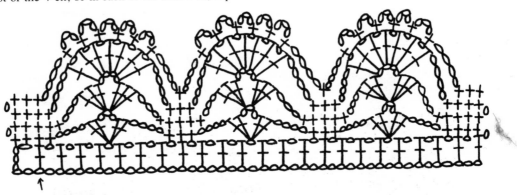

167. Chain multiples of 12 plus 5.

Row 1: Dc in the 7th ch, *ch 1 and dc in the 2nd dc, rep from *, ending row with dc in the last ch, ch 1 and turn.

Row 2: Sc in the 1st dc, and sc in the 1-ch, * ch 4, dc in the 3rd 1-ch, ch 5, dc in the 1-ch just used, ch 4, sc in the 3rd 1-ch, rep from *, ending row with 2 sc in the turning ch, ch 1 and turn.

Row 3: Sc in each of the 1st 2 sc, *ch 5, work 2 dc in the 5-ch, ch 5, work another 2 dc in the same 5 dc, ch 5, sc in the next sc, rep from *, ending row with sc in each of the last 2 sc, ch 1 and turn.

Row 4: Sc in each of the 1st 2 sc, * ch 6, work 2 dc in the 2nd 5-ch, ch 5, work 2 dc in the same 5-ch, ch 6, sc in the next sc, rep from *, ending row with sc in each of the last 2 sc.

Row 5: Sc in each of the 1st sc, * ch 7, work 2 dc around the 5-ch, ch 5, work 2 dc in the same 5-ch, ch 7, work 1 sc in the next sc, rep from *, ending row with sc in the last 2 sc.

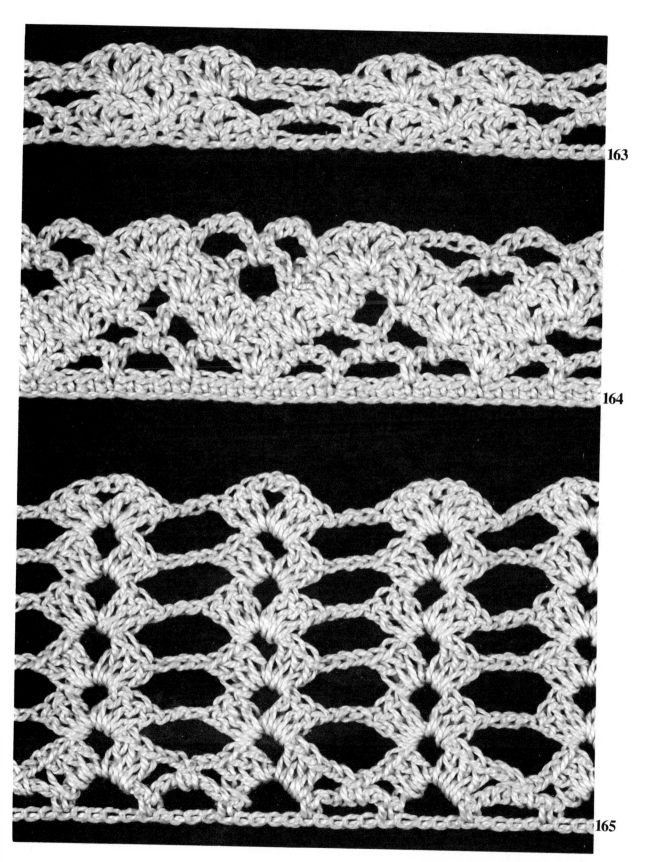

163

164

165

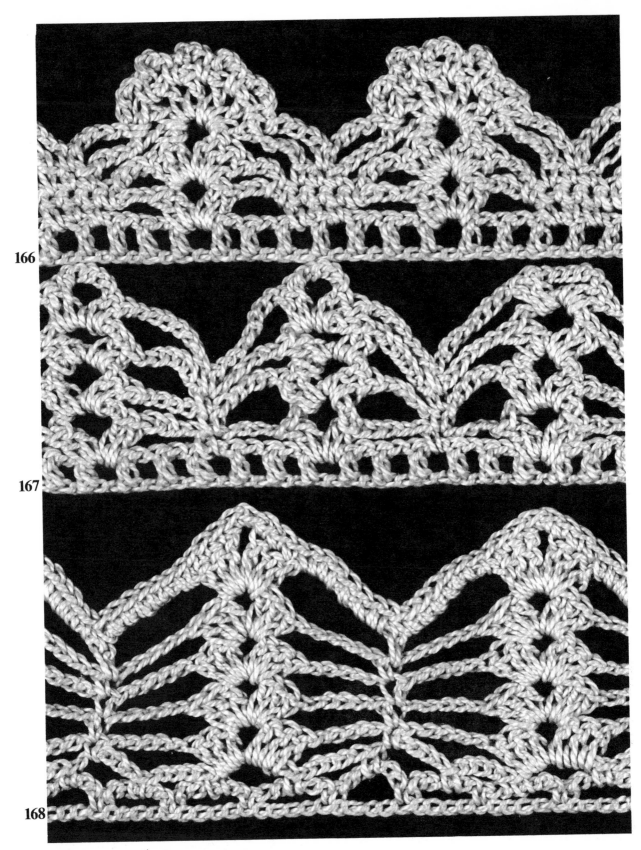

166

167

168

128   Simple Filet and Shells in Grid

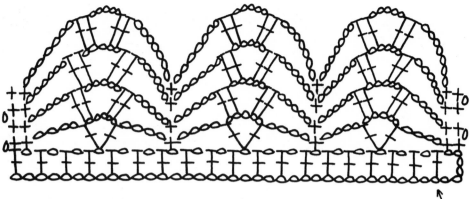

168. Chain multiples of 21 plus 2.

Row 1: Sc in the 2nd ch, *ch 5 and sc in the 5th ch, rep from *, ending row with sc in the last ch, ch 6 and turn.

Row 2: *sc in the middle of the 5-ch, ch 5, rep from *, ending row with last sc, ch 2 and dc in the last sc, ch 1 and turn.

Row 3: Sc in the dc, *ch 5, work 3 dc in the 2nd 5-ch, ch 2 and work another 3 dc in the same 5-ch, ch 5 and sc in the 2nd 5-ch, rep from *, ending row with sc in the turning ch, ch 1 and turn.

Row 4: Sc in the sc, * ch 5, work 3 dc in the 2-ch, ch 2 and work another 3 dc in the same 2-ch, ch 5 and sc in the next sc, rep from *, ending row with last sc, ch 1 and turn.

Rows 5–6: Same as row 4, ch 1 and turn.

Row 7: * sc in the sc, ch 7 and work 3 dc in the 2-ch, ch 3 and work another 3 dc in the same 2-ch, ch 7, rep from *, ending row with last sc, ch 1 and turn.

Row 8: Sc in the 1st sc, *work 7 sc around the 7-ch, work 1 sc in each of the 3 dc, 2 sc in the 3-ch, sc in each of the 3-dc, 7 sc around the 7-ch, rep from *, ending row with sc in last sc.

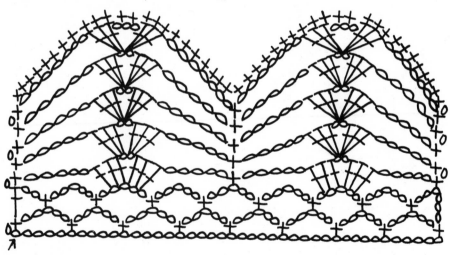

169. Chain multiples of 10 plus 2.

Row 1: Sc in the 2nd ch, *ch 3 and work 2 dc in the 5th ch, ch 2 and work another 2 dc in the same ch, ch 3 and sc in the 5th ch, rep from *, ending row with last sc, ch 6 and turn.

Row 2: *work 2 dc in the 2-ch, ch 2 and another 2 dc in the same 2-ch, ch 4, rep from *, ending row with last set, ch 2 and trc in the last sc, ch 1 and turn.

Row 3: Sc in the trc, *ch 3 and work 2 dc in the 2nd 2-ch, ch 2 and work another 2 dc in the same 2-ch, ch 3 and sc in the middle of the 4-ch, rep from *, ending row with sc in the turning ch, ch 6 and turn.

Row 4: Same as row 2, ch 1 and turn.

Row 5: Same as row 3, ch 6 and turn.

Row 6: Same as rows 2 and 4, ch 1 and turn.

Row 7: Sc in the trc, *ch 3 and dc in the 3-ch and work 3-ch picot, rep 4 more times, another dc in the same 3-ch, ch 3 and sc in the middle of the 4-ch, rep from *, ending row with the last sc.

Simple Filet and Shells in Grid   129

169

170

130   **Simple Filet and Shells in Grid**

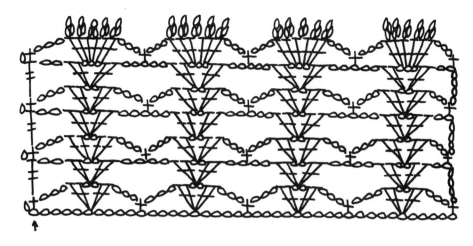

170. Chain multiples of 12 plus 7.

Row 1: Dc in the 10th ch, dc in each of the next 6 chs, *ch 2 and dc in the 3rd ch, ch 2 and dc in the 3rd ch, dc in each of the next 6 chs, rep from *, ending row with dc in the last ch, ch 3 and turn.

Row 2: Dc in the 1st dc, *ch 2 and dc in the space between the 1st and next dc, work 1 dc between each of the next 5 sets of dc, ch 2 and dc in the 2nd dc, ch 2 and dc in the same dc, rep from *, ending row with dc, 2 chs and dc in the turning ch, ch 4 and turn.

Row 3: Dc in the 2-ch, *ch 3 and dc just after the next dc, work 4 more dc between the next 4 sets of dc, ch 3 and dc in the 2nd 2-ch, ch 2 and dc in the same 2-ch, rep from *, ending row with dc, 2 chs and dc in the turning ch, ch 3 and turn.

Row 4: Dc in the 2-ch, ch 2 and dc in the same 2-ch, *ch 4 and dc in the space after the 2nd dc, work 1 dc in the space between each of the next 3 sets of dc, ch 4 and dc in the 2-ch, ch 2 and dc in the same 2-ch, rep from *, ending row with dc in the turning ch, ch 2 and dc in the same turning ch, ch 3 and turn.

Row 5: Dc in the 2-ch, ch 2 and dc in the same 2-ch, *ch 4 and dc in the space after the next dc, dc in between the next 2 sets of dc, ch 4 and dc in the next 2-ch, ch 2 and dc in the same 2-ch, ch 2 and dc in the same 2-ch, rep from *, ending row with last set, ch 5 and turn.

Row 6: Dc in the 3rd dc, ch 2 and dc in the same dc, *ch 4 and dc in the space after the next dc, dc after the next dc, ch 4 and dc in the 2nd dc, ch 2 and dc in the same dc, ch 2 and dc in the 2nd dc, ch 2 and dc in the same dc, rep from *, ending row with 4 chs, dc in the turning ch, ch 5 and turn.

Row 7: Work 4-ch picot and dc in the 1st dc, ch 2, * sc in the 2nd dc, ch 5 and dc in the space between the next 2 dc, ch 5 and sc in the 2nd dc, ch 2 and dc in the 2nd 2-ch, work 4-ch picot, dc in the same 2-ch, 4-ch picot, dc in the same 2-ch and 4-ch picot, dc in the same 2-ch, ch 2, rep from *, ending row with dc, picot and dc in the turning ch.

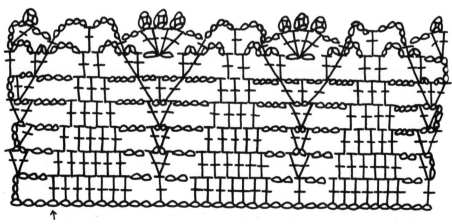

· 11 ·
Inverted V-Stitch and Inverted Shell

171. Chain multiples of 15 plus 2.

Row 1: Sc in the 2nd ch and the 5 chs following, * ch 3, finish 3 dc together, one in each of the next 3 chs, ch 3, sc in the next ch and in the 5 chs following, work 4-ch picot, sc in the next ch and the 5 chs following, rep from *, ending row with 6 sc.

172. Chain multiples of 4 plus 6.

Row 1: Finish 2 dc together in the 7th ch and the 4th ch, * ch 5, finish 2 dc together in the ch just used and the 4th ch, rep from *, ending row with last set, 2 chs and 1 trc in the ch just used.

173. Chain multiples of 6 plus 6.

Row 1: Sc in the 2nd ch and in each ch all across the row, ch 6 and turn.
Row 2: Finish 2 dc together, in the 1st sc and the 3rd sc, *ch 7 and finish 2 dc together in the 3rd sc and the 3rd sc, rep from *, ending row with last set, ch 3 and dc in the last sc, ch 1 and turn.
Row 3: Sc in the dc, work 3 sc in the 3-ch, * work 8 sc in each 7-ch, rep from *, ending row with 4 sc in the turning ch.

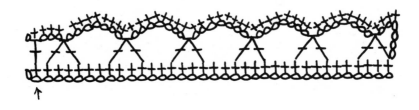

132

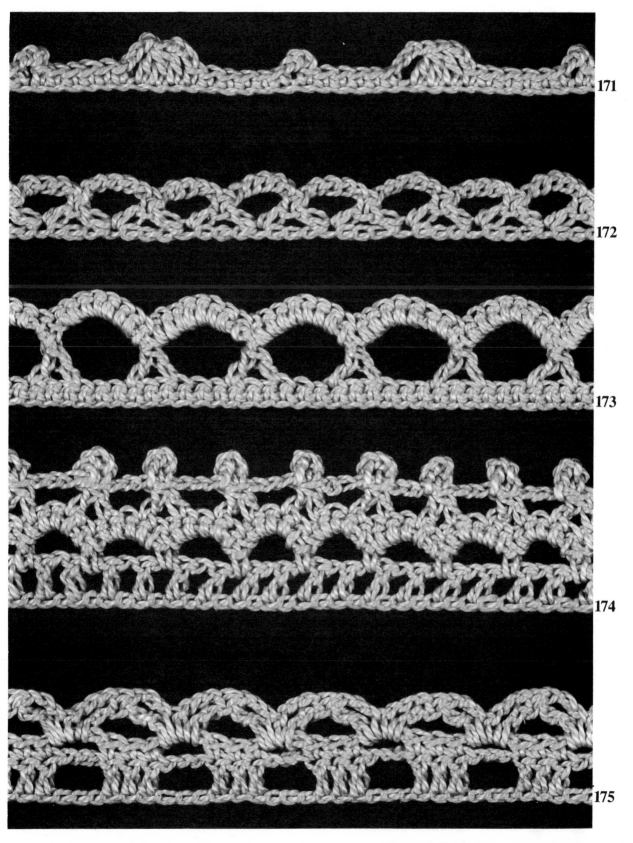

171

172

173

174

175

Inverted V-Stitch and Inverted Shell 133

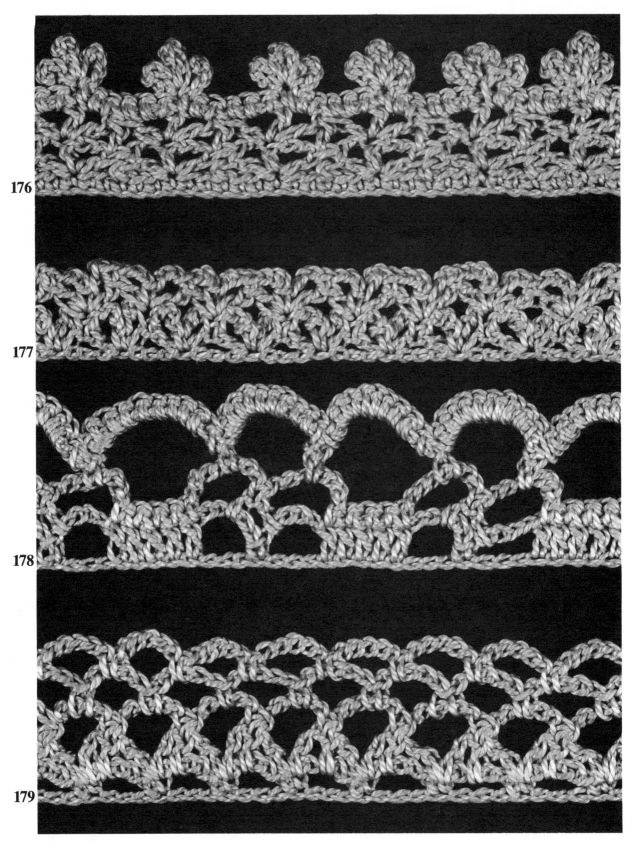

176

177

178

179

134   Inverted V-Stitch and Inverted Shell

174. Chain multiples of 4 plus 4.

Row 1: 1 dc in the 5th ch, *ch 1, dc in the 2nd dc, rep from *, ending row with 1 dc in the ch after last dc, ch 1 and turn.

Row 2: 1 sc in the 1st dc, *ch 5, 1 sc in the 2nd 1-ch, rep from *, ending row with sc in the turning ch, ch 1 and turn.

Row 3: Sc in the sc, *1 sc in each of the next 5 chs, rep from *, ending row with sc in the last sc, ch 3 and turn.

Row 4: 1 dc in the 3rd sc, * work 1 5-ch picot, ch 3, finish 2 dc together in the 2nd sc, and the 3rd sc, rep from *, ending row with last picot.

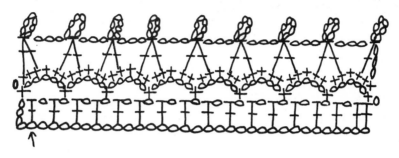

175. Chain multiples of 6 plus 6.

Row 1: 1 dc in the 6th ch, *ch 3, 1 dc in the 4th ch, 1 dc in each of the next 2 chs, rep from *, ending row with dc in the 4th ch and the ch after that, ch 1 and turn.

Row 2: 1 sc in each of the dc, *ch 3, 1 sc in each of the dc, rep from *, ending row with 1 sc in the last dc and 1 in the turning ch, ch 3 and turn.

Row 3: Work 1 trc in the 1st of the 3-ch, *ch 3, 1 sc in the middle of the 3-ch, ch 3, work 1 trc in the last of the 3-ch, finish together with a trc in the 1st of the next 3-ch, rep from *, ending row with 1 trc in the last of 3-ch finished together with dc in last sc.

176. Chain multiples of 6 plus 1.

Row 1: 1 sc in the 2nd ch and in each ch all across the row, ch 3 and turn.

Row 2: 1 dc in the 4th sc, *ch 2, 1 dc in the sc just used, ch 2, 1 dc in the sc just used, finished together with a dc formed in the 3rd sc and the next 3rd sc, rep from *, ending row with 2 dc finished together in the 3rd sc and the next 3rd sc, ch 3 and turn.

Row 3: Dc in the single standing dc, *ch 2, dc in the same dc just used, ch 2, dc in the dc just used, worked together with a dc formed in the 3 dc worked together, and a dc worked in the next single standing dc, rep from *, ending row with 2 dc finished together in the last single standing dc and the turning ch, ch and turn.

Row 4: 1 sc in the 2 dc finished together, 3 sc in the 2-ch, *work 3 5-ch picot, 2 sc in the 2-ch, 1 sc in the top of the 3 dc finished together, 2 sc in the 2-ch, rep from *, ending row with 1 sc in the turning ch.

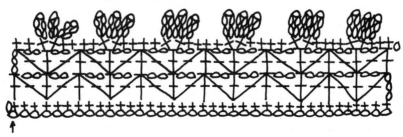

177. Chain multiples of 4 plus 2.

Row 1: Sc in the 2nd ch, *ch 3, finish 2 dc together, 1 in the ch just used, and 1 in the 4th ch, ch 3 and sc in the ch just used, rep from *, ending row with sc in the last ch, ch 4 and turn.

Row 2: Dc in the top of the 2 dc finished together, *ch 3, sc in the same dc, ch 3, dc in the stitch just used, finished together with a dc in the next 2 dc, rep from *, ending row with trc in the last sc.

178. Chain multiples of 12 plus 2.

Row 1: Sc in the 2nd ch, *ch 5 and dc in the 4th ch, dc in each of the next 4 dc, ch 5 and sc in the 4th ch, rep from *, ending row with sc in the last ch, ch 3 and turn.
Row 2: Dc in the beginning of the 5-ch, *ch 7 and sc in each of the next 5 dc, ch 7 and finish 2 dc together formed in the next 5-ch and the 5-ch after that, rep from *, ending row with last 7-ch and finish 2 dc to-

gether in the last 5-ch and 1 in the last sc, ch 2 and turn.
Row 3: *sc in the 7-ch, ch 10 and sc in the next 7-ch, ch 10, rep from *, ending row with last sc, ch 3 and dc in the top of the turning ch, ch 1 and turn.
Row 4: Work 1 sc in the 1st dc and work 4 sc in the 3-ch, *work 10 sc around the next 10-ch, rep from *, ending row with sc in the last sc.

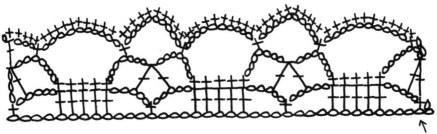

179. Chain multiples of 4 plus 2.

Row 1: Sc in the 2nd ch, * ch 5 and sc in the 4th ch, rep from *, ending row with last sc, ch 5 and turn.
Row 2: *finish 1 trc in the 1st sc, together with 1 dc in the middle of the 5-ch, together with 1 trc in the next sc, ch 5, rep from *, ending row with last set, 1 ch and 1 trc in the same sc, ch 1 and turn.

Row 3: Sc in the 1st trc, *ch 5, sc around the middle of the 5-ch, rep from *, ending row with sc in the turning ch, ch 6 and turn.
Row 4: *sc around the middle of the 5-ch, ch 5, and rep from *, ending row with last sc, ch 2 and trc in the last sc.

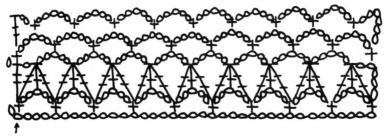

180. Chain multiples of 3 plus 4.

Row 1: Dc in the 5th ch and dc in each ch all across the row, ch 3 and turn.
Row 2: Dc in the 2nd dc, *ch 1 and dc in the same dc, dc in the 3rd dc, rep from *, ending row with last set and dc in the turning ch, ch 4 and turn.
Row 3: Sk 1st dc, *finish 2 dc together, 1 in each of the

next 2 dc, ch 2 and rep from *, ending row with last set, ch 1 and dc in the turning ch, ch 1 and turn.
Row 4: Sc in dc, sc in 1-ch, ch 2 and sc in 1st of next 2-ch, *ch 3 and sc in 1st of the next 2-ch, work another sc in the same ch, and rep from *, ending row with sc in the turning ch, ch 2 and sc in the same turning ch.

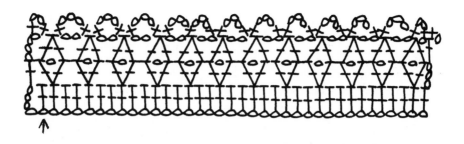

181. Chain multiples of 4 plus 4.

Row 1: Dc in the 5th ch and in each ch all across the row, ch 3 and turn.

Row 2: Dc in the 2nd dc, *ch 3 and finish 2 dc together, 1 in the dc just used, and 1 in the 4th dc, rep from *, ending row with last set, ch 2 and dc in the turning ch, ch 1 and turn.

Row 3: Sc in the dc, sc in the 2-ch, work 3-ch picot, work another sc in the same 2-ch, *sc in the top of the 2 dc finished together, work 2 sc in the beginning of the 3-ch, work 3-ch picot, sc in the last of the 3-ch, rep from *, ending row with sc in the turning ch.

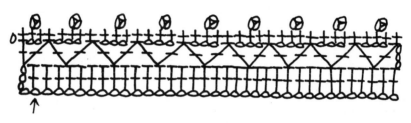

182. Chain multiples of 14 plus 7.

Row 1: Dc in the 5th ch and dc in each of the next 2 chs, *ch 5 and dc in the 5th ch and in the next ch, ch 5 and dc in the 5th ch and in each of the next 3 chs, rep from *, ending row with 1 dc in each of the last 4 chs, ch 4 and turn.

Row 2: *finish 2 dc together in the 1st dc and the 3rd dc, ch 5, dc in the middle of the next 2 dc, ch 3, dc in the same space, ch 5, rep from *, ending row with 2 dc

finished together, 1 ch and 1 dc in the turning ch, ch 2 and turn.

Row 3: *sc in the top of the 2 dc finished together, ch 5, work 1 trc in the 3-ch, ch 3, work another trc in the same 3-ch, ch 3, and work another trc in the same 3-ch, ch 5, rep from *, ending row with sc in the last 2 dc finished together, ch 1 and sc in the turning ch.

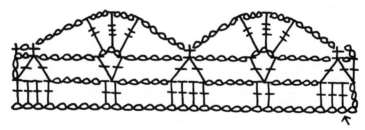

183. Chain multiples of 4 plus 2.

Row 1: Sc in 2nd ch and in each ch all across the row, ch 5 and turn.

Row 2: *finish 3 trc together in the 2nd sc and the 2 sc following that, ch 3, rep from *, ending row with last set, 1 ch and 1 trc in the last sc, ch 4 and turn.

Row 3: *work 3 trc in the top of the 3 trc finished to-

gether, ch 1, rep from *, ending row with last set and one trc in the turning ch, ch 1 and turn.

Row 4: Sc in 1st trc, sc in next trc, *ch 5, sc in 2nd trc, sc in 1-ch, sc in next trc, rep from *, ending row with sc in the last trc.

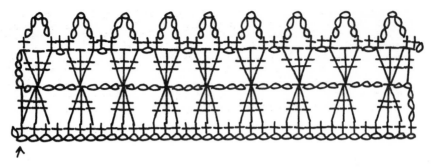

184. Chain multiples of 9 plus 10.

Row 1: Dc in the 5th ch, *dc in each of the next 5 chs, ch 3 and dc in the 4th ch, rep from *, ending row with 1 additional dc in the ch after the last 6 chs, ch 1 and turn.
Row 2: Sc in the 1st dc, *ch 5, finish 3 trc together in each of the next 3 dc, ch 5, finish 3 trc together, one in each of the next 3 dc, ch 5, sc around the middle of the next 3-ch, rep from *, ending row with last 3 trc, ch 2 and 1 dc in the last sc, ch 3 and turn.
Row 3: Work 12 trc in the next 5-ch, * work 12 trc in the 3rd 5-ch, rep from *, ending row with last set and dc in the last ch.

185. Chain multiples of 8 plus 5.

Row 1: Finish 2 dc together, 1 in the 5th ch, and 1 in the 4th ch, *ch 3 and finish 2 dc together, 1 in the ch just used, and 1 in the 4th ch, rep from *, ending row with last set, ch 1 and dc in the ch just used, ch 3 and turn.
Row 2: Dc in the top of the 2 dc finished together, *ch 3 and finish 2 dc together, 1 in the top of the last 2 dc finished together, 1 in the top of the next 2 dc finished together, rep from *, ending row with 2 dc finished together in the top of the last 2 dc and the turning ch, ch 1 and turn.
Row 3: Sc in the top of the 1st 2 dc finished together, ch 2, *sc in the middle of the 3-ch, ch 8, sc in the middle of the next 3-ch, ch 5, rep from *, ending row with last sc, ch 2 and sc in the turning ch, ch 1 and turn.
Row 4: *work 23 dc around the 8-ch, sc in the middle of the 5-ch, rep from *, ending row with sc in the last sc.

186. Chain multiples of 16 plus 2.

Row 1: Sc in 2nd ch and in each ch all across the row.
Row 2: Dc in 2nd sc, *ch 3, dc in the 4th sc, rep from *, ending row with last dc and 1 dc in the next and last sc, ch 1 and turn.

Row 3: Sc in 1st dc, * ch 6, work 3 trc together in the 2nd dc, and the 1st and next ch, ch 4, work 3 trc together in the ch just used and the next ch and the dc, ch 6, sc in the 2nd group of 3-ch, rep from *, ending row with sc in the turning ch.

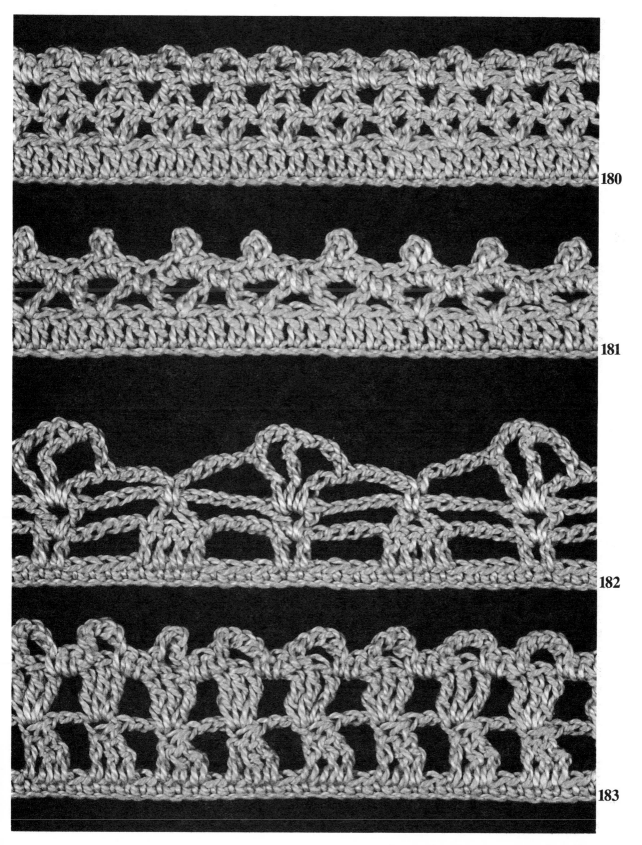

180

181

182

183

Inverted V-Stitch and Inverted Shell   139

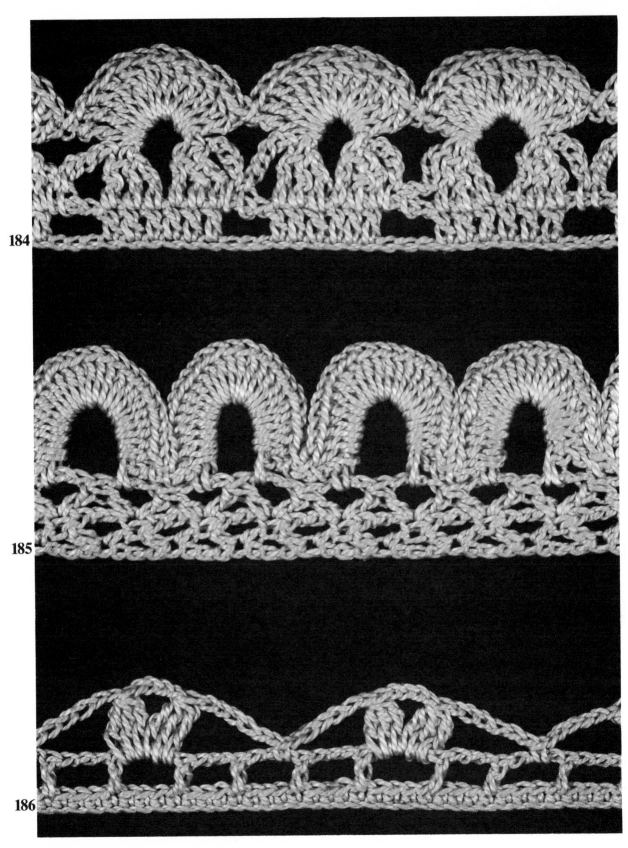

184

185

186

140 Inverted V-Stitch and Inverted Shell

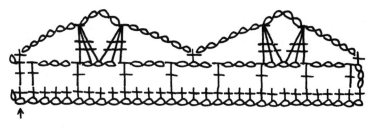

187.   Chain multiples of 8 plus 6.

Row 1: Work 2 dc in the 5th ch, * sc in the 4th ch, 2 dc in the 4th ch, ch 3, 2 dc in the ch just used, rep from *, ending row with 2 dc in the 4th ch, ch 1, 1 dc in the ch just used, ch 1 and turn.

Row 2: Sc in the 1st dc, *ch 4, work 4-ch picot, finish 4 dc together 1 in each of the next 4 dc, ch 4, 4-ch picot, 1 sc in the middle of the 3-ch, rep from *, ending row with 4-ch picot and 1 sc in the turning ch.

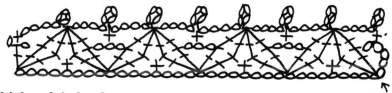

188.   Chain multiples of 6 plus 2.

Row 1: Sc in the 2nd ch and in each ch all across the row, ch 2 and turn.
Row 2: Work 2 dc in the 1st sc, *sc in the 3rd sc, work 5 dc in the 3rd sc, rep from *, ending row with 3 dc in the last sc, ch 1 and turn.
Row 3: Sc in the top of the dc, *ch 2, finish 5 dc together,

in the next dc, the dc after that, the sc, and in each of the next 2 dc, ch 2 and sc in the next dc, rep from *, ending row with sc in the turning ch, ch 1 and turn.
Row 4: Sc in the sc, * work sc in each of the 2-ch, work 5-ch picot, sc in each of the next 2-ch, rep from *, ending row with extra sc in the last sc.

189.   Chain multiples of 4 plus 4.

Row 1: Dc in the 5th ch and in each ch all across the row, ch 5 and turn.
Row 2: Work 1 Y-stitch with a heading of 4 dc in the 3rd dc, *ch 3, work 1 Y-stitch with a heading of 4 dc in the 4th dc, rep from *, ending row with last Y-stitch, 1 ch and 1 trc in the turning ch, ch 4 and turn.

Row 3: Work 2 dc together in the next 2 dc, * ch 3, work 3-ch picot, ch 3, work 4 dc together, 2 in the last 2 dc of the last set of dc in the Y-stitch, work the other 2 dc in the 1st 2 dc of the Y-stitch of the next set, rep from *, ending row with 3 dc worked together in the last 2 dc of the last Y-stitch and a 3rd one in the turning ch.

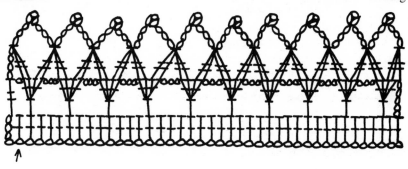

190. Chain multiples of 11 plus 4.

Row 1: 1 dc in the 5th ch, *ch 3, 5 dc in the 5th ch, ch 3, finish 2 dc together in the 5th and next ch, rep from *, ending row with 2 dc finished together, ch 1 and turn.

Row 2: *sc in the top of the 2 dc finished together, ch 3, dc in each of the next 3 dc, ch 3, dc in the last dc just used and dc in each of the next 2 dc, ch 3, rep from *, ending row with sc in the turning ch, ch 4 and turn.

Row 3: Finish 3 dc together, worked in each of the next 3 dc, *ch 3, sc in the beginning of the 3-ch, ch 5, sc in the last of the 3-ch, ch 3, finish 3 dc together worked in the next 3 dc, and 3 dc worked in the next 3 dc, rep from *, ending row with last set and 1 trc in the last sc.

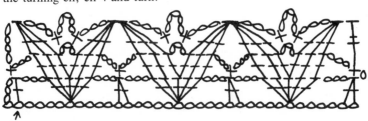

191. Chain multiples of 12 plus 2.

Row 1: Sc in the 2nd ch, * ch 4 and dc in the 6th ch, ch 5 and dc in the same ch, ch 4 and sc in the 6th ch, rep from *, ending row with sc in the last ch, ch 5 and turn.

Row 2: *work 5 dc in the beginning of the 5-ch, ch 3 and work another 5 dc in the same 5-ch, ch 2 and dc in the next sc, ch 2, rep from *, ending row with dc in the last sc, ch 5 and turn.

Row 3: Sk 1st dc, *finish 5 dc together, worked 1 in each of the next 5 dc, work 5 dc in the 3-ch, finish 5 dc together, once in each of the next 5 dc, ch 2 and dc in the next dc, ch 2, rep from *, ending row with dc in the turning ch, ch 1 and turn.

Row 4: Sc in the dc, *ch 3 and sc in the top of the 5 dc finished together, ch 5 and finish 5 dc together worked 1 in each of the next 5 dc, ch 5 and sc in top of the next 5 dc finished together, ch 3 and sc in the 2-ch, ch 3 and sc in the next 2-ch, rep from *, ending row with sc in the last 5 dc finished together, ch 3 and sc in the turning ch.

192. Chain multiples of 8 plus 6.

Row 1: Dc in the 8th ch, *ch 1 and dc in the 2nd ch, rep from *, ending row with dc in the last ch, ch 3 and turn.

Row 2: Work 3 dc in the 1st 1-ch, *ch 3, work 3 dc in the 2nd 1-ch, rep from *, ending row with dc in the turning ch, ch 6 and turn.

Row 3: Sk 1st dc, *sc in the 2nd dc, ch 4, finish 3 dc together 1 in the 2nd dc and 1 in each of the next 2 dc, ch 4, rep from *, ending row with 3 dc finished together and 1 dc in the turning ch.

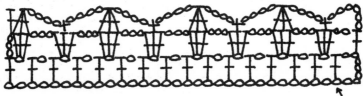

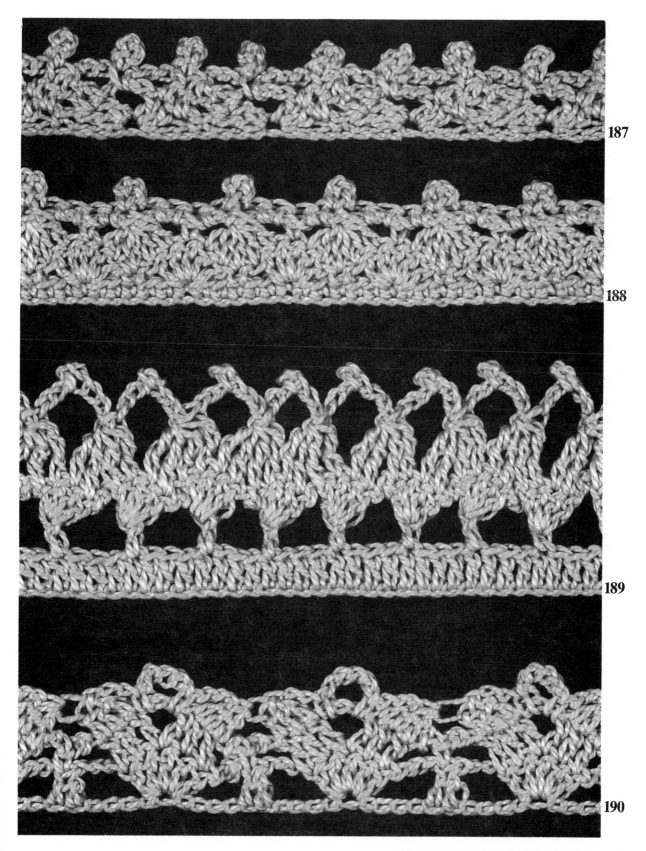

187

188

189

190

Inverted V-Stitch and Inverted Shell 143

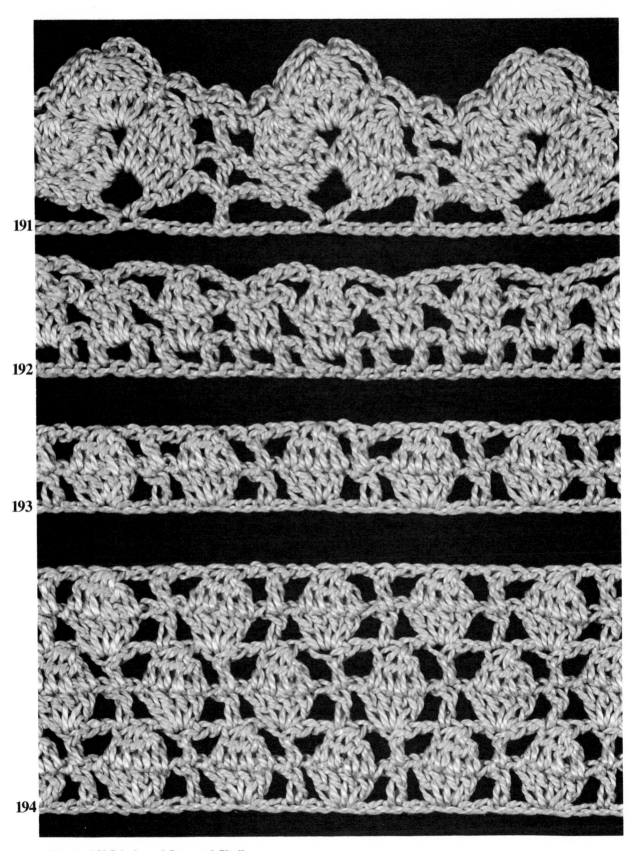

191

192

193

194

144 Inverted V-Stitch and Inverted Shell

193. Chain multiples of 6 plus 5.

Row 1: 4 dc in the 8th ch, *ch 1, dc in the 3rd ch, ch 1, 4 dc in the 3rd ch, rep from *, ending row with dc in the last ch, ch 5 and turn.

Row 2: Sk 1st dc, *finish 4 dc together, worked once in each of the next 4 dc, ch 2, dc in the next dc, ch 2, rep from *, ending row with dc in the turning ch.

194. Chain multiples of 6 plus 5.

Row 1: 4 dc in the 8th ch, *ch 1, dc in the 3rd ch, ch 1, 4 dc in the 3rd ch, rep from *, ending row with dc in the 3rd and last ch, ch 5 and turn.

Row 2: Sk 1st dc, *finish 4 dc together in each of the next 4 dc, ch 2, dc in the next dc, ch 2, rep from *, ending row with 2 chs and 1 dc in the turning ch, ch 3 and turn.

Row 3: Dc in the 1st dc, *ch 1, dc on the top of the 4 dc finished together, ch 1, 4 dc in the next dc, rep from *, ending row with 2 dc in the turning ch, ch 3 and turn.

Row 4: Dc in 2nd dc, * ch 2, dc in the next dc, ch 2, finish 4 dc together, 1 in each of the next 4 dc, rep from *, ending row with dc in the last dc and 1 in the turning ch, ch 4 and turn.

Row 5: Sk 1st 2 dc finished together, * work 4 dc in the next dc, ch 1, dc in the top of the 4 dc finished together, ch 1, rep from *, ending row with dc in the turning ch, ch 5 and turn.

Row 6: Sk 1st dc, finish 4 dc together, 1 formed in each of the next 4 dc, ch 2, dc in the next dc, ch 2, rep from *, ending row with dc in the turning ch.

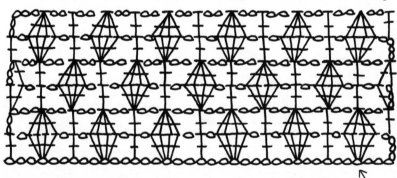

195. Chain multiples of 8 plus 5.

Row 1: 1 dc in the 7th ch, *ch 1, dc in the 2nd ch, rep from *, ending row with dc, ch 4 and turn.

Row 2: Work 5 dc in the 3rd dc, *ch 1, dc in the 2nd dc, ch 1, work 5 dc in the 2nd dc, rep from *, ending row with dc in the turning ch, ch 6 and turn.

Row 3: Sk 1st dc, * finish 5 dc together, 1 in each of the next 5 dc, ch 3, dc in the next dc, ch 3, rep from *,

ending row with dc in the turning ch, ch 1 and turn.

Row 4: Sc in the 1st dc, * 1 sc in each of the 3 chs, 1 sc in the top of the 5 dc finished together, work 3 5-ch picot into the sc just formed, sl st together, sc in each of the next 3 chs, rep from *, ending row with 1 extra sc in the turning ch.

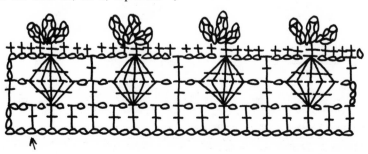

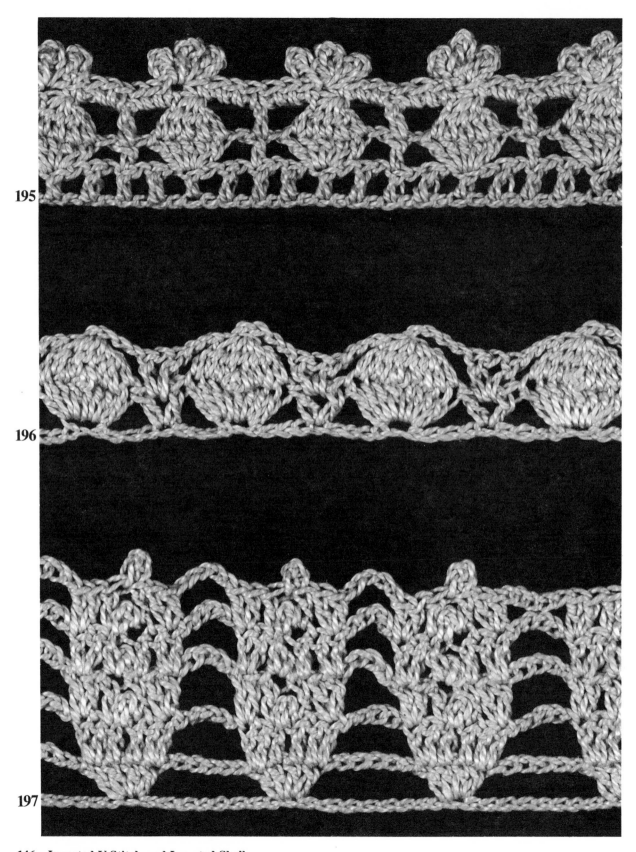

195

196

197

146　Inverted V-Stitch and Inverted Shell

196. Chain multiples of 10 plus 4.

Row 1: Dc in the 4th ch, *4 dc in the 5th ch, work 3-ch picot, 4 dc in the ch just used, dc in the 5th ch, ch 1, dc in the same ch, rep from *, ending row with 2 dc in the last ch, ch 3 and turn.

Row 2: 1 dc in the 1st dc, *ch 3, finish 8 dc together, 1 in each of the next 8 dc, ch 5, dc in the 1-ch, ch 1, dc in the same 1-ch, rep from *, ending row with 2 dc in the turning ch.

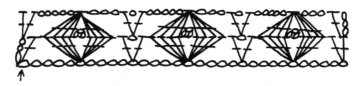

197. Chain multiples of 9 plus 4 plus 4.

Row 1: Work 3 dc in the 4th ch, * ch 6 and work 4 dc in the 9th ch, rep from *, ending row with 4 dc in the last ch, ch 3 and turn.

Row 2: Dc in the 1st dc, *dc in the next dc, work 3-ch picot, dc in the next dc, work 2 dc in the next dc, ch 5 and work 2 dc in the next dc, rep from *, ending row with last set and 2 dc in the turning ch, ch 4 and turn.

Row 3: *dc back in the 1st dc, finished together with dc in the 2nd dc, work 3-ch picot, dc in the next dc, finished together with a dc in the 2nd dc, ch 1 and dc in the same dc, ch 4 and dc in the next dc, ch 1, rep from *, ending row with last set, ch 5 and turn.

Row 4: Dc in the 1st dc, finished together with a dc in the top of the 2 dc finished together, *work 3-ch picot, finish 2 dc together in the next 2 dc finished together, and the next dc, ch 2 and dc in the same dc, ch 4 and dc in the next dc, ch 2 and finish 2 dc together in the dc just used and in the top of the next 2 dc finished together, rep from *, ending row with last set.

Row 5: Same as row 4.

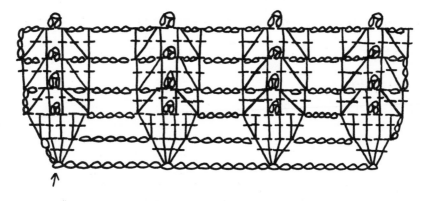

·12·
Small Shells

198.   **Chain multiples of 3 plus 6.**

Row 1: 1 dc in the 9th ch, *ch 2, 1 dc in the 3rd ch, rep from *, ending row with last dc, ch 5 and turn.
Row 2: Sk 1st dc, *dc in the dc, ch 2, rep from *, ending row with dc in the turning ch, ch 4 and turn.
Row 3: Dc in 1st dc, ch 1, dc in the same dc, *ch 1, 1 dc in the next dc, 1 ch, 4 times, dc in the same dc, rep from *, ending row with a dc, ch, dc, ch and a dc in the turning ch.
Bottom Row: Sc in each ch and in each dc all across the row.

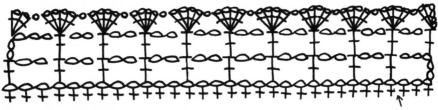

199.   **Chain multiples of 9 plus 2.**

Row 1: Sc in the 2nd ch, *dc in the 4th ch, ch 2, dc in the dc just used, dc in the next ch, ch 2, dc in the ch just used, sc in the 4th ch, rep from *, ending row with sc in the last ch, ch 1 and turn.
Row 2: *sc in the sc, work 1 hdc and 1 dc into the 1st ch and 2 dc in the next ch, work 2 dc into the ch after the 2 dc, work 1 dc and 1 hdc into the next ch, rep from *, ending row with sc in the last sc.

200.   **Chain multiples of 12 plus 6.**

Row 1: Dc in the 6th ch, *sc in the 4th ch and sc in each of the next 4 chs, dc in the 4th ch, ch 2, dc in the ch just used, ch 2, dc in the ch just used, rep from *, ending row with dc in the 4th ch, ch 2 and dc in the same ch, ch 3 and turn.
Row 2: Work 4 dc around the 2-ch, *sc in the 2nd sc and sc in each of the next 2 sc, work 4 dc in the next 2-ch, dc in the dc, work 4 dc in the next 2-ch, rep from *, ending row with 5 dc in the turning ch.

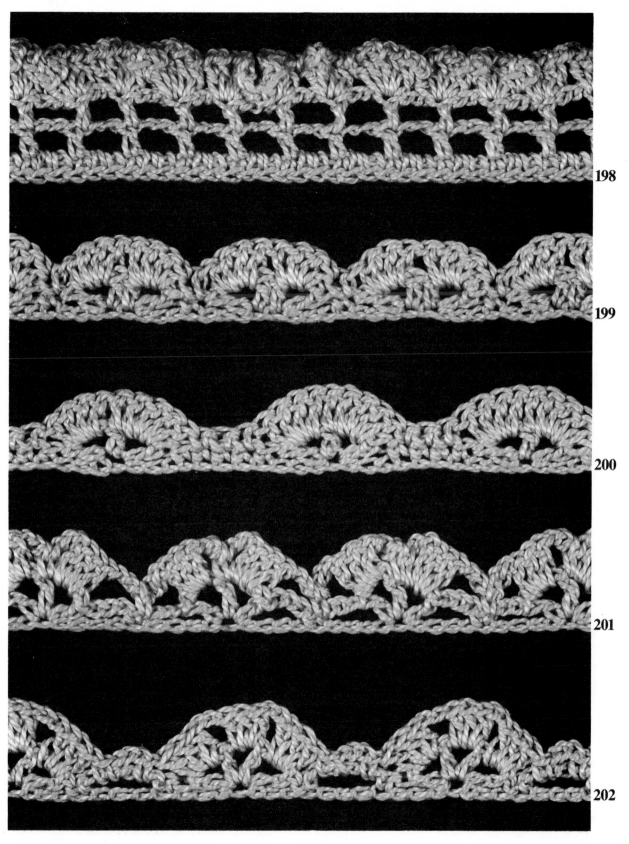

198

199

200

201

202

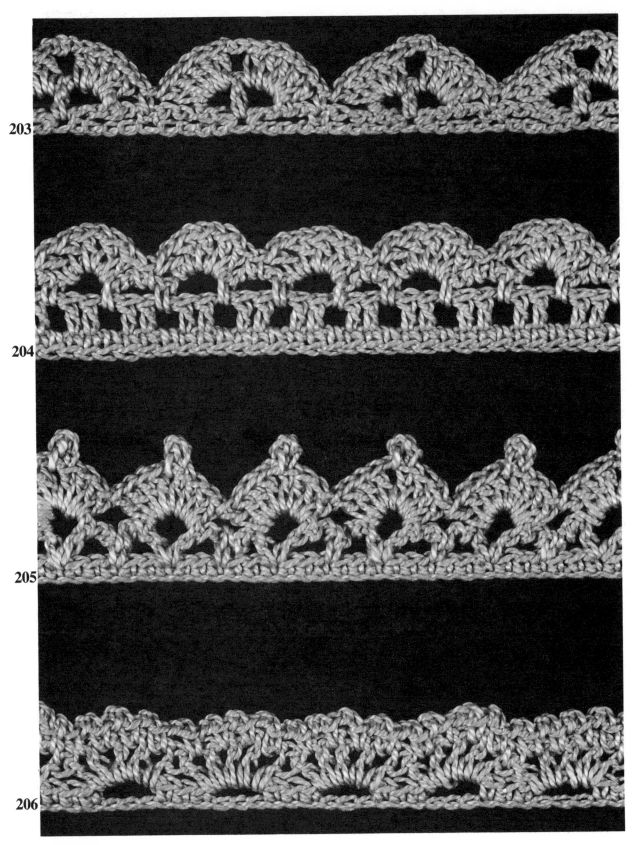

203

204

205

206

150 Small Shells

201.   Chain multiples of 10 plus 2.

Row 1: Sc in the 2nd ch, *ch 3, dc in the 5th ch, ch 3, dc in the ch just used, ch 3, dc in the same ch, ch 3, sc in the 5th ch, rep from *, ending row with sc in the last ch, ch 1 and turn.

Row 2: * sc in the sc, ch 3, 3 dc in the 2nd 3-ch, ch 3, sc in the next dc, ch 3, 3 dc in the next 3-ch, ch 3, rep from *, ending row with sc in the last sc.

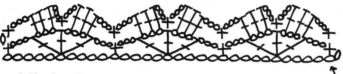

202.   Chain multiples of 12 plus 6.

Row 1: Sc in the 8th ch, * work 1 dc in the 4th ch, ch 2, dc in the same ch, ch 2, dc in the same ch, ch 2, dc in the same ch, sc in the 4th ch, ch 5, sc in the 4th ch, rep from *, ending row after last set with 2 chs and 1 dc in the 2nd ch, ch 4 and turn.

Row 2: Sc in the last part of the 2-ch, *3 dc around the next 2-ch, ch 2, work 3 dc around the next 2-ch, ch 2, work 3 dc around the next 2-ch, sc in the beginning of the next 5-ch, ch 3, sc in the last part of the 5-ch, rep from *, ending row with last sc, ch 1 and hdc in the turning ch.

203.   Chain multiples of 10 plus 2.

Row 1: 1 sc in the 2nd ch, *ch 2, 1 dc in the 5th ch, ch 3, 1 dc in the ch just used, ch 3, 1 dc in the ch just used, ch 2, sc in 5th ch, rep from *, ending row after last set with 2 chs and a sc in the 5th and last ch, ch 1 and turn.

Row 2: * 1 sc in the sc, 5 dc in the 3-ch, ch 3, 5 dc in the next 3-ch, rep from *, ending row with sc of the last set.

204.   Chain multiples of 6 plus 4.

Row 1: Dc in the 5th ch, *ch 1, 1 dc in the 2nd ch and the ch after that, rep from *, ending row with the last 2 dc, ch 5 and turn.
Row 2: *sc in the 1-ch, ch 5, rep from *, ending row with last sc, ch 2 and 1 dc in the turning ch, ch 1 and turn.

Row 3: Sc in the dc, * work 1 dc and ch 1 into the 5-ch 4 times, 1 dc in the same 5-ch, sc in the next 5-ch, rep from *, ending row with sc in the turning ch.
Bottom Row: Sc in the 2nd ch and in each ch all across the row.

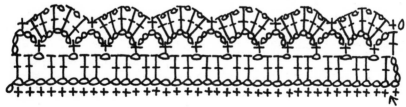

205.   Chain multiples of 6 plus 2.

Row 1: Sc in the 2nd ch and in each ch all across the row, ch 1 and turn.
Row 2: Sc in the 1st sc, * ch 3, dc in the 3rd sc, ch 4, dc in sc just used, ch 3, sc in the 3rd sc, rep from *, ending row with sc in the last sc, ch 3 and turn.

Row 3: * 4 dc around the 4-ch, ch 1, work 4-ch picot, sc in the 1-ch just formed, 4 dc around the 4-ch just used, rep from *, ending row with dc in the last sc.

206.　Chain multiples of 6 plus 2.

Row 1: Sc in the 2nd ch and in each of the next 2 chs, *ch 4, sc in the 4th ch and in each of the next 2 chs, rep from *, ending row with sc in the last ch, ch 2 and turn.

Row 2: Work dc in the beginning of the 4-ch, *ch 1 and dc in the 4-ch 3 times, ch 1 and finish 2 dc together, 1 in the 4-ch just used, 1 in the beginning of the next 4-ch, rep from *, ending row with last set and 1 dc in the last sc, ch 1 and turn.

Row 3: Sc in the 1st dc, ch 1, * sc in the next 1-ch, ch 2 and sc in the next 1-ch 3 times, rep from *, ending row with last set and 1 sc in the turning ch.

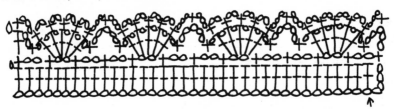

207.　Chain multiples of 9 plus 4.

Row 1: 1 dc in 5th ch and in each ch all across the row, ch 1 and turn.

Row 2: 1 sc in next dc, * ch 2, 1 sc in 3rd dc, rep from *, ending row with 1 sc in turning ch, ch 5 and turn.

Row 3: * 1 sc in next 2-ch, ch 1, dc in the next 2-ch, ch 1, and dc in the same 2-ch 4 times, ch 1, 1 sc in the next 2-ch, ch 5, rep from *, ending row with 1 sc in the last 2-ch, ch 2, 1 dc in the last sc, ch 1 and turn.

Row 4: 1 sc in 1st dc, * ch 3, sc in next dc, 2 chs 4 times, sc in next dc, ch 3, 1 sc in the middle of the 5-ch, rep from *, ending row with 1 sc in the turning chain.

208.　Chain multiples of 11 plus 2.

Row 1: Sc in the 2nd ch and in each ch all across the row, ch 1 and turn.

Row 2: Sc in the 2nd sc and the next sc, *ch 3, work 1 trc in the 5th sc, ch 1 and trc in the same sc 4 times, ch 3 and sc in the 5th sc, sc in the next sc, rep from *, ending row with sc in each of the last 2 sc, ch 1 and turn.

Row 3: Sc in the 1st sc, * work 4 sc in the 3-ch, ch 3, sc in the 1-ch 4 times, ch 3, and work 4 sc in the 3-ch, rep from *, ending row with sc in the last sc.

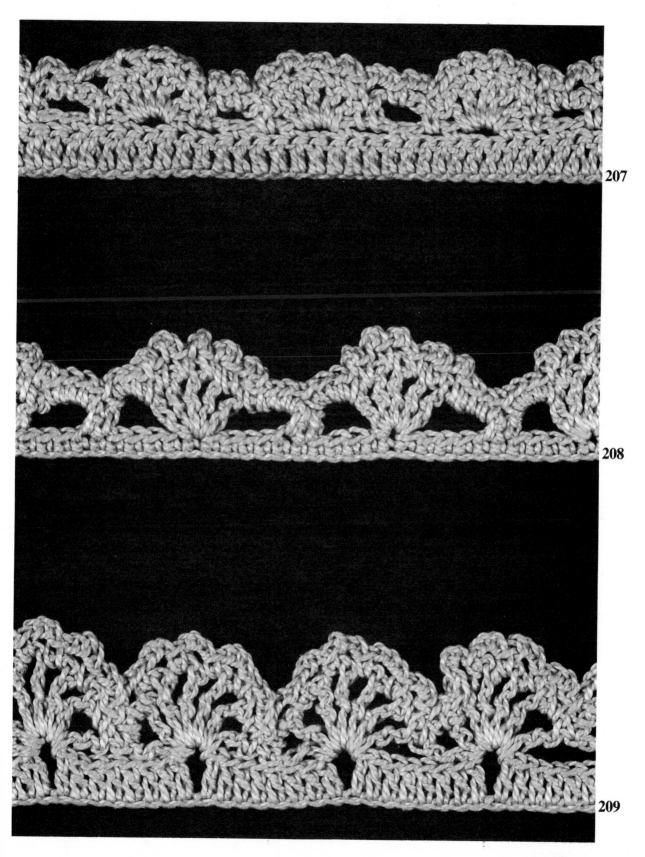

207

208

209

210

211

212

154   Small Shells

209. Chain multiples of 8 plus 4.

Row 1: Dc in the 5th ch and each of the next 3 chs, *ch 3, and dc in the next ch and dc in each of the next 7 chs, rep from *, ending row with dc in each of the last 5 chs, ch 1 and turn.

Row 2: Sc in the 1st dc, *work trc in the next 3-ch, ch 2 and trc in the same 3-ch 6 more times, rep from *, ending row with last set and sc in the turning ch, ch 1 and turn.

Row 3: Sl st in the sc, * sc in the next 2-ch, ch 3 and sc in the next 2-ch 5 times, rep from *, ending row with last set and sl st in the last sc.

210. Chain multiples of 6 plus 6.

Row 1: Dc in the 8th ch, *ch 1 and dc in the 2nd ch, rep from *, ending row with last dc, ch 1 and turn.

Row 2: Sl st in the 1st dc, the ch, and in the next dc, * ch 5, sl st in the next dc, the 1-ch, the dc, 1-ch, and in the

dc, rep from *, ending row with 3 sl st, the last 2 in the turning ch, ch 1 and turn.

Row 3: * work 5 dc in the 5-ch, ch 5, work another 5 dc in the same 5-ch, rep from *, ending row with last set.

211. Chain multiples of 8 plus 5.

Row 1: 1 dc in the 7th ch, *ch 1, and dc in the 2nd ch, rep from *, ending row with last dc, ch 3 and turn.

Row 2: *sc in the next 1-ch, ch 3, rep from *, ending row with 2 chs and 1 hdc in the turning ch, ch 1 and turn.

Row 3: Sc in the hdc, ch 2, dc in the 2nd 3-ch, *ch 1 and dc in the same 3-ch 4 times, ch 1, sc in the 2nd 3-ch, ch 1, dc in the 2nd 3-ch, rep from *, ending row with sc in the turning ch, ch 4 and turn.

Row 4: Sc in the 2nd 1-ch, *ch 3, sc in the next 1-ch and 3 chs 3 times, sc in the 3rd 1-ch, rep from *, ending row with 3 chs and a dc in the last sc, ch 5 and turn.

Row 5: *sc in the 2nd 3-ch, ch 3, sc in the next 3-ch, ch 3, sc in the next 3-ch, ch 5, rep from *, ending row with 2 chs and 1 dc in the turning ch.

212. Chain multiples of 8 plus 5.

Row 1: Dc in the 5th ch and in each ch all across the row, ch 1 and turn.

Row 2: Sc in 1st dc, * 2 dc in 3rd dc, ch 3, sc in next dc, rep from *, ending row with sc in the turning ch, ch 5 and turn.

Row 3: * sc in the top of the 3-ch, dc in the next sc, ch 3, dc in the sc just used, sc in the next 3-ch, ch 6, rep from *, ending row with sc in the top of the last 3-ch, ch 2, work 1 trc in the last sc, ch 3 and turn.

Row 4: Work 3-ch picot, 5 dc in 2-ch, *sc in the middle of the 3-ch, work 5 dc in the 1st half of the 6-ch, work 5-ch picot, 5 dc in the last half of the 6-ch, rep from *, ending row with 5 dc in the turning ch, ch 2, work 1 trc in the same turning ch.

213. Chain multiples of 5 plus 1.

Row 1: 1 sc in the 2nd ch and in each ch all across the row, ch 1 and turn.

Row 2: 1 sc in the 1st sc and in each sc all across the row, ch 1 and turn.

Row 3: Sc in the 1st sc, *ch 2, dc in the next sc, ch 3, work 5 dc around the dc just formed, making a perpendicular angle, sc in the 4th sc, rep from *, ending row with the last sc, ch 1 and turn.

Row 4: Sc in the 1st sc, ch 2, * sc in the 3rd dc, ch 2, sc in the next dc, ch 2, sc in the next dc, ch 2, sc in the middle of the 3-ch, ch 2, sc in the top of the perpendicular dc, rep from *, ending row with dc in the last sc.

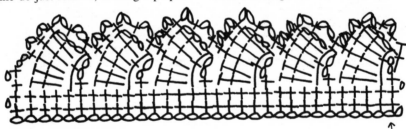

214. Chain multiples of 10 plus 4.

Row 1: Dc in the 4th ch and in each ch all across the row, ch 1 and turn.

Row 2: Sc in each of the next 3 dc, * ch 3, work 2 dc in the 3rd dc, ch 2, work 2 dc in the same dc, ch 3, sc in the 3rd dc and each of the next 4 dc, rep from *, ending row with sc in each of the last 3 dc, ch 1 and turn.

Row 3: Sc in 1st sc and next sc, *ch 3, work 3 dc in the 2-ch, ch 2, work 3 dc in the same 2-ch, ch 3, sc in the 2nd sc and in each of the next 2 sc, rep from *, ending row with sc in each of the last 2 sc, ch 1 and turn.

Row 4: Sc in the 1st sc, *ch 3, work 4 dc in the 2-ch, ch 2, work 4 dc in the same 2-ch, ch 3, sc in the 2nd sc, rep from *, ending row with sc in the last sc.

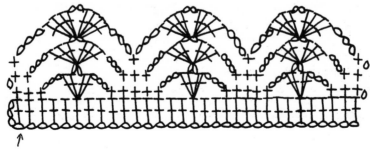

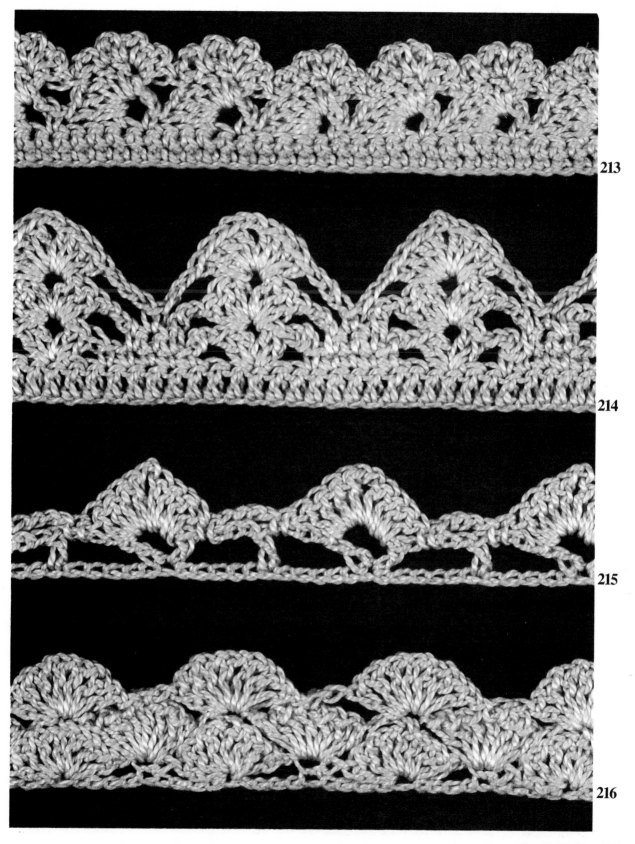

213

214

215

216

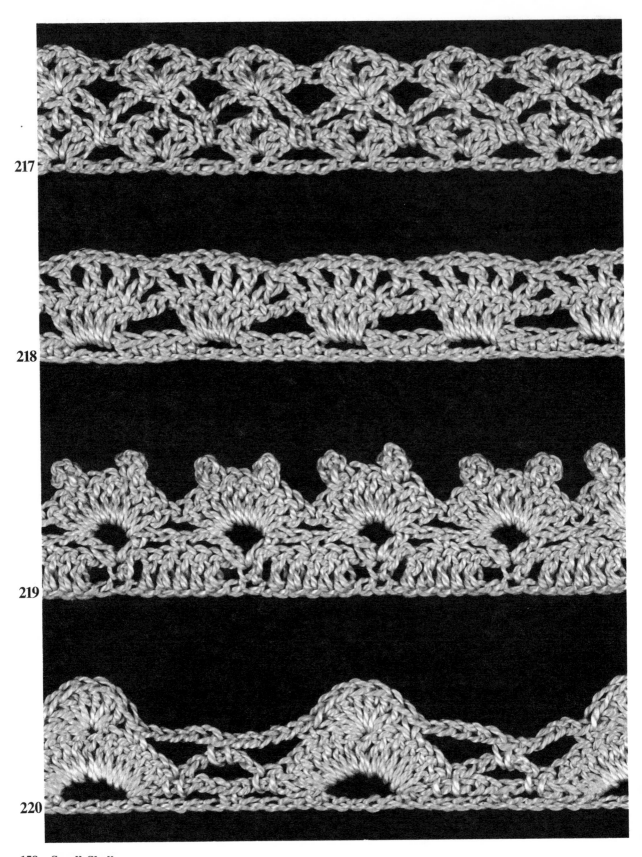

217

218

219

220

158 Small Shells

215. Chain multiples of 13 plus 5.

Row 1: 1 dc in the 5th ch, * ch 4, dc in the 6th ch, ch 4, dc in the 7th ch, ch 4 and dc in the same ch, rep from *, ending row with dc in the last ch, ch 5 and turn.
Row 2: * sc around the 4-ch, 4 dc around the next 4-ch, ch 2, work another 4 dc around the same 4-ch, sc around the next 4-ch, ch 4, rep from *, ending row with 4 dc in the turning ch and 1 trc.

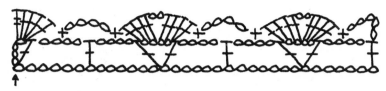

216. Chain multiples of 10 plus 2.

Row 1: Sc in the 2nd ch, *ch 1, and work 1 dc in the 5th ch, ch 1, 7 times, sc in the 5th ch, rep from *, ending row with dc and ch in the last ch 3 times and 1 other dc in the last ch, ch 1 and turn.
Row 2: Sc in the 1st dc, *ch 1 and dc in the sc 7 times, ch 1 and sc in the 4th dc, rep from *, ending row with dc and ch 3 times, 1 other dc in last sc, ch 1 and turn.
Row 3: Sc in the 1st dc, *ch 1 and dc in the sc 7 times, ch 1 and sc in the 4th dc, rep from *, ending row with dc and 1 ch 3 times, 1 additional dc in the last sc.

217. Chain multiples of 6 plus 3.

Row 1: 2 dc in the 6th ch, * ch 2, 2 dc in the same ch, 2 dc in the 6th ch, rep from *, ending row with last set and 1 dc in the 3rd and last ch, ch 1 and turn.
Row 2: Sc in the dc, *ch 3, dc in the 2-ch, ch 3, sc between the 2 sets of shells, rep from *, ending row with sc in the turning ch, ch 4 and turn.
Row 3: *2 dc in the dc, ch 2, 2 dc in the dc just used, rep from *, ending row with last set and 1 trc in the last sc.

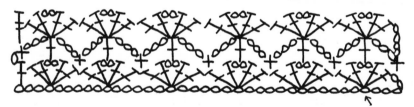

218. Chain multiples of 7 plus 2.

Row 1: Sc in the 2nd ch and each of the next 2 chs, * ch 3, sc in the 4th ch and each of the next 3 chs, rep from *, ending row with sc in each of the last 3 chs, ch 4 and turn.
Row 2: * work 5 dc in the next 3-ch, ch 3, rep from *, ending row with last set, 1 ch and dc in the turning ch, ch 3 and turn.
Row 3: Sk 1st dc, *dc in the next dc, ch 1, 4 times, dc in the next dc, rep from *, ending row with an extra dc in the turning ch.

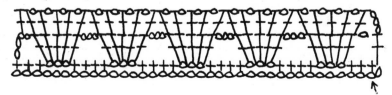

219. Chain multiples of 7 plus 4.

Row 1: Dc in the 5th ch and dc in the next ch, * ch 2, sc in the 2nd ch, ch 2, dc in the 2nd ch and in each of the next 4 chs, rep from *, ending row with dc in each of the last 3 chs, ch 1 and turn.

Row 2: Sc in 1st dc, *ch 1, dc in the sc, ch 3, dc in the same sc, ch 1, sc in the 3rd dc, rep from *, ending row with sc in the turning ch, ch 3 and turn.

Row 3: * work 3 dc in the beginning of the 3-ch, work 3-ch picot, work 3 dc in the middle of the same 3-ch, work 3-ch picot, work 3 more dc in the same 3-ch, rep from *, ending row with last set and dc in the last sc.

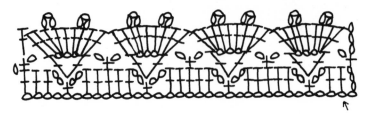

220. Chain multiples of 15 plus 2.

Row 1: Sc in the 2nd ch, *ch 5 and sc in the 5th ch, rep from *, ending row with last sc, ch 5 and turn.

Row 2: *sc around the next 5-ch, work 13 dc around the next 5-ch, sc in the next 5-ch, ch 5, rep from *, ending row with sc and 3 dc in the last sc, ch 1 and turn.

Row 3: Sc in the 1st dc, *ch 5, sc in the middle of the 5-ch, ch 5, sc in the 4th dc, work 7 dc in the 3rd dc, sc in the 3rd dc, rep from *, ending row with sc in the turning ch.

221. Chain multiples of 10 plus 4.

Row 1: Dc in the 4th ch and in each ch all across the row, ch 4 and turn.

Row 2: Dc in the 2nd dc, *ch 1 and dc in the 2nd dc, rep from *, ending row with dc in the turning ch, ch 4 and turn.

Row 3: Sk 1st dc, dc in next dc, *ch 1 and dc in the next dc, rep from *, ending row with dc in the turning ch, ch 3 and turn.

Row 4: Sk 1st dc, dc in each ch and in each dc all across the row, ending row with 2 dc in the turning ch, ch 1 and turn.

Row 5: Sl st in 1st dc, *ch 1 and work double trc in 5th dc 7 times, ch 1 and sl st in 5th dc, rep from *, ending row with sl st in the turning ch, ch 1 and turn.

Row 6: Sl st in 1st ch, work 3-ch picot and sc in next 1-ch 6 times, work 3-ch picot and sl st in next 1-ch, sl st in next 1-ch, rep from *, ending row with sl st in the last dc.

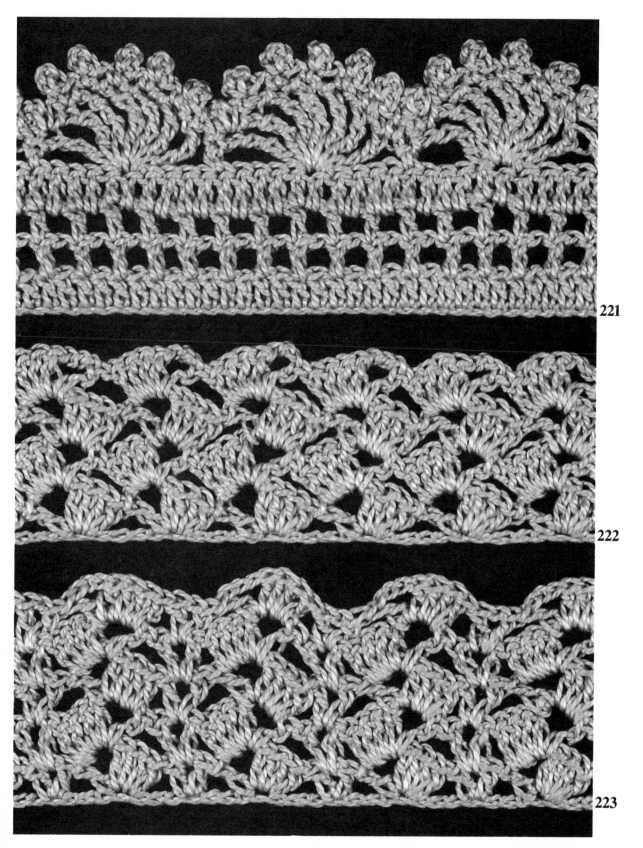

221

222

223

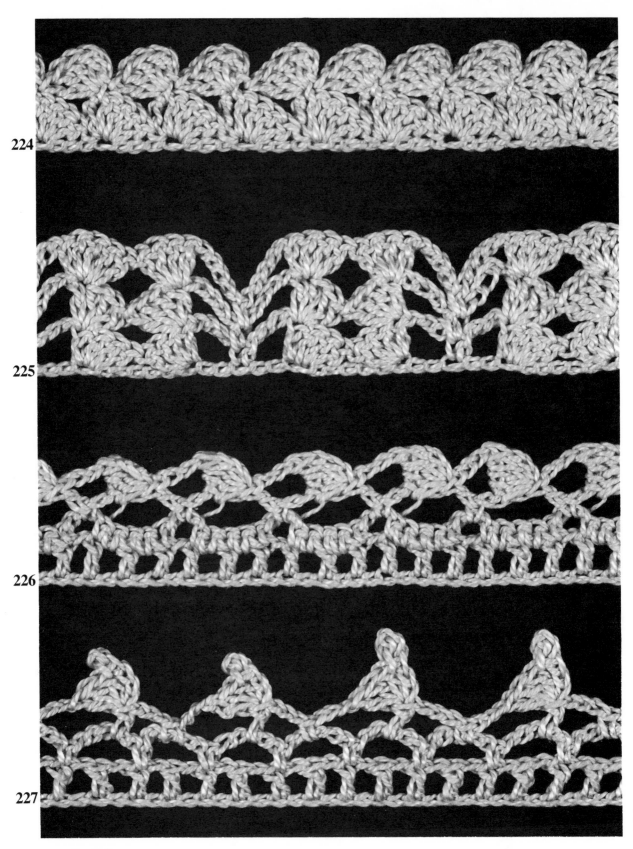

224

225

226

227

162 Small Shells

222. Chain multiples of 5 plus 4.

Row 1: Work 4 dc in the 7th ch, *ch 3, 1 dc in the ch just used, 4 dc in the 5th ch, rep from *, ending row with last set and 1 dc in the 3rd ch, ch 3 and turn.

Row 2: * 4 dc in the 3-ch, ch 3, 1 dc in the same 3-ch, rep from *, ending row with last set and 1 dc in the turning ch, ch 3 and turn.

Rows 3–4: Same as row 2.

223. Chain multiples of 8 plus 4.

Row 1: Dc in the 4th ch, * 4 dc in the 4th ch, ch 3, 1 dc in the ch just used, dc in the 4th ch, ch 1, dc in the same ch, rep from *, ending row with last set and 2 dc in the last ch, ch 3 and turn.

Row 2: Dc in the 1st dc, * 4 dc in the 3-ch, ch 3, dc in the 3-ch just used, dc in the 1-ch, ch 1, dc in the same 1-ch, rep from *, ending row with last set and 2 dc in the turning ch, ch 3 and turn.

Rows 3–5: Same as row 2.

224. Chain multiples of 4 plus 2.

Row 1: Sc in the 2nd ch, * ch 2, 4 dc in the sc just formed, sc in the 4th ch, rep from *, ending row with sc in the last ch, ch 3 and turn.

Row 2: 2 dc in the sc, * sc in the top of the next 2-ch, ch 2, 4 dc in the sc just formed, rep from *, ending row with last set and 2 dc in the last sc.

225. Chain multiples of 12 plus 4.

Row 1: 3 dc in the 4th ch, * 4 dc in the 6th ch, ch 4, sc in the 3rd ch, ch 4, 4 dc in the 3rd ch, rep from *, ending row with last sc, ch 4 and dc in the 3rd ch, ch 8 and turn.

Row 2: *sc in the sc, ch 5, 4 dc in the 1st dc, 4 dc in the 7th dc, ch 5, rep from *, ending row with 4 dc in the turning ch, ch 3 and turn.

Row 3: 3 dc in the 1st dc, * 4 dc in the 7th dc, ch 6, sc in the next sc, ch 6, 4 dc in the next dc, rep from *, ending row with 1 dc in the turning ch.

226. Chain multiples of 6 plus 5.

Row 1: Dc in the 5th ch, * ch 1, dc in the 2nd ch, rep from *, ending row with 1 dc in the ch after the last dc, ch 3 and turn.

Row 2: 1 sc in the 2nd dc, *sc in the next 1-ch, sc in the next dc, sc in the next 1-ch, sc in the next dc, ch 3, sc in the next dc, rep from *, ending row with last set, ch 1 and work 1 hdc in the turning ch, ch 1 and turn.

Row 3: Sc in the hdc, *ch 7, work 1 dc back in the sc, ch 3, work 4 dc back in the top of the dc, sc in the top of the 3-ch, sl st back in each of the 4 dc, ch 3, dc in sc, rep from *, ending row with sc in the turning ch.

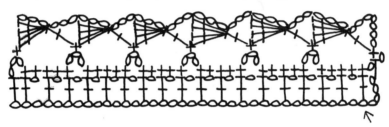

227. Chain multiples of 8 plus 5.

Row 1: 1 dc in the 7th ch, * ch 1, 1 dc in the 2nd ch, rep from *, ending row with last dc, ch 5 and turn.

Row 2: *1 sc in the 2nd dc, ch 5, rep from *, ending row with sc in the last dc, ch 2, 1 dc in the turning ch, ch 1 and turn.

Row 3: Sc in the dc, * ch 3, dc in the next 5-ch, ch 4, work 4-ch picot, 3 dc in the 1st of the 4-ch just made, ch 3, sc in the next 5-ch, rep from *, ending row with sc in the turning ch.

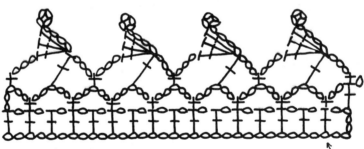

·13·
Shells—Large Patterns

228. Chain multiples of 11 plus 2.

Row 1: Sc in the 2nd ch and in each of the next 4 chs, *ch 3, sc in the 3rd ch and each of the next 8 chs, rep from *, ending row with sc in each of the last 5 chs, ch 1 and turn.

Row 2: Sc in the 1st sc, *ch 4, work 7 dc in the 3-ch, ch 4, sc in the 5th sc, rep from *, ending row with sc in the last sc, ch 1 and turn.

Row 3: *sc in the sc, ch 4, dc in each dc, ch 4, rep from *, ending row with sc in the last sc, ch 1 and turn.

Row 4: *sc in the sc, ch 4, dc in the next dc and ch 1, 6 times, dc in the next dc, ch 4, rep from *, ending row with sc in the last sc, ch 7 and turn.

Row 5: Work sc in the next dc and next ch 6 times, sc in the next dc, ch 3 and rep from *, ending row with last sc, ch 2 and double trc in the last sc.

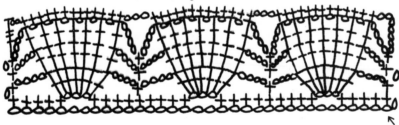

229. Chain multiples of 36 plus 2.

Row 1: Sc in the 2nd ch and in each ch all across the row, ch 5 and turn.

Row 2: Dc in the 4th sc, * ch 2, dc in the 3rd sc, rep from *, ending row with dc in the last sc, ch 5 and turn.

Row 3: Dc in the 2nd dc, ch 2 and dc in the next dc 3 times, * ch 4, work sc in the 2nd dc, ch 5, sc in the next dc, ch 4, dc in the 2nd dc, ch 2 4 times, rep from *, ending row with last dc in turning ch, ch 5 and turn.

Row 3: Dc in the 2nd dc, ch 2 and dc in the next dc 2 times, * ch 5, double trc and ch 1 in the 5-ch 4 times, and work 1 more double trc in the same 5-ch, ch 5, dc in the 2nd dc, ch 2 and dc in the next dc 2 times, ch 2 and dc in the turning ch, rep from *, ending row with dc in the turning ch, ch 5 and turn.

Row 4: Dc in the 2nd dc, ch 2 and dc in the next dc, * ch 5, work 1 double trc, ch 1 and work another double trc and ch 3 in each of the next 4 double trc, work another double trc, ch 1 and double trc in the same double trc, ch 5, dc in the 2nd dc, ch 2 and dc in the next dc, ch 2 and dc in the turning ch, ch 5 and turn.

Row 5: Dc in the 2nd dc, * ch 5, work 3 double trc in the next 1-ch, followed by 2 chs, work 3-ch picot, and 2 chs 4 times, work another double trc in the next 1-ch, ch 5, dc in the 2nd dc, ch 2 and dc in the turning ch.

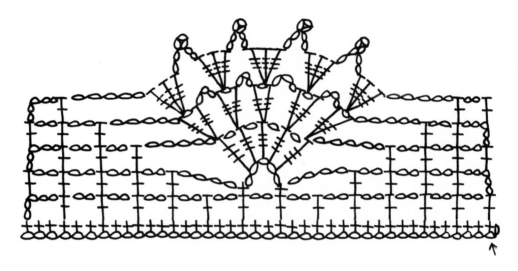

230. Chain multiples of 18 plus 4.

Row 1: Dc in the 5th ch, * ch 2 and dc in the 3rd ch, rep from *, ending row with last dc and 1 dc in the ch after that, ch 4 and turn.

Row 2: 3 dc in the 1st 2-ch, * ch 3, work 3 dc in the 2nd 2-ch, rep from *, ending row with last 3 dc, ch 1, 1 dc in the turning ch, ch 3 and turn.

Row 3: Dc in the 1-ch, * ch 3, 3 dc in the next 3-ch, ch 5, work 3 dc in the next 3-ch, ch 3, 3 dc in the next 3-ch, rep from *, ending row with 2 dc in the turning ch, ch 1 and turn.

Row 4: Sc in the 1st dc, ch 1, * sc in the beginning of the 3-ch, ch 3, work 3 dc in the 1st part of the 5-ch, ch 5, work 3 dc in the last part of the 5-ch, ch 3, sc in the last part of the next 3-ch, ch 3, rep from *, ending row with sc in the last part of the 3-ch, ch 1 and sc in the turning ch, ch 1 and turn.

Row 5: Sc in the 1st sc and sc in the 1-ch, * ch 2, dc in each of the next 3 dc, work 3 dc in the beginning of the 5-ch, ch 3, work 3 dc in the last part of the 5-ch, dc in each of the next 3 dc, ch 2, work 3 sc around the 3-ch, rep from *, ending row with sc in the last 1-ch and sc in the last sc, ch 1 and turn.

Row 6: Sc in 1st sc, *ch 3, dc in each of the next 6 dc, work 6 dc around the next 3 chs, work 1 dc in each of the next 6 dc, ch 3, sc in the 2nd sc, rep from *, ending row with sc in the last sc, ch 5 and turn.

Row 7: Dc in the 1st dc, * ch 1, dc in the 2nd dc 4 times, ch 2, dc in the next dc, ch 1 and dc in the 2nd dc 3 times, ch 1 and finish 2 dc together in the 2nd dc and the next dc, rep from *, ending row with 1 ch and 1 double trc in the last sc, ch 1 and turn.

Row 8: Sc in the double trc, * work 2 sc in each of the next 4 1-chs, 3 sc in the next 1-ch, 2 sc in each of the next 4 1-chs, rep from *, ending row with sc in the last dc.

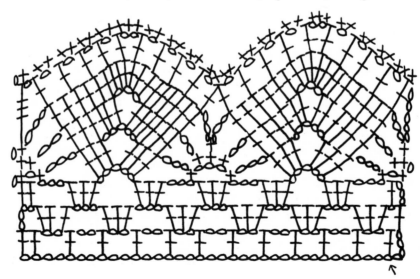

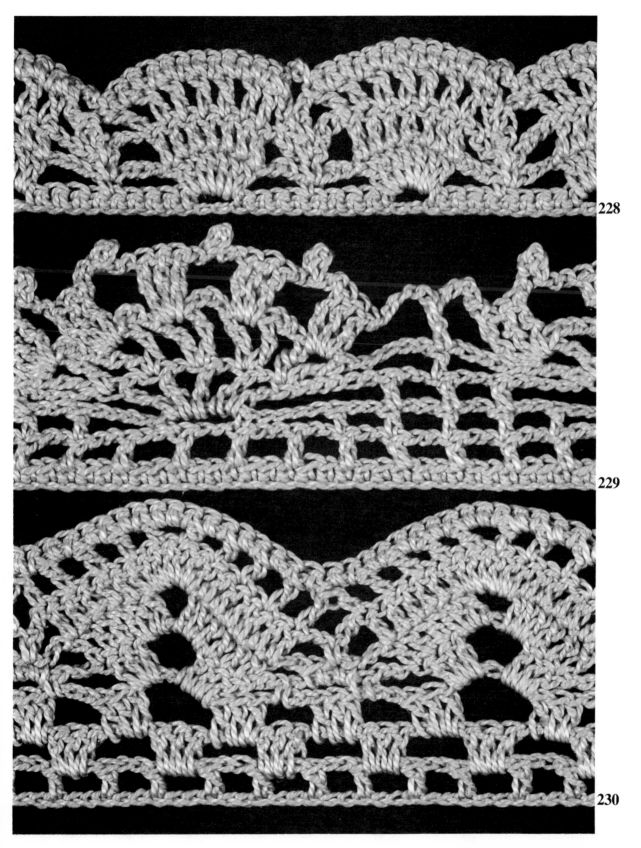

228

229

230

Shells—Large Patterns 167

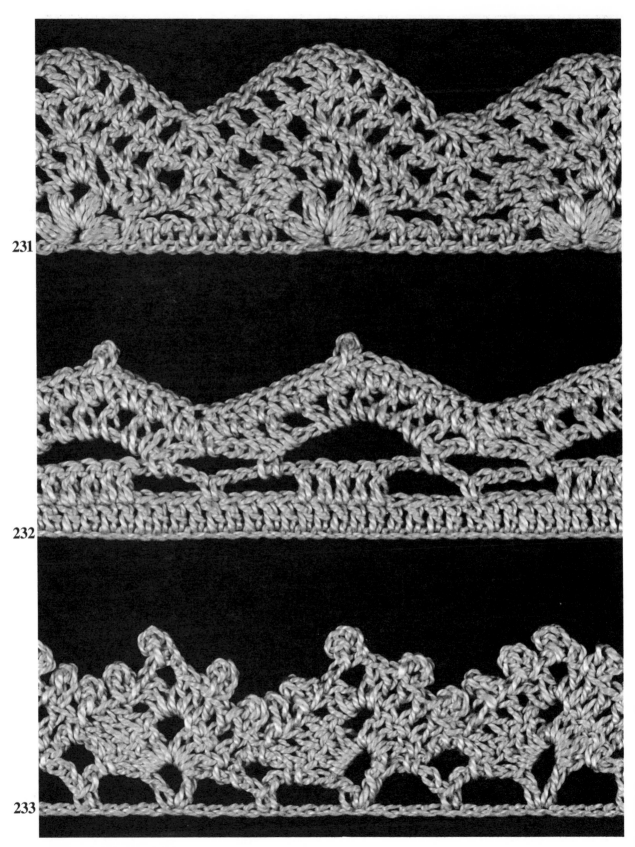

231

232

233

168   Shells—Large Patterns

231. Chain multiples of 14 plus 2.

Row 1: Sc in the 2nd ch, sc in the next ch, * ch 2, sc in the 2nd ch, ch 2, work 3-looped puff stitch in the 4th ch, ch 3, work 3-looped puff stitch in the same ch, ch 3, work another 3-looped puff stitch in the same ch, ch 3, work another 3-looped puff stitch in the same ch, ch 2, sc in 4th ch, ch 2, sc in 2nd ch, ch 2, sc in 2nd ch, rep from *, ending row with sc in the last ch, ch 1 and turn.

Row 2: Sc in the 1st sc, *ch 2, work 1 dc in the next 3-ch, ch 1, dc in the same 3-ch, ch 1, dc in the same 3-ch, ch 1 and dc in the next 3-ch, ch 1 and dc in the same 3-ch, ch 1 and dc in the same 3-ch, ch 1 and dc in the next 3-ch, ch 1 and dc in the same 3-ch, ch 1 and dc in the same 3-ch, ch 2, sc in the 3rd 2-ch, rep from *, ending row with sc in the last sc, ch 4 and turn.

Row 3: Dc in 1st dc, * ch 1 and dc in the next dc 3 times, ch 1 and dc in the next 1-ch, ch 1 and dc in the next dc, ch 1 and dc in the next 1-ch, ch 1 and dc in the next dc 3 times, ch 2, finish 3 dc together 1 in the next dc, 1 in the sc and 1 in the next dc, rep from *, ending row with 2 dc finished together in the last dc and the sc, ch 3 and turn.

Row 4: Sk 2 dc finished together, dc in the next dc, ch 2, * dc in the next dc and ch 1 3 times, dc in the 1-ch and ch 1, dc in the next dc, ch 1, dc in the 1-ch, ch 1, dc in the next dc and 1 ch, 2 times, dc in the next dc and ch 2, finish 3 dc together in the next dc, the 3 dc finished together and the next dc, rep from *, ending row with 2 dc finished together, the last in the turning ch.

232. Chain multiples of 16 plus 4.

Row 1: Dc in the 5th ch and in each ch all across the row, ch 1 and turn.

Row 2: Sc in the 1st dc, *ch 5 and dc in the 5th dc, dc in each of the next 5 dc, ch 5 and sc in the 5th dc, rep from *, ending row with sc in the turning ch, ch 6 and turn.

Row 3: * sc towards the end of the 5-ch, ch 10, and sc towards the beginning of the next 5-ch, ch 7, rep from *, ending row with sc, ch 3 and dc in the last sc, ch 1 and turn.

Row 4: Sc in the dc, * ch 1 and dc in the 10-ch 8 times, ch 1 and sc around the 7-ch, rep from *, ending row with sc in the turning ch, ch 1 and turn.

Row 5: Work 2 hdc in the 1-ch, * work 2 hdc in each of the next 3 1-chs, work 1 hdc in the next 1-ch, work 3-ch picot, work 2 hdc in the same 1-ch, work 2 hdc in each of the next 3 1-chs, finish 2 hdc finished together in each of the next 2 1-chs, rep from *, ending row with sc in the last sc.

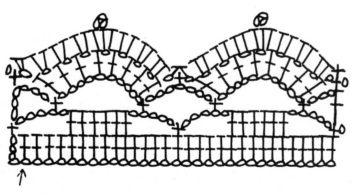

233. Chain multiples of 10 plus 2.

Row 1: Sc in the 2nd ch, *ch 5 and dc in the 5th ch, ch 5 and dc in the same ch, ch 5 and sc in the 5th ch, rep from *, ending row with last sc, ch 6 and turn.

Row 2: *sc in the middle of the 5-ch, work 3 dc towards the beginning of the 2nd 5-ch, ch 3 and work another 3 dc towards the end of the same 5-ch, sc in the middle of the next 5-ch, ch 5 and rep from *, ending row with sc in the last 5-ch, ch 2 and turn.

Row 3: *dc in the 1st dc and work 5-ch picot, dc in each of the next 2 dc and another 5-ch picot, work 2 dc in the 3-ch and another 5-ch picot, work another 2 dc in the 3-ch and 5-ch picot, dc in each of the next 2 dc and 5-ch picot, dc in the next dc and sc in the next 5-ch, rep from *, ending row with last set.

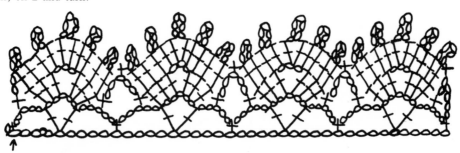

234. Chain multiples of 22 plus 6.

Row 1: Dc in the 8th ch, * ch 1 and dc in the 2nd ch, rep from *, ending row with last dc, ch 1 and turn.

Row 2: Sc in the 1st dc, sc in the ch and dc 3 times, * ch 3 and dc in the 3rd 1-ch, ch 2 and dc in the same 1-ch, ch 3 and sc in the 3rd dc, sc in the ch and sc in the dc 5 times, rep from *, ending row with last 7 sc, the last 2 in the turning ch, ch 1 and turn.

Row 3: Sc in each of the next 6 sc, * ch 3 and dc in the next dc, ch 1 and dc in the 2-ch, ch 3 and dc in the same 2-ch, ch 1 and dc in the next dc, ch 3 and sc in the 2nd sc and in each of the next 8 sc, rep from *, ending row with last 6 sc, ch 1 and turn.

Row 4: Sc in each of the next 5 sc, * ch 3, dc in the next dc and ch 1, dc in the next dc and ch 1, dc in the 3-ch, ch 3, dc in the same 3-ch, ch 1 and dc in the next dc, ch 1 and dc in the next dc, ch 3 and sc in the 2nd sc, sc in each of the next 6 sc, rep from *, ending row with sc in each of the last 5 sc, ch 1 and turn.

Row 5: Sc in the 1st sc and sc in each of the next 3 sc, * ch 3 and dc in the next dc, ch 1 and dc in the next dc, ch 1 and dc in the next dc, ch 1 and dc in the 3-ch, ch 3 and dc in the same 3-ch, ch 1 and dc in the next dc 3 times, ch 3 and sc in the 2nd sc and sc in each of the next 4 sc, rep from *, ending row with sc in each of the last 4 sc, ch 1 and turn.

Row 6: Sc in each of the next 3 sc, * ch 3 and dc in the next dc, ch 1 and dc in the next dc 3 times, ch 1 and dc in the 3-ch, ch 3 and dc in the same 3-ch, ch 1 and dc in the next dc 4 times, ch 3 and sc in the 2nd sc, sc in each of the next 2 sc, rep from *, ending row with sc in each of the 3 last sc, ch 6 and turn.

Row 7: * sc in the dc and ch 3 5 times, sc in the 3-ch, ch 3 and sc in the next dc 5 times, work 4-ch picot, rep from *, ending row with last sc, ch 2 and trc in the last sc.

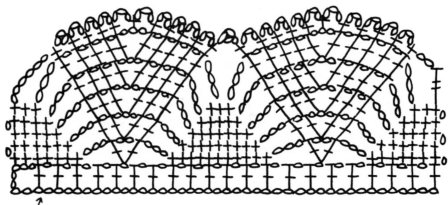

235. Chain multiples of 20 plus 2.

Row 1: Sc in the 2nd ch and in each ch all across the row, ch 1 and turn.

Row 2: Sc in the 1st sc, * ch 4 and sc in the 4th sc, rep from *, ending row with last sc, ch 6 and turn.

Row 3: * sc around the 4-ch, ch 4, sc around the next 4-ch, ch 3, work 2 dc around the middle of the next 4-ch, ch 3, sc around the next 4-ch, ch 4, sc around the 4-ch, ch 4 and rep from *, ending row with last sc, ch 2 and trc in the last sc, ch 1 and turn.

Row 4: Sc in the trc, * ch 4, sc around the 4-ch, ch 4, dc in the last of the 3-ch, dc in each of the next 2 dc, dc in the beginning of the next 3-ch, ch 4, sc around the 4-ch, ch 4 and sc around the middle of the 4-ch, rep from *, ending row with sc in the turning ch, ch 6 and turn.

Row 5: * sc around the 4-ch, ch 5, dc in the end of the next 4-ch, dc in each of the next 4 dc, dc in the beginning of the next 4-ch, ch 5, sc around the next 4-ch, ch 4, rep from *, ending row with sc in the last 4-ch, ch 2 and trc in the last sc, ch 1 and turn.

Row 6: Sc in the trc, * ch 5, work 1 trc in the dc, and work 4-ch picot 5 times, trc in the last dc, ch 5 and sc around the 4-ch, rep from *, ending row with sc in the turning ch.

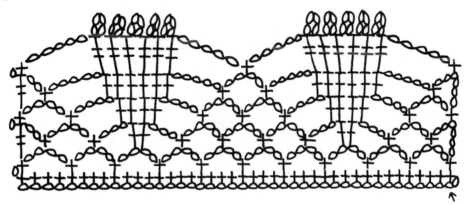

236. Chain multiples of 16 plus 6.

Row 1: Sc in the 8th ch, * ch 5, sc in the 4th ch, rep from *, ending row with last sc, ch 2 and dc in the 2nd ch, ch 1 and turn.

Row 2: Sc in 1st dc, ch 5, *sc around the middle of the 5-ch, ch 5, sc around the middle of the next 5-ch, work 8 dc around the middle of the 5-ch, sc around the middle of the next 5-ch, ch 5, rep from *, ending row with sc in the turning ch, ch 5 and turn.

Row 3: * sc around the middle of the 5-ch, ch 4, dc in the 2nd dc and in the next 5 dc, ch 4, sc around the middle of the next 5-ch, ch 5 and rep from *, ending row with sc around the 5-ch, ch 2 and dc in the last sc, ch 1 and turn.

Row 4: Sc in the dc, * ch 5, sc around the middle of the 5-ch, ch 5, sc around the 4-ch, ch 3, dc in the 2nd dc and in each of the next 3 dc, ch 3, sc around the 4-ch, rep from *, ending row with sc in the turning ch, ch 5 and turn.

Row 5: * sc around the middle of the 5-ch, ch 5, sc in the end of the 3-ch, ch 3, dc in the 2nd dc and the next dc, ch 3, sc in the beginning of the next 3-ch, ch 5, sc in the next 5-ch, ch 5, and rep from *, ending row with last sc, ch 2 and dc in the last sc.

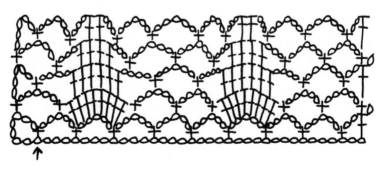

237. Chain multiples of 43 plus 4.

Row 1: Dc in the 5th ch and all across the row, ch 4 and turn.

Row 2: Dc in the 3rd dc, * ch 4 and dc in the 6th ch, ch 1 and dc in the 2nd dc, rep from *, ending row with dc, ch 1 and dc in the turning ch, ch 6 and turn.

Row 3: Work 1 dc in each of the 4-chs, ch 4 and 1 dc in each of the next 4-chs, ch 1 and work 9 trc in the next 4-ch, ch 1 and 1 dc in each of the next 4-chs, ch 4 and 1 dc in each of the next 4-chs, ch 3 and dc in the turning ch, ch 4 and turn.

Row 4: Work 2 dc in 3-ch, ch 4 and 1 dc in each of the 4-chs, ch 1 and trc in the trc, ch 1 and trc in the trc 8 times, ch 1 and 1 dc in each of the 4-chs, ch 4 and 3 dc in the turning ch, ch 6 and turn.

Row 5: Work 1 dc in each of the 4-chs, ch 1 and work 2 trc in the 2nd 1-ch, ch 2 and 2 trc in the next 1-ch 7 times, ch 1 and work 1 dc in each of the next 4-chs, ch 3 and dc in the turning ch, ch 4 and turn.

Row 6: 2 dc in the 3-ch, ch 2, work 3-ch picot, work 1 trc in the 2-ch, work 3-ch picot, and work 2 trc in the same 2-ch, work another 3-ch picot, work trc, picot, 2 trc, picot 6 more times, ch 2 and 3 dc in the turning ch.

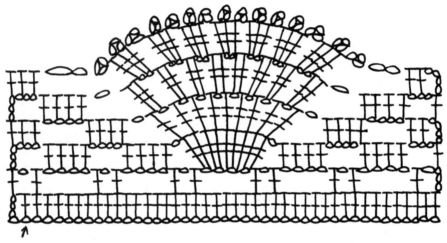

238. Chain multiples of 22 plus 2.

Row 1: Sc in the 2nd ch and in each ch all across the row, ch 1 and turn.

Row 2: Sc in the 1st sc and the next 3 sc, work another sc in the same sc, * ch 6, dc in the 6th sc, and each of the next 3 sc, ch 6, work 2 sc in the 6th sc, and sc in each of the next 6 sc, work another sc in the same sc, rep from *, ending row with 5 sc, ch 1 and turn.

Row 3: Sc in the 1st 4 sc, * ch 6, 2 dc in the 1st dc, dc in the next dc, ch 3, dc in the next dc, 2 dc in the next dc, ch 6, sc in the 2nd sc and sc in each of the next 6 sc, rep from *, ending row with sc in the last 4 sc, ch 1 and turn.

Row 4: Sc in the 1st 3 sc, * ch 6, 1 dc in each of the 1st 3 dc, ch 3, dc in the 3-ch, ch 3, dc in the same 3-ch, ch 3, dc in each of the next 3 dc, ch 6 and sc in the 2nd sc and each of the next 4 sc, rep from *, ending row with 3 sc, ch 1 and turn.

Row 5: Sc in each of the 1st 2 sc, * ch 6, dc in each of the next 3 dc, ch 3, dc in the next dc, ch 3, dc in the next 3-ch, ch 3, dc in the same 3-ch, ch 3, dc in the dc, ch 3, dc in the next dc, dc in the next 2 dc, ch 6, sc in the 2nd sc and the next 2 sc, rep from *, ending row with 2 sc, ch 1 and turn.

Row 6: Sc in the 1st sc, * ch 6, dc in each of the next 3 dc, ch 3 and dc in the next dc 2 times, ch 3, dc in the 3-ch, ch 3 and dc in the same 3-ch, ch 3 and dc in the next dc 3 times, dc in the next 2 dc, ch 6 and sc in the 2nd sc, rep from *, ending row with sc, ch 8 and turn.

Row 7: * dc in each of the next 3 dc, ch 3 and dc in the next dc 3 times, ch 3 and dc in the 3-ch, ch 3 and dc in the same 3-ch, ch 3 and dc in the next dc 4 times, dc in the next 2 dc, ch 3 and rep from *, ending row with double trc in the last sc, ch 5 and turn.

Row 8: Dc in 1st dc, * dc in each of the next 2 dc, ch 3 and dc in the dc 4 times, ch 3 and dc in the 3-ch, ch 3 and dc in the same 3-ch, ch 3 and dc in the next dc 5 times, dc in the next dc, finish it together with a dc in the 3-ch and dc in the next dc, rep from *, ending row with 2 dc finished together in the last dc and the turning ch, ch 1 and turn.

Row 9: Sc in each of the 1st dc, * work 2 sc around the beginning of the 3-ch, work 3-ch picot, work 2 other sc around the same 3-ch, sc in each dc in between sets, rep from *, ending row with sc in the last 3 dc and the turning ch.

234

235

236

237

238

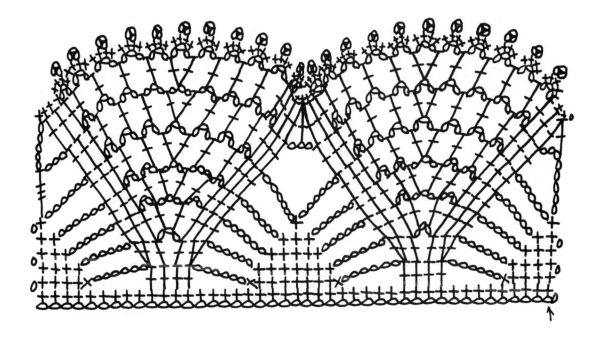

239. **Chain multiples of 16 plus 2.**

Row 1: Sc in the 2nd ch and in each ch all across the row, ch 3 and turn.

Row 2: Dc in the 3rd sc, ch 1, dc in the sc just used, * dc in the 3rd sc, ch 1, dc in the sc just used, rep from *, ending row with last set and 1 dc in the 2nd sc, ch 5 and turn.

Row 3: Sc in the 1-ch, *ch 5, sc in the next 1-ch, rep from *, ending row with 2 chs and 1 dc in the turning ch, ch 3 and turn.

Row 4: 3 dc around the 2-ch, * sc in the middle of the 5-ch, ch 5, sc in the next 5-ch, ch 5, sc in the middle of the next 5-ch, work 7 dc around the next 5-ch, rep from *, ending row with 4 dc in the turning ch, ch 4 and turn.

Row 5: Sk 1st dc, dc in the next dc and ch 1 3 times, *sc in the middle of the next 5-ch, ch 5, sc in the middle of the next 5-ch, ch 5, sc in the middle of the next 5-ch, ch 1 and dc in the next dc 7 times, ch 1, rep from *, ending row with dc and ch in each of the last dc, 1 dc in the turning ch, ch 5 and turn.

Row 6: Sk 1st dc, dc in next dc and ch 2 3 times, *sc in the middle of the next 5-ch, ch 5, sc in the middle of the next 5-ch, ch 2 and dc in the next dc 7 times and ch 2, rep from *, ending row with dc in the turning ch, ch 3 and turn.

Row 7: 3-ch picot, * dc in each 2-ch and 3-ch picot, work 1 sc in 5-ch and 3-ch picot, rep from *, ending row with dc in turning ch.

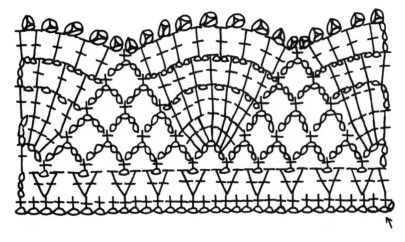

240.   Chain multiples of 25 plus 6.

Row 1: Dc in the 8th ch, * ch 1 and dc in the 2nd ch, rep from *, ending row with dc in the last ch, ch 1 and turn.

Row 2: Sc in the 1st dc, ch, dc, ch and dc, * ch 3 and dc in the 3rd dc, dc in the next ch, the dc, the ch and the dc, ch 3 and sc in the 3rd dc, the ch, the dc, the ch, the dc, the ch, the dc, the ch and the dc, rep from *, ending row with sc in the last dc, ch, and dc, 2 in the turning ch, ch 1 and turn.

Row 3: Sc in each of the 1st 4 sc, * ch 3, dc in each of the next 3 dc, ch 2, and dc in the dc just used, dc in each of the next 2 dc, ch 3, sc in the 2nd sc and sc in each of the next 6 sc, rep from *, ending row with sc in each of the last 4 sc, ch 1 and turn.

Row 4: Sc in each of the 1st 3 sc, * ch 3 and dc in each of the next 3 dc, ch 2 and sc in the 2-ch, ch 2 and dc in each of the next 3 dc, ch 3 and sc in the 2nd sc, sc in each of the next 4 sc, rep from *, ending row with sc in each of the last 3 sc, ch 1 and turn.

Row 5: Sc in each of the 1st 2 sc, * ch 3 and dc in each of the next 3 dc, ch 1 and sc in the dc just used, ch 10 and sc in the next dc, ch 1 and dc in the dc just used, dc in each of the next 2 dc, ch 3 and sc in the 2nd sc and each of the next 2 sc, rep from *, ending row with sc in each of the last 2 sc, ch 1 and turn.

Row 6: Sc in the 1st sc, * ch 3, dc in each of the next 3 dc, work 16 dc in the middle of the 10-ch, dc in each of the next 3 dc, ch 3 and sc in the 2nd sc, rep from *, ending row with sc in the last sc, ch 9 and turn.

Row 7: Sk 1st 3 dc, * work 1 trc in the next dc, work another trc in the 2nd dc, ch 2, work trc in the dc just used, work trc in the 2nd dc, rep 6 more times, ch 2 and dc in the sc, ch 2 and rep from *, ending row with dc in the last 3-ch, ch 1 and turn.

Row 8: Sl st in the dc, sl st in the 2-ch, sl st in the 1st trc, * sc in the 2-ch, work 4-ch picot, rep 5 more times, sc in the next 2-ch, sl st and rep from *, ending row with last set and sl st 3 times in the turning ch.

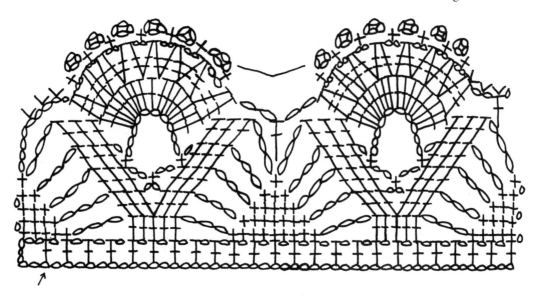

241.   Chain multiples of 26 plus 2.

Row 1: Sc in the 2nd ch and in each ch all across the row, ch 7 and turn.

Row 2: Trc in the 5th sc, * ch 1 and trc in the 2nd sc, ch 1 and trc in the 2nd sc, ch 2 and trc in the 5th sc, ch 7 and trc in the same sc, ch 2 and trc in the 5th sc, ch 1 and trc in the 2nd sc, ch 1 and trc in the 2nd sc, ch 7 and trc in the 8th sc, and rep from *, ending row with trc in the last sc, ch 1 and turn.

Row 3: Sc in the 1st trc, * ch 7 and sc in the 2nd trc, ch 2 and work 11 dc around the 7-ch, ch 2 and sc in the 2nd trc, ch 7 and sc around the middle of the 7-ch, rep from *, ending row with sc in the turning ch, ch 7 and turn.

Row 4: * sc around the middle of the 7-ch, ch 3 and finish 3 trc together in each of the next 3 dc, ch 7 and finish 3 trc together, 1 in the dc just used and 1 in each of the next 2 dc, rep 3 more times, ch 4 and sc around the middle of the 7-ch, ch 7, rep from *, ending row with last sc, ch 3 and trc in the last sc, ch 5 and turn.

Row 5: *sc in the middle of the 7-ch, ch 8 3 times, sc in the next 7-ch, ch 4 and sc around the 7-ch, ch 4, rep from *, ending row with sc in the turning ch.

239

240

241

242

243

178   Shells—Large Patterns

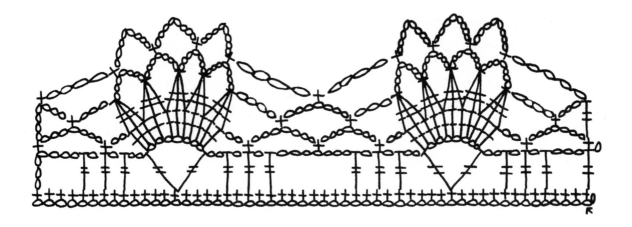

242. Chain multiples of 9 plus 6.

Row 1: Sc in the 8th ch, * work 6 dc in the 3rd ch, sc in the 3rd ch, ch 5 and sc in the 3rd ch, rep from *, ending row with sc after the last set, ch 2 and dc in the 2nd ch, ch 1 and turn.

Row 2: Sc in the dc, * ch 2 and dc in the next dc 6 times, ch 2 and sc in the middle of the 5-ch, rep from *, ending row with sc in the turning ch, ch 4 and turn.

Row 3: Dc in the dc and ch 3 all across the row, dc in the last sc after the last dc, ch 1 and turn.

Row 4: Sk 1st dc, * sc in the dc, work 3 dc in the 3-ch, rep from *, ending row with sc in the turning ch.

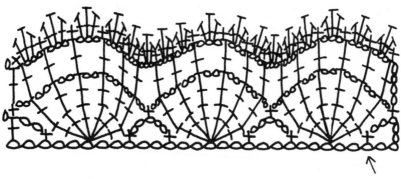

243. Chain multiples of 9 plus 4.

Row 1: Sc in the 5th ch, * ch 3 and sc in the 2nd ch, rep from *, ending row with last sc, ch 1 and hdc in the last ch, ch 1 and turn.

Row 2: Sc in the hdc, * ch 3, sc in the middle of the next 3-ch, work 7 trc around the middle of the next 3-ch, sc around the middle of the next 3-ch, ch 3 and sc in the middle of the next 3-ch, rep from *, ending row with sc in the turning ch, ch 4 and turn.

Row 3: * sc around the middle of the 3-ch, work 2 trc in each trc, sc around the middle of the 3-ch, ch 3, rep from *, ending row with sc, ch 1 and hdc in the sc, ch 1 and turn.

Row 4: * work 2 trc in the 1st trc, and 1 trc in the next trc 3 times, then 2 trc in each trc 2 times, 1 trc in the next trc and 2 trc in the next trc 3 times, ch 2, rep from *, ending row with sc.

Shells—Large Patterns 179

244. Chain multiples of 16 plus 4.

Row 1: Dc in the 5th ch and dc in each of the next 6 chs, * ch 1 and dc in the 2nd ch, dc in each of the next 14 chs, rep from *, ending row with 1 dc in each of the last 8 chs, ch 1 and turn.

Row 2: Sc in the dc, * ch 5 and sc in the 4th dc, ch 3 and work 5 dc in the 1-ch, ch 3 and sc in the 4th dc, ch 5 and sc in the 4th dc, rep from *, ending row with sc in the turning ch, ch 5 and turn.

Row 3: * sc in the 5-ch, ch 3, dc in the dc, ch 1, dc in the dc, ch 1, dc in the dc, ch 1, dc in the dc just used, ch 1, dc in the next dc, ch 1, dc in the next dc, ch 3, sc in the next 5-ch, ch 5, rep from *, ending row with last sc, ch 2 and dc in the last sc, ch 1 and turn.

Row 4: Sc in the dc, * ch 3 and dc in the 3-ch, ch 1 and dc in the 1-ch 5 times, ch 1 and dc in the beginning of the next 3-ch, ch 3 and sc in the middle of the 5-ch, rep from *, ending row with sc in the turning ch, ch 4 and turn.

Row 5: * work 2 trc in the 3-ch and work 3-ch picot, work 2 trc in the next 1-ch and work 3-ch picot 6 times, work 2 trc in the next 3-ch, rep from *, ending row with trc in the sc.

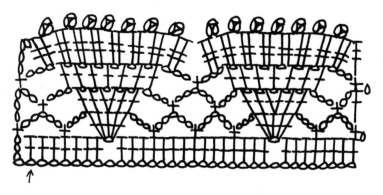

245. Chain multiples of 19 plus 6.

Row 1: Dc in the 8th ch, ch 1 and dc in the 2nd ch, * ch 3 and dc in the 4th ch, dc in the next ch, ch 3 and dc in the 4th ch, ch 1 and dc in the 2nd ch 5 times, rep from *, ending row with dc in each of the last 2 chs, ch 1 and turn.

Row 2: Sc in the 1st dc, ch 3 and sc in the 1-ch, ch 3 and sc in the next 1-ch, * ch 3 and dc in each of the next 2 dc, ch 3 and sc in the next 1-ch, ch 3 and sc in the 1-ch 4 more times, rep from *, ending row with sc in the turning ch, ch 3, another sc in the turning ch, ch 3 and turn.

Row 3: Sc in the 3-ch, ch 3 and sc in the next 3-ch, * ch 3 and work 2 dc in the next dc, ch 3 and work another 2 dc in the next dc, ch 3 and sc in the 3-ch, ch 3 and sc in the next 3-ch, ch 3 and sc in the next 3-ch, ch 3 and sc in the next 3-ch, rep from *, ending row with sc in the last 3-ch, ch 3 and hdc in the last sc, ch 1 and turn.

Row 4: Sc in the 3-ch, ch 3 and sc in the next 3-ch, * ch 3 and work 1 dc in each of the next 2 dc, ch 7, dc in each of the next 2 dc, ch 3 and sc in the next 3-ch, ch 3 and sc in the next 3-ch, ch 3 and sc in the next 3-ch, rep from *, ending row with sc in the hdc, ch 1 and turn.

Row 5: Sc in the hdc, ch 3 and sc in the sc, *ch 3, dc in each of the next 2 dc, ch 2 and trc in the 7-ch, ch 1 and trc in the 7-ch 5 more times, ch 2 and dc in each of the next 2 dc, ch 3 and sc in the 2nd 3-ch, ch 3 and sc in the next 3-ch, rep from *, ending row with sc, ch 3 and turn.

Row 6: Sc in the 3-ch, * ch 3 and dc in each of the next 2 dc, ch 4 and sc back into the 1st ch, work trc into the next trc ch 4 and sc in the 1st ch 6 more times, dc in each of the next 2 dc, ch 3 and sc in the 2nd 3-ch, rep from *, ending row with sc in the last 3-ch, ch 8 and turn.

Row 7: * work 3-ch picot, ch 2, finish 2 dc together in the next 2 dc, ch 2 and work 3-ch picot, ch 2 and trc in the next trc 6 times, ch 2, work 3-ch picot, ch 2 and finish 2 dc together in the next 2 dc, rep from *, ending row with double trc in the turning ch.

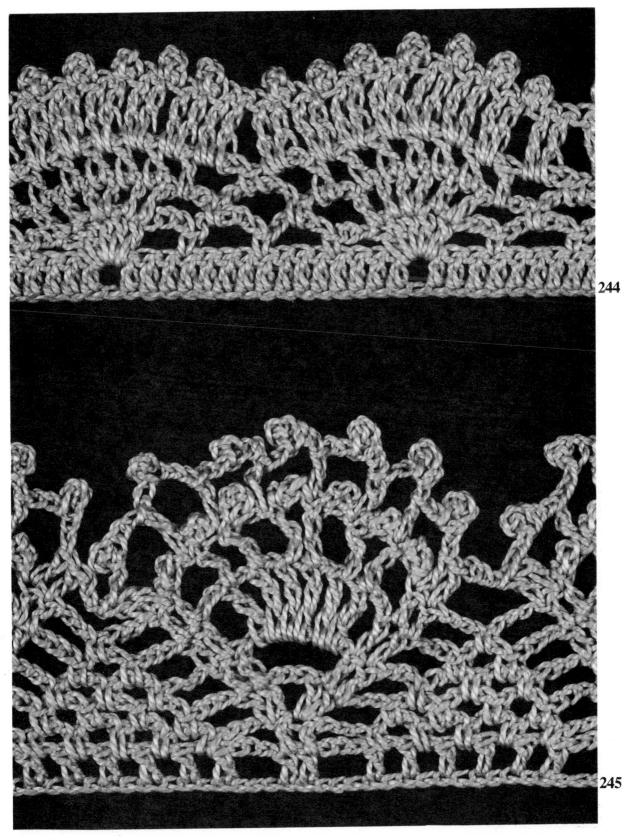

244

245

246

247

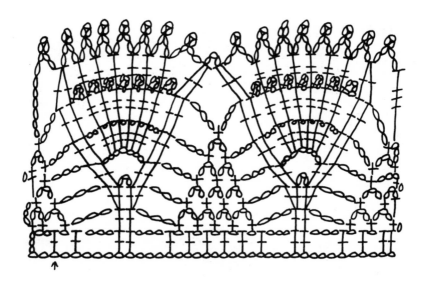

246.   Chain multiples of 29 plus 4.

Row 1: Dc in the 5th ch and in each ch all across the row, ch 5 and turn.

Row 2: Dc in the 4th dc, ch 2 and dc in the 3rd dc, ch 2 and dc in the 3rd dc, * ch 5 and trc in the 5th dc, ch 5 and dc in the 5th dc, ch 2 and dc in the 3rd dc 6 more times, rep from *, ending row with dc in the turning ch, ch 4 and turn.

Row 3: Dc in the middle of the 2-ch, ch 2 and dc in the middle of the next 2-ch, ch 2 and dc in the middle of the next 2-ch, * ch 5 and sc in the last of the 5-ch, sc in the trc, sc in the beginning of the 5-ch, ch 5 and dc in the 2-ch, ch 2 and dc in the next 2-ch 5 more times, rep from *, ending row with 2 dc in the turning ch, ch 5 and turn.

Row 4: Dc in the 2-ch, ch 2 and dc in the next 2-ch, * ch 5 and sc in last of the 5-ch, sc in each of next 3 sc, sc in beginning of next 5-ch, ch 5 and dc in next 2-ch, ch 2 and dc in the next dc 4 more times, rep from *, ending row with dc in the turning ch, ch 4 and turn.

Row 5: Dc in the 2-ch, ch 2 and dc in the next 2-ch, * ch 6 and sc in the end of the 5-ch, sc in each of the next 5 sc, sc in the beginning of the next 5-ch, ch 6 and dc in the 2-ch, ch 2 and dc in the next 2-ch 3 more times, rep from *, ending row with 2 dc in the turning ch, ch 5 and turn.

Row 6: 1 dc in the 2-ch, * ch 6 and sc in the last of the 6-ch, ch 7 and sc in the beginning of the next 6-ch, ch 6 and dc in the 2-ch, ch 2 and dc in the 2-ch 2 more times, rep from *, ending row with dc in the turning ch, ch 4 and turn.

Row 7: Dc in the 2-ch, * ch 2, work 2 double trc in the 7-ch, ch 1 and work 2 double trc in the 7-ch, 5 more times, ch 2 and dc in the 2-ch, ch 2 and dc in the 2-ch, rep from *, ending row with 2 dc in the turning ch, ch 7 and turn.

Row 8: * finish 2 dc together in the 2-ch and the next 1-ch, ch 3 and finish 2 dc together in the last 1-ch and the next 1-ch 5 more times, ch 3 and dc in the 2-ch, ch 3, rep from *, ending row with dc in the turning ch.

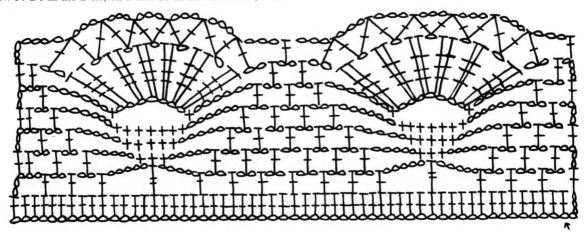

247. Chain multiples of 14 plus 4.

Row 1: Sc in the 5th ch, ch 3, sc in the 2nd ch, * ch 2, work 2 dc in the 4th ch, ch 2, 2 dc in the same ch, ch 2, sc in the 4th ch, ch 3, sc in the 2nd ch, ch 3, sc in the 2nd ch, ch 3, sc in the 2nd ch, rep from *, ending row with last sc, and 1 hdc in the next ch, ch 1 and turn.

Row 2: Sc in the 1st hdc, ch 3, sc in the next 3-ch, * ch 2, 2 dc in the next 2-ch, ch 2, 2 dc in the same 2-ch, ch 2, 2 dc in the same 2-ch, ch 2, sc in the 3-ch, ch 3, sc in the next 3-ch, ch 3, sc in the next 3-ch, rep from *, ending row with sc in the turning ch, ch 3 and turn.

Row 3: Sc in the 1st 3-ch, * ch 2, 2 dc in the 2-ch, ch 2, work another 2 dc in the same 2-ch, ch 1, 2 dc in the next 2-ch, ch 2, 2 dc in the same 2-ch, ch 2, sc in the next 3-ch, ch 3, and sc in the next 3-ch, rep from *, ending row with sc in the last 3-ch, ch 1 and hdc in the last sc, ch 1 and turn.

Row 4: Sc in the hdc, ch 2, * 2 dc in the 2nd 2-ch, ch 2, 2 dc in the same 2-ch, ch 2, sc in the next 1-ch, ch 2, 2 dc in the next 2-ch, ch 2, 2 dc in the same 2-ch, ch 2, sc in the next 3-ch, rep from *, ending row with sc in the turning ch.

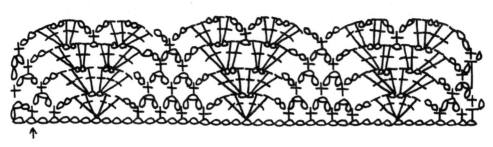

248. Chain multiples of 16 plus 2.

Row 1: Sc in the 2nd ch, * ch 5 and sc in the 4th ch, rep from *, ending row with sc in the last ch, ch 7 and turn.

Row 2: * sc around the middle of the 5-ch, ch 5 and rep from *, ending row with last sc, ch 3 and dc in the last sc, ch 1 and turn.

Row 3: Sc in the dc, * ch 5 and sc around the middle of the 5-ch, ch 3 and work 3 dc in the middle of the next 5-ch, ch 3 and sc around the middle of the next 5-ch, ch 5 and sc around the middle of the 5-ch, rep from *, ending row with sc in the turning ch, ch 6 and turn.

Row 4: * sc in the middle of the 5-ch, ch 3, work 2 dc in the next dc, dc in the next dc, 2 dc in the next dc, ch 3 and sc in the middle of the next 5-ch, ch 5, rep from *, ending row with sc in the last dc, ch 1 and turn.

Row 5: Sc in the 1st dc, * ch 3, work 2 dc in the next dc, dc in each of the next 3 dc, work 2 dc in the next dc, ch 3 and sc in the middle of the next 5-ch, rep from *, ending row with sc in the turning ch, ch 1 and turn.

Row 6: * sc in the sc, ch 3, dc in the next dc and work 3-ch picot 6 times and dc in the next dc, ch 3 and rep from *, ending row with sc in the last sc.

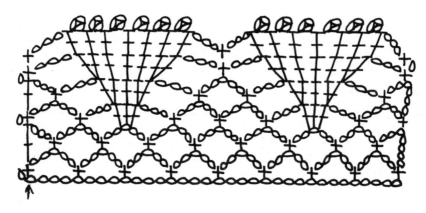

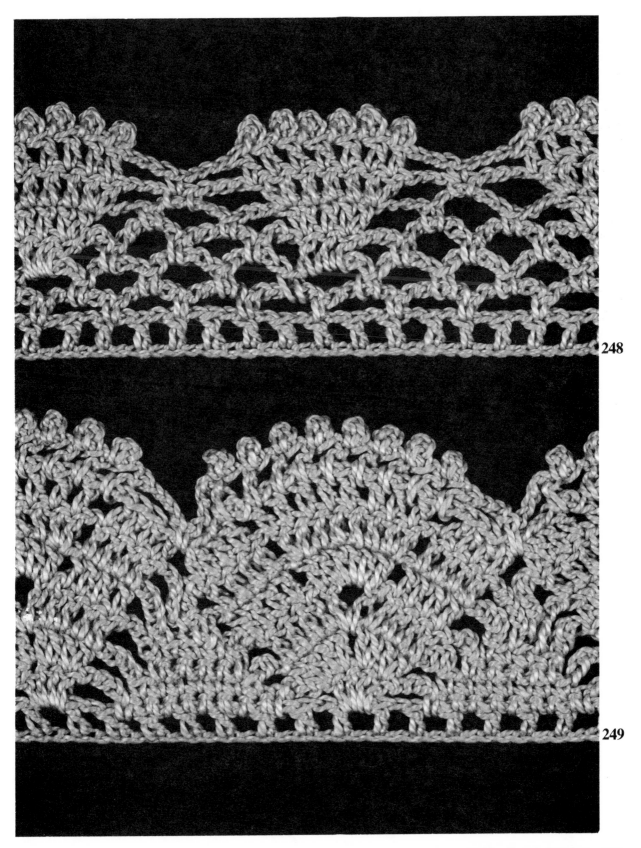

248

249

249. Chain multiples of 14 plus 5.

Row 1: Dc in the 7th ch, *ch 1 and dc in the 2nd ch, rep from *, all across the row, ch 1 and turn.

Row 2: Sc in the dc, ch, dc, ch and dc, * ch 4, dc in the next dc, work 2 dc in the 1-ch, dc in the next ch, ch 4 and sc in the dc and ch 4 times, sc in the next dc (totalling 9), rep from *, ending row with 5 sc, ch 1 and turn.

Row 3: Sc in each of the next 4 sc, * ch 4, work 2 dc in the next dc, work another 2 dc in the next dc, ch 1 and 2 dc in the next dc, 2 dc in the next dc, ch 4 and sc in the 2nd sc, sc in each of the next 6 sc, rep from *, ending row with 4 sc, ch 1 and turn.

Row 4: Sc in each of the next 3 sc, * ch 4, dc in each of the next 4 dc, ch 1 and dc in the 1-ch, ch 3 and dc in the same 1-ch, ch 1 and dc in each of the next 4 dc, ch 4 and sc in the 2nd sc, and sc in each of the next 4 sc, rep from *, ending row with 3 sc, ch 1 and turn.

Row 5: Sc in each of the next 2 sc, * ch 5 and dc in each of the next 4 dc, ch 1 and dc in the next dc, work 4 dc in the 3-ch, dc in the next dc, ch 1 and dc in each of the next 4 dc, ch 5 and sc in the 2nd sc and in each of the next 2 sc, rep from *, ending row with 2 sc, ch 1 and turn.

Row 6: Sc in the 1st sc, *ch 5, dc in each of the next 4 dc, ch 2 and work 2 dc in the next dc, dc in each of the next 4 dc, work 2 dc in the next dc, ch 2 and dc in each of the next 4 dc, ch 5 and sc in the 2nd sc, rep from *, ending row with last sc, ch 8 and turn.

Row 7: * finish 2 dc together in the top of the 5-ch and in the dc, dc in each of the next 3 dc, ch 2 and dc in the next dc, ch 1 and dc in the next dc 7 times, ch 2 and dc in each of the next 3 dc, finish 2 dc together, 1 in next dc and 1 in dc after that, rep from *, ending row with last 1 dc finished together with 1 triple triple stitch in the sc, ch 1 and turn.

Row 8: Sc in the triple triple stitch, *ch 4, dc in the 2-ch, ch 1 and work 3-ch picot, dc in the next 1-ch ch 1 and work 3-ch picot 7 more times, dc in the 2-ch, ch 4 and sc in the top of the 2 dc finished together, rep from *, ending row with sc in the turning ch.

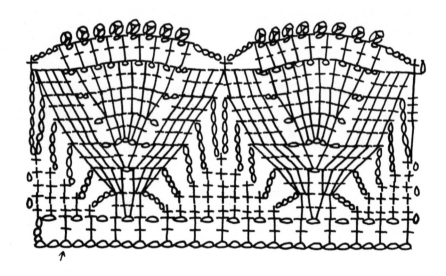

·14·
Lace Patterns

250.   Chain multiples of 15 plus 2.

Row 1: Sc in each of the next 5 chs, * ch 5 and sc in the 5th ch, sc in each of the next 10 chs, rep from *, ending row with sc in each of the last 6 chs, ch 1 and turn.

Row 2: Sc in each of the next 5 sc, * work 2-looped cluster in the 5-ch, ch 3 and work 2-looped cluster 4 more times, sc in the 2nd sc and in each of the next 8 sc, rep from *, ending row with sc in each of the last 4 sc, ch 3 and turn.

Row 3: Work double X-stitch in 1st and next sc, * work 2-looped cluster after the sc, ch 1 and work another 2-looped cluster in the same stitch, ch 3 and sc in the 3-ch, ch 3 and sc in the next 3-ch 3 more times, ch 3 and 2-looped cluster just before the sc, ch 1 and 2-looped cluster in the same stitch, work double X-stitch in the 3rd sc and the next sc, work another X-stitch in each of the next 2 sc, and another X-stitch in each of the next 2 sc, rep from *, ending row with dc in the last sc, ch 4 and turn.

Row 4: Work 2-looped cluster in the 1-ch, ch 1 and work another 2-looped cluster in the same 1-ch, ch 3 and sc in the 3-ch, ch 3 and sc in the next 3-ch 4 times, ch 3 and work 2-looped cluster in the 1-ch, ch 1 and work another 2-looped cluster in the same 1-ch, ch 2, rep from *, ending row with dc in the turning ch, ch 5 and turn.

Row 5: * work 2-looped cluster in the 1-ch, ch 1 and work another 2-looped cluster in the same 1-ch, ch 3 and sc in the 2nd 3-ch, ch 3 and sc in the next 3-ch 3 times, ch 3 and work 2-looped cluster in the 1-ch, ch 1 and work another 2-looped cluster in the same 1-ch, ch 1 and rep from *, ending row with trc after the last cluster, ch 5 and turn.

Row 6: * work 2-looped cluster in the 1-ch, ch 1 and work another 2-looped cluster in the same 1-ch, ch 3 and sc in the next 3-ch, ch 3 and sc in the next 3-ch, ch 3 and sc in

the next 3-ch, ch 3 and work 2-looped cluster in the next 1-ch, ch 1 and work another 2-looped cluster in the same 1-ch, ch 6 and rep from *, ending row with last cluster, ch 1 and dc in the turning ch, ch 8 and turn.

Row 7: * work 2-looped cluster in the 1-ch, ch 1 and work another 2-looped cluster in the same 1-ch, ch 3 and sc in the 2nd 3-ch, ch 3 and sc in the next 3-ch, ch 3 and work 2-looped cluster in the next 1-ch, ch 1 and work another 2-looped cluster in the same 1-ch, ch 8, rep from *, ending row with last cluster, ch 3 and trc in the turning ch, ch 8 and turn.

Row 8: * work 2-looped cluster in the 1-ch, ch 1 and work another 2-looped cluster in the same 1-ch, ch 3 and sc in the 2nd 3-ch, ch 3 and work 2-looped cluster in the next 1-ch, ch 1 and work another 2-looped cluster in the same 1-ch, ch 10, rep from *, ending row with 5 chs and dc in the turning ch, ch 3 and turn.

Row 9: Dc in the 2nd ch, * ch 3 and finish 2 dc together in the same ch as the last dc and the 3rd ch, ch 3 and work 2-looped cluster in the 1-ch, ch 1 and work another 2-looped cluster in the same 1-ch, work 2-looped cluster in the next 1-ch, ch 1 and work another 2-looped cluster in the same 1-ch, ch 3 and finish 2 dc together in the 1st ch and the 3rd ch, ch 3 and finish another 2 dc together in the last ch used and the 3rd ch, rep from *, ending row with 3 chs and dc in the turning ch, ch 1 and turn.

Row 10: Sc in the dc, work 4-ch picot, 3 sc in the 3-ch and 4-ch picot, * work 4 sc in the next 3-ch, sc in the 1st cluster and sc in the 1-ch, work 4-ch picot, sc in the 1-ch, sc in the next cluster, 4 sc in each 3-ch and 4-ch picot 3 times, rep from *, ending row with picot and sc in the turning ch.

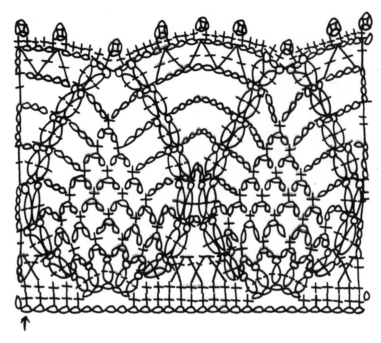

251. Chain multiples of 8 plus 2.

Row 1: Sc in the 2nd ch, * ch 5 and sc in the 4th ch, rep from *, ending row with sc in the last ch, ch 7 and turn.

Row 2: * sc in the middle of the next 5-ch, ch 5, rep from *, ending row with last sc, ch 2 and trc in the last sc, ch 1 and turn.

Row 3: Sc in the trc, * ch 5 and sc in the 5-ch, rep from *, ending row with sc in the turning ch, ch 1 and turn.

Row 4: Sc in the sc, * ch 2 and sc in the middle of the 5-ch, ch 3 and sc in the middle of the same 5-ch, ch 2 and sc in the next 5-ch, ch 11 and sc in the same 5-ch, ch 11 and sc in the same 5-ch, ch 11 and sc in the same 5-ch, ch 11 and sc in the same 5-ch, rep from *, ending row with 2 sets of 11 chs and hdc in the last sc, ch 6 and turn.

Row 5: * sc in the middle of the 11-ch, ch 3 and sc in the middle of the next 11-ch, sc in the next 11-ch, ch 3 and sc in the middle of the next 11-ch, ch 3, and rep from *, ending row with sc in the last 11-ch, ch 1 and turn.

Row 6: Sc in the 1st sc, ch 2, * sc in the 3-ch, ch 3 and sc in the next 3-ch, ch 3 and sc in the next 3-ch, ch 3, rep from *, ending row with sc in the last 3-ch, ch 2 and sc in the last sc, ch 1 and turn.

Row 7: Work 2 sc in the 2-ch, * work sc, 1 hdc, 5 dc, 1 hdc and 1 sc in the 3-ch, work 4 sc around the next 3-ch, 4 sc around the next sc, rep from *, ending row with last set.

Bottom Row: * work 2 sc in the ch, sc in the next ch, ch 3 and sc in the same ch, work 2 sc in the next ch, sk next ch, rep from *, ending row with last sc.

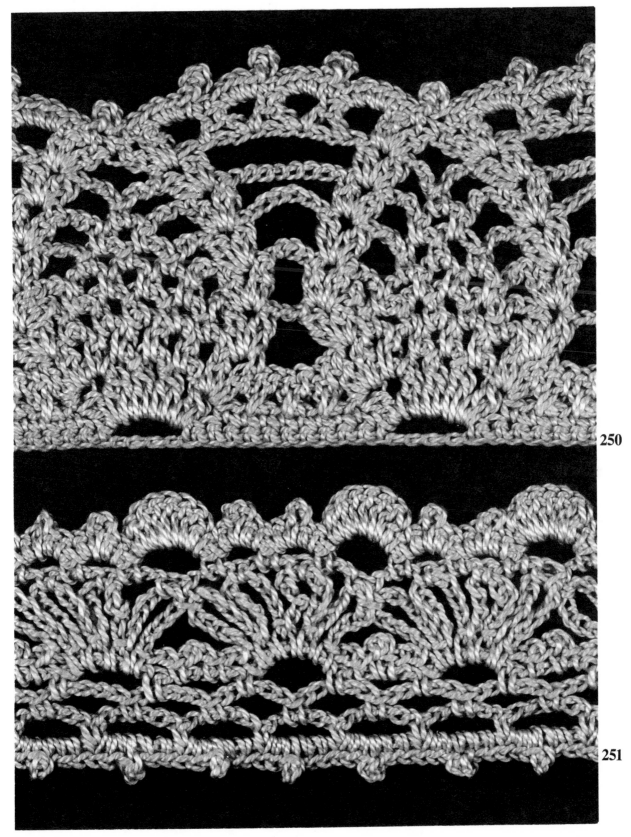

250

251

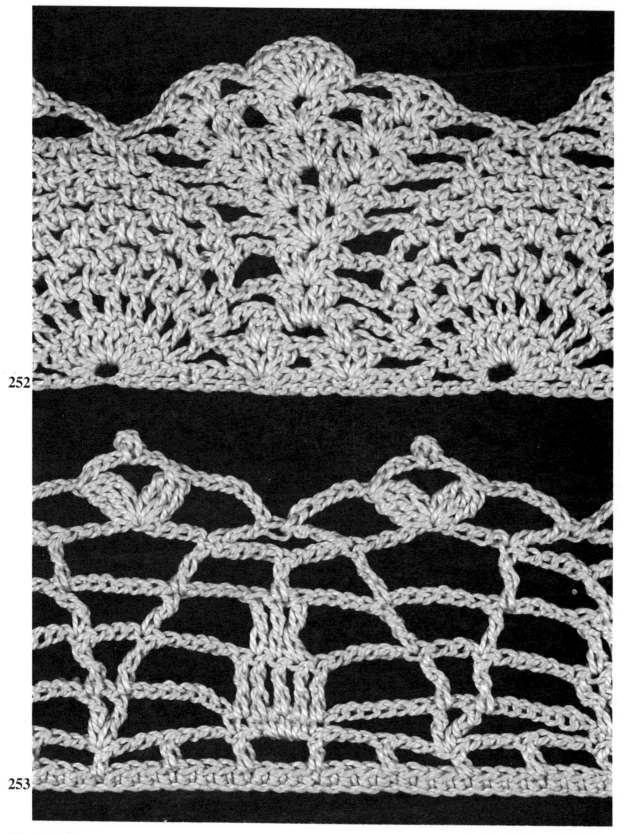

252

253

252. Chain multiples of 24 plus 4.

Row 1: Work 4 dc in the 4th ch, * ch 1 and sc in the 5th ch, ch 3 and sc in the 4th ch, ch 4 and sc in the 5th ch, ch 3 and sc in the 4th sc, ch 1 and work 9 dc in the 5th ch, and rep from *, ending row with 5 dc in the last ch, ch 4 and turn.

Row 2: Sk 1st dc, dc in each dc and ch 1 4 times, * work 2 dc in the 2nd sc, ch 1 and work 2 dc in the same sc, work 2 dc in the next sc, ch 1 and work 2 dc in the same sc, ch 1 and dc in the dc and ch 1 9 times, ch 1 and rep from *, ending row with dc in the last dc, ch 4 and turn.

Row 3: Sc in the 1-ch and ch 3 4 times, * 2 dc in the 2nd 1-ch, ch 1 and work 2 dc in the next 1-ch, ch 3 and sc in the 2nd 1-ch, ch 3 and sc in the next 1-ch 7 times, ch 3, rep from *, ending row with sc in the turning ch, ch 1 and dc in the turning ch, ch 1 and turn.

Row 4: Sc in the dc, ch 3 and sc in the 3-ch 3 times, * ch 3 and work 2 dc in the 1-ch, ch 1 and work another 2 dc in the same 1-ch, ch 3, sc in the 3-ch 7 times, rep from *, ending row with sc in the turning ch, ch 4 and turn.

Row 5: Sc in the 3-ch, ch 3 and sc in the sc, ch 3 and sc in the sc, * ch 3 and work 2 dc in the 1-ch, ch 1 and work 2 dc in the same 1-ch, ch 3 and work sc in the 2nd 3-ch, ch 3 and sc in the next 3-ch 5 times, rep from *, ending row with sc in the last 3-ch, ch 1 and dc in the sc, ch 1 and turn.

Row 6: Sc in the dc, ch 3 and sc in the 3-ch, ch 3 and sc in the next 3-ch, * ch 3 and work 2 dc in the 1-ch, ch 1 and work 2 dc in the same 1-ch, ch 1 and work another 2

dc in the same 1-ch, ch 3 and sc in the 2nd 3-ch, ch 3 and sc in the next 3-ch 4 times, rep from *, ending row with sc in the turning ch, ch 4 and turn.

Row 7: Sc in the 3-ch, ch 3 and sc in the next 3-ch, * ch 3 and work 2 dc in the 1-ch, ch 1 and work 2 dc in the same 1-ch, ch 1 and work 2 dc in the next 1-ch, ch 1 and work another 2 dc in the same 1-ch, ch 3 and sc in the 2nd 3-ch, ch 3 and sc in the next 3-ch 3 times, rep from *, ending row with sc in the last 3-ch, ch 1 and dc in the last sc, ch 1 and turn.

Row 8: Sc in the dc, ch 3 and sc in the next 3-ch, * ch 3 and 2 dc in the next 1-ch, ch 1 and 2 dc in the same 1-ch, 2 dc in the next 1-ch, ch 1 and 2 dc in the same 1-ch, 2 dc in the next 1-ch, ch 1 and 2 dc in the same 1-ch, ch 3 and sc in the 2nd 3-ch, ch 3 and sc in the next 3-ch, rep from *, ending row with sc in the turning ch, ch 4 and turn.

Row 9: Sc in the 3-ch, * ch 3 , work 2 dc in the next 1-ch, ch 1 and work another 2 dc in the same 1-ch, ch 2 and work 2 dc in the next 1-ch, ch 1, work 2 dc in the same 1-ch, ch 2, work 2 dc in the next 1-ch, ch 1 and work 2 dc in the same 1-ch, ch 3 and sc in the 2nd 3-ch, ch 3 and sc in the next 3-ch, rep from *, ending row with sc in the last 3-ch, ch 1 and dc in the last sc, ch 1 and turn.

Row 10: Sc in the dc, * ch 3, work 2 dc in the next 1-ch, ch 1, work 2 dc in the same 1-ch, ch 2, work 9 dc in the next 1-ch, ch 2 and work 2 dc in the next 1-ch, ch 1 and work 2 dc in the same 1-ch, ch 3 and sc in the 2nd 3-ch, rep from *, ending row with sc in the turning ch.

253. Chain multiples of 20 plus 2.

Row 1: Sc in 2nd ch and in each ch all across the row, ch 4 and turn.

Row 2: Dc in the 3rd sc, * ch 3, dc in the 4th sc, rep from *, ending row with last dc, 1 ch and dc in the 2nd sc, ch 1 and turn.

Row 3: Sc in the 1st dc, ch and the next dc, * ch 7, work trc in the 2nd dc, ch 1, work another trc in the same dc, ch 7, sc in the 2nd dc, sc in each of the 3-ch, and sc in the next dc, rep from *, ending row with sc in the dc, 2 sc in the turning ch and ch 4 and turn.

Row 4: Work 1 trc in the 2nd sc and the next sc, * ch 5, work trc in next trc, ch 3, and work trc in next trc, ch 5, work 1 trc in each of next 5 sc, rep from *, ending row with 1 trc in each of the last 3 sc, ch 4 and turn.

Row 5: Trc in the 2nd trc, * ch 4, trc in the 2nd trc, ch 6, work another trc in the next trc, ch 4, work trc in the 2nd trc, trc in the next 2 trc, rep from *, ending row with trc in the last trc, and trc in the turning ch, ch 6 and turn.

Row 6: Sk 1st 2 trc, * trc in the next trc, ch 9, work trc in the next trc, ch 3, dc in the 2nd trc, ch 3, rep from *, ending row with dc in the turning ch, ch 5 and turn.

Row 7: Trc in the next trc, * ch 6, work 3-looped triple cluster in the 5th ch, ch 3, work 3-ch picot, ch 3, work 3-looped triple cluster in the ch just used, ch 6, finish 2 trc together, 1 in the last trc, and 1 in the next trc, rep from *, ending row with 2 trc finished together in the last trc and in the turning ch.

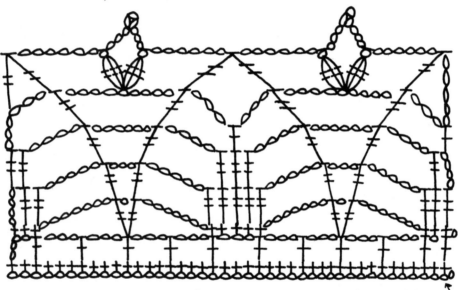

254. Chain multiples of 30 plus 4.

Row 1: Dc in the 4th ch and dc in each ch all across the row, ch 8 and turn.

Row 2: Work 1 trc in the 5th dc, * ch 7 and trc in the 7th dc, trc in each of the next 8 dc, ch 7, trc in the 7th dc, ch 7, trc in the 7th dc, rep from *, ending row with last trc, ch 3, trc in the turning ch, ch 11 and turn.

Row 3: * work 4 trc in the last part of the 7-ch, trc in the next trc, ch 15 and trc in the 8th trc, work 4 trc in the beginning of the next 7-ch, ch 7 and trc in the middle of the next 7-ch, ch 7, rep from *, ending row with 5 trc, ch 7 and trc in the turning ch, ch 7 and turn.

Row 4: * work 4 trc towards the end of the 7-ch, trc in the next trc, ch 3 and trc in the beginning of the 15-ch, ch 3 and trc towards the middle of the 15-ch, ch 7 and trc

towards the latter middle of the 15-ch, ch 3 and trc towards the end of the 15-ch, ch 3 and trc in the 5th trc, 4 trc in the 1st part of the 7-ch, ch 7, rep from *, ending row with last set of 5 trc, ch 3 and trc in the turning ch, ch 4 and turn.

Row 5: Work 3 trc in the 3-ch, trc in the next trc, * ch 3, trc in the 5th trc, work 5-ch picot, ch 3 and trc in the next trc, work 5-ch picot, and ch 3, work trc in the middle of the 7-ch, ch 3 and work another 5-ch picot, ch 4, work trc in the ch just used, work 5-ch picot, ch 3, work trc in the next trc, 5-ch picot, ch 3, trc in the next trc, 5-ch picot, ch 3, work trc in the 5th trc, work 7 trc in the next 7-ch, trc in the next trc, rep from *, ending row with trc in the last trc and 4 trc in the turning ch.

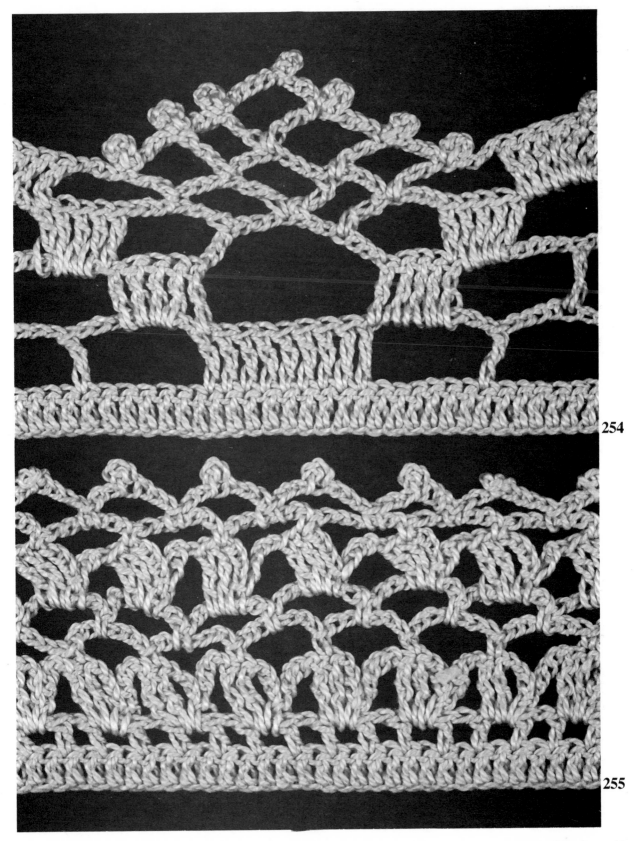

254

255

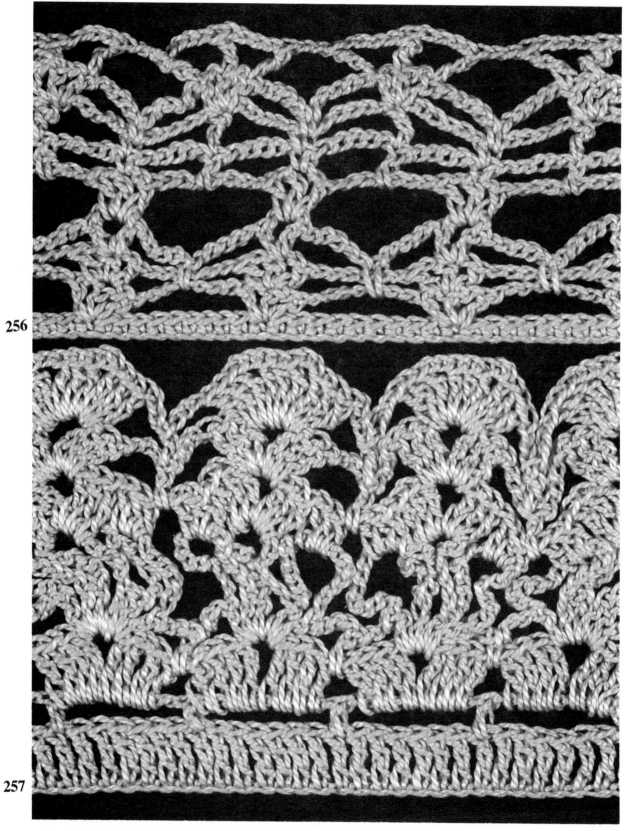

256

257

194 Lace Patterns

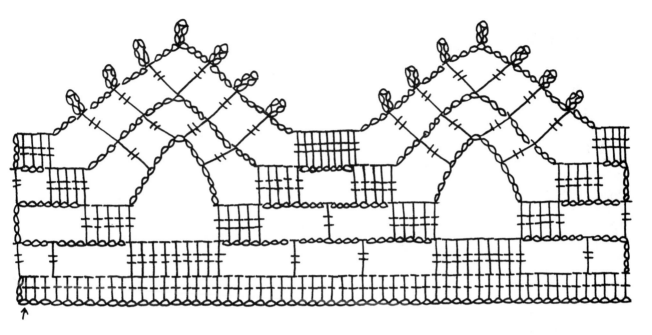

255. Chain multiples of 4 plus 4.

Row 1: Dc in the 5th ch and in each ch all across the row, ch 5 and turn.

Row 2: Dc in the 3rd dc, * ch 1 and dc in the 2nd dc, rep from *, ending row with dc in the turning ch, ch 1 and turn.

Row 3: Sc in the 1st 1-ch, * ch 4, work 2 trc in the same 1-ch, ch 5, sc in the 2nd 1-ch, rep from *, ending row with sc in the turning ch, ch 12 and turn.

Row 4: * sc in the top of the 1st 4-ch, ch 7 and rep from *, ending row with last sc, ch 9 and turn.

Row 5: * sc in the middle of the 7-ch, ch 7, rep from *, ending row with last sc, ch 3 and double trc in the turning ch, ch 3 and turn.

Row 6: Trc in the beginning of the 3-ch, ch 4 and sc in the same ch, * ch 5 and work 2 trc in the middle of the next 7-ch, ch 4 and sc in the same ch, rep from *, ending row with last sc, ch 5 and turn.

Row 7: * sc in the top of the 4-ch, ch 6, rep from *, ending row with the sc in the last 4-ch, ch 5 and turn.

Row 8: * work 3-ch picot, ch 3, sc around the 6-ch, ch 3, rep from *, ending row with last 3-ch, picot and dc in the last sc.

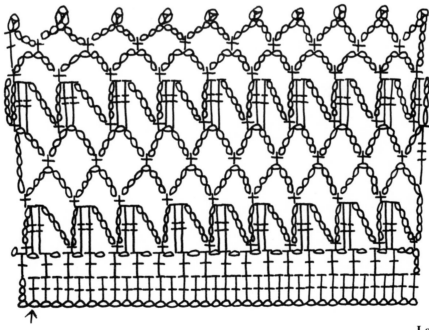

256. Chain multiples of 10 plus 2.

Row 1: 1 sc in the 2nd ch and in each ch all across the row, ch 4 and turn.

Row 2: 1 dc in the 1st sc, * ch 7, 1 dc in the 10th sc, ch 1, 1 dc in the sc just used, ch 1, dc in the sc just used, rep from *, ending row with 1 dc, 1 ch and 1 dc, ch 4 and turn.

Row 3: 1 dc in the 1st dc, * ch 6, 1 dc in the middle dc of the 3 dc worked together, ch 1, dc in the dc just used, ch 1, dc in the dc just used, rep from *, ending row with dc, ch and 1 dc in the turning ch, ch 4 and turn.

Row 4: 1 dc in the 1st dc, * ch 5, sl st around the middle of the 2 2-ch rows below, ch 5, dc in the 2nd dc, ch 3, 1 dc in the dc just used, rep from *, ending row with 1 dc, 1 ch and 1 dc in the turning ch, ch 4 and turn.

Row 5: 1 dc in the 1st dc, * ch 7, 1 dc in the 3-ch, ch 1, dc in the 3-ch, ch 1, dc in the same 3-ch, rep from *, ending

row with 1 dc, 1 ch and 1 dc in the turning ch, ch 1 and turn.

Row 6: 1 sc in the 1st dc, * ch 5, work 1 dc around the middle of the 7-ch, ch 5, sc in the 2nd dc of the 3 dc set, rep from *, ending row with sc in the turning ch, ch 1 and turn.

Row 7: Sc in the 1st sc, * ch 6, trc in the next dc, ch 6, sc in the next sc, rep from *, ending row with sc in the last sc, ch 1 and turn.

Row 8: * sc in the sc, ch 5, dc in the trc, ch 1, dc in the same trc, ch 1, dc in the same trc, ch 5, rep from *, ending row with sc in the last sc, ch 1, sl st in the next 5 chs, ch 8 and turn.

Row 9: Trc in the 2nd dc, * ch 4, trc in the next dc, ch 2, trc in the next dc, ch 4, trc in the next dc, rep from *, ending row with trc in the last dc.

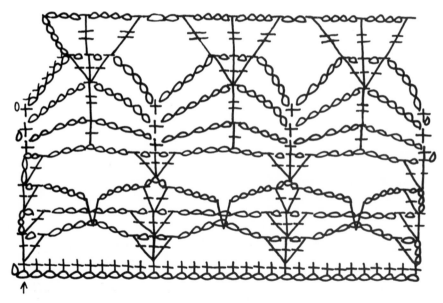

257. Chain multiples of 7 plus 5.

Row 1: Trc in the 5th ch, trc in each ch all across the row, ch 9 and turn.

Row 2: Dc in the 8th trc, * ch 6 and trc in the 7th trc, rep from *, ending row with dc in the turning ch, ch 4 and turn.

Row 3: * work 4 trc in the beginning of the 6-ch, ch 2 and work another 4 trc in last part of the same 6-ch, rep from *, ending row with last set, ch 6 and turn.

Row 4: * dc in the 2-ch, ch 15 and dc in the same 2-ch, ch 15 and dc in the same 2-ch, ch 15 and dc in the same 2-ch, ch 3 and dc after the 4th trc, rep from *, ending row with dc in the turning ch, ch 11 and turn.

Row 5: * work 3 dc in the middle of the 15-ch, work 3 trc

in the middle of the next 15-ch, ch 2 and work another 3 trc in the same 15-ch, work 3 dc in the middle of the next 15-ch, rep from *, ending row with last set, ch 6 and turn.

Row 6: * work 3 trc in the 2-ch, ch 2 and work another 3 trc in the same 2-ch, ch 3 and dc in the space after the 3rd dc, ch 3, rep from *, ending row with dc in the turning ch, ch 5 and turn.

Row 7: * work 3 trc in the 2-ch, ch 2, work another 3 trc in the same 2-ch, ch 2 and work another 3 trc in the same 2-ch, ch 3, dc in the next dc, ch 3, rep from *, ending row with last set, ch 1 and dc in the turning ch.

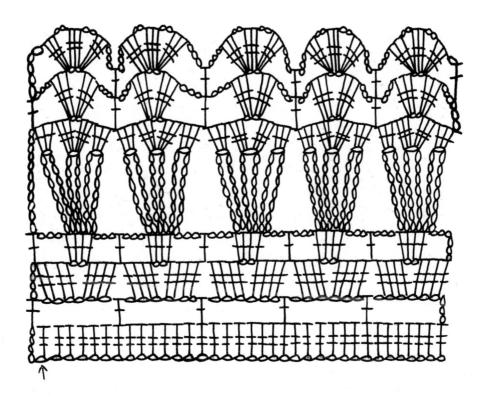

258. Chain multiples of 18 plus 2.

Row 1: Sc in the 2nd ch and in each ch all across the row, ch 3 and turn.

Row 2: Dc in the 2nd sc and in each of the next 2 sc, * ch 3 and work 2 dc in the 6th sc, ch 2 and dc in the same sc, ch 3 and dc in the 6th sc, and dc in each of the next 6 sc, rep from *, ending row with dc in each of the last 4 sc, ch 3 and turn.

Row 3: Dc in the 2nd dc and in each of the next 2 dc, * ch 3 and work 3 dc in the 2-ch, ch 3 and work another 3 dc in the same 2-ch, ch 3 and dc in the 2nd dc and each of the next 5 dc, rep from *, ending row with dc in the last 2 dc and dc in the turning ch.

Row 4: Dc in the 2nd dc and the next dc, * ch 3, work 4 dc in the 2nd 3-ch, ch 5 and work another 4 dc in the same 3-ch, ch 3 and dc in the 2nd dc, and dc in each of the next 4 dc, rep from *, ending row with 1 dc in each of the last 2 dc and dc in the turning ch.

Row 5: Dc in the 2nd dc and dc in the next dc, * ch 3, work 4 dc in the beginning of the 5-ch, ch 5 and sc in the middle of the 5-ch, ch 5 and work 4 dc in the end of the same 5-ch, ch 3, dc in the 2nd dc and dc in each of the next 3 dc, rep from *, ending row with dc in the last dc and dc in the turning ch, ch 3 and turn.

Row 6: Dc in the 2nd dc, * ch 3 and work 4 dc in the 5-ch, ch 5 and sc in the end of the next 5-ch, ch 5, sc in end of next 5-ch, ch 5 work 4 dc in the same 5-ch, ch 3 and dc in the 2nd dc, dc in each of the next 2 dc, rep from *, ending row with dc in the last dc and dc in the turning ch, ch 3 and turn.

Row 7: Dc in the 2nd dc, * ch 2, work 4 dc in the top of the 5-ch, ch 5, sc in the top of the same 5-ch, ch 5 and sc in the middle of the 5-ch, ch 5 and sc in the top of the next 5-ch, ch 5 and work 4 dc in the top of the same 5-ch, ch 2 and dc in the 2nd dc, dc in the next dc, rep from *, ending row with dc in the last dc and dc in the turning ch, ch 4 and turn.

Row 8: * work 4 dc in the top of the 1st 5-ch, ch 5 and sc in the top of the same 5-ch, ch 5 and sc in the middle of the next 5-ch, ch 5 and sc in the middle of the next 5-ch, ch 5 and sc in last of next 5-ch, ch 5 and work 4 dc in the top of the same 5-ch, ch 1 and dc in the 2nd dc, ch 1 and rep from *, ending row with 1 ch and 1 dc in the turning ch, ch 6 and turn.

Row 9: * work 5 dc around the 5-ch, sc around the middle of the next 5-ch, work 5 dc around the middle of the next 5-ch, sc around the middle of the next 5-ch, work 5 dc around the middle of the next 5-ch, ch 5, rep from *, ending row with last set, ch 1 and work trc in the turning ch.

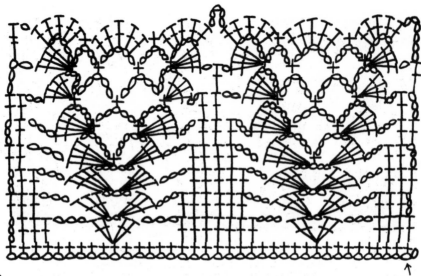

259. Chain 4.

Row 1: Trc in the 1st ch, * ch 4 and trc in the 1st ch, rep from *, ending row with last set, ch 3 and turn.

Row 2: * work 4 dc in next 4-ch, ch 3 and work another 4 dc in the same 4-ch, ch 3 and sc in the next 4-ch, ch 5 and sc in the 4-ch, ch 3, rep from *, ending row with last set and dc in the last ch, ch 3 and turn.

Row 3: Work 4 dc in the 3-ch, * ch 3 and work another 4 dc in the same 3-ch, ch 5 and sc in the next 5-ch, ch 5 and work 4 dc in the 2nd 3-ch, rep from *, ending row with last set and trc in the turning ch, ch 3 and turn.

Row 4: * work 4 dc in the 3-ch, ch 3 and work another 4 dc in the same 3-ch, ch 3 and sc around the 5-ch, ch 5 and sc in the next 5-ch, ch 3 and rep from *, ending row with last set and dc in the turning ch, ch 3 and turn.

Row 5: * work 4 dc in the 3-ch, ch 3 and work another 4 dc in the same 3-ch, ch 5 and sc in the 5-ch, ch 5 and rep from *, ending row with last set and dc in the dc, ch 1 and turn.

Row 6: Sc in the dc, ch 4, * sc in the 3-ch, ch 9 and sc in the sc, ch 9, rep from *, ending row with sc in the turning ch, ch 3 and turn.

Row 7: * work 3 dc in the 2nd sc, ch 3, and work 3 dc in the same sc, ch 12, rep from *, ending row with last set and dc in the last sc, ch 4 and turn.

Row 8: * sc in the 3-ch, work 4-ch picot and sc in same 3-ch, work 4 dc in the beginning of the 12-ch, work 4-ch picot, work another 4 dc in the middle of the same 12-ch, work another 4-ch picot, work another 4 dc in the middle of the same 12-ch, work 4-ch picot, work another 4 dc towards the end of the 12-ch, rep from *, ending row with last set, ch 1 and hdc in the turning ch.

258

259

260

261

260. Chain multiples of 22 plus 2.

Row 1: Sc in the 2nd ch and sc in each ch all across the row, ch 5 and turn.

Row 2: Dc in the 4th sc, * ch 2 and dc in the 3rd sc, rep from *, ending row with dc in the last sc, ch 3 and turn.

Row 3: Work 3 dc in each of the next 3 2-chs, * ch 13, sk 1–2 chs, work 3 dc in each of the next 6 2-chs, rep from *, ending row with an extra dc in the turning ch, ch 4 and turn.

Row 4: Work 3 dc between the 1st 2 sets of 3 dc, work another 3 dc between the next 2 sets of dc, * ch 6, sc in the middle of the 13-ch, ch 6 and work 3 dc between the next 2 sets of 3 dc, rep 4 more times, rep from *, ending row with 2 dc in the turning ch, ch 3 and turn.

Row 5: Work 3 dc after the 1st 2 dc, work another 3 dc between the next 2 sets of 3 dc, * ch 6 and sc in the last of the 6-ch of the row below, sc in the sc, sc in the 1st of the next 6-ch, ch 6, work 3 dc after the next set of dc, rep 3 more times, rep from *, ending row with 1 extra dc in the turning ch, ch 4 and turn.

Row 6: Dc in the top of the 2 dc, work 3 dc between the next 2 sets of 3 dc, * ch 6 and sc in the last of the 6-ch, sc in each of the next 3 sc, sc in the beginning of the next 6-ch, ch 6, work 3 dc after the next 3 dc, rep two times, rep from *, ending row with 2 dc in the turning ch, ch 3 and turn.

Row 7: Work 3 dc after the 2 dc, * ch 6 and sc in the last of the 6-ch, sc in each of the next 5 sc, sc in the 1st of the next 6-ch, ch 6, work 3 dc after the 1st set of 3 dc, work another 3 dc after the next set of 3 dc, and rep from *, ending row with dc in the turning ch, ch 4 and turn.

Row 8: Dc in the 1st dc, * ch 6 and sc in the last of the 6-ch, sc in each of the next 7 sc, sc in the 1st of the next 6-ch, ch 6 and work 3 dc in the middle of the 2 sets of 3 dc, rep from *, ending row with 2 dc in the turning ch, ch 3 and turn.

Row 9: 3 dc in the 2nd dc, * ch 6 and sc in the 2nd sc, sc in each of the next 6 sc, ch 6 and 3 dc in the next dc and 3 dc in the 2nd dc, rep from *, ending row with dc in the turning ch, ch 4 and turn.

Row 10: Dc in the 1st dc, work 3 dc in the last 3 dc of the set, * ch 6 and sc in the 2nd sc and in each of the next 4 sc, ch 6, 3 dc in the next dc, work 3 dc in the middle of the 2 sets of 3 dc, work 3 dc in the 3rd dc, rep from *, ending row with 2 dc in the turning ch, ch 3 and turn.

Row 11: Work 3 dc after the 2 dc, work 3 dc in the 3rd dc, * ch 6, sc in the 2nd sc and in each of the next 2 sc, ch 6 and work 3 dc in the next dc, work 3 dc in the middle of the next 2 sets, work 3 dc in the last dc, rep from *, ending row with 1 dc in the turning ch, ch 4 and turn.

Row 12: Dc in the 1st dc, work 3 dc in between the next 2 sets, work 3 dc in the 3rd dc, * ch 6 and sc in the 2nd sc, ch 6 and work 3 dc in the next dc, work 3 dc in between the sets of 3 dc 3 times, 3 dc in the 3rd dc, rep from *, ending row with 2 dc in the turning ch, ch 1 and turn.

Row 13: Sc in 1st dc, ch 2, sc between next 2 sets of 3 dc, ch 4, sc between the next set of 3 dc and ch 4, sc in last dc, * ch 7 and sc in last dc, ch 4 and sc between the sets 4 times, ch 4 and sc in the last dc, rep from *, ending row with sc between last sets, ch 2 and sc in the turning ch.

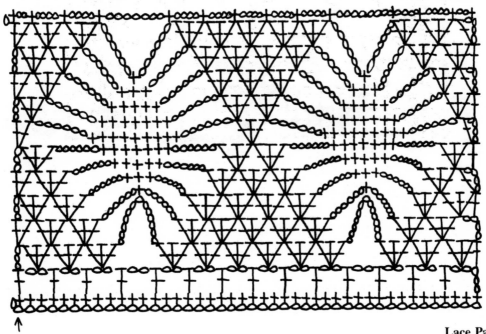

261. Chain multiples of 15 plus 8.

Row 1: Work 3 dc in the 6th ch, ch 3 and work another 3 dc in the ch just used, * dc in the 3rd ch and in each of the next 9 chs, work 3 dc in the 3rd ch, ch 3 and work another 3 dc in the same ch, rep from *, ending row with last set and 1 dc in the 3rd ch, ch 3 and turn.

Row 2: * work 3 dc in the 3-ch, ch 3 and work another 3 dc in the same 3-ch, work dc in each of the next 4 dc, ch 1 and dc in the 3rd dc and in each of the next 3 dc, rep from *, ending row with last set and dc in the turning ch, ch 3 and turn.

Row 3: * work 3 dc in the 3-ch, ch 3 and work another 3 dc in the same 3-ch, ch 2 and dc in each of the next 3 dc, work another dc in the 3rd dc, and dc in each of the next 2 dc, ch 2, rep from *, ending row with last set and dc in the turning ch, ch 3 and turn.

Row 4: * work 3 dc in the 3-ch, ch 3 and work another 3 dc in the same 3-ch, ch 4 and dc in each of the next 2 dc, dc in the 3rd dc and dc in the next dc, ch 4, rep from *, ending row with last set and dc in the turning ch, ch 3 and turn.

Row 5: * work 3 dc in the 3-ch, ch 3 and work another 3 dc in the same 3-ch, ch 12 and finish 2 dc together in the 5th dc and the next dc, ch 12 and rep from *, ending row with last set and dc in the turning ch, ch 3 and turn.

Row 6: * work 3 dc in the 3-ch, ch 3 and work another 3 dc in the same 3-ch, ch 5 and sc in the middle of the 12-ch, ch 15, sc in the middle of the next 12-ch, ch 5 and rep from *, ending row with dc in the turning ch, ch 3 and turn.

Row 7: * work 3 dc in the 3-ch, ch 3 and work another 3 dc in the same 3-ch, ch 3 and work another 3 dc in the same 3-ch, ch 5 and work 3 dc around the beginning of the 15-ch, ch 3 and work another 3 dc towards the middle of the same 15-ch, ch 3 and work 3 dc around the middle of the 15-ch, ch 3 and work 3 dc after the middle of the 15-ch, ch 3 and work 3 dc towards the end of the 15-ch, ch 5, rep from *, ending row with last set and dc in the turning ch, ch 3 and turn.

Row 8: * work 3 dc in the 3-ch, work 4-ch picot, rep from *, all across row, ending with dc in the turning ch.

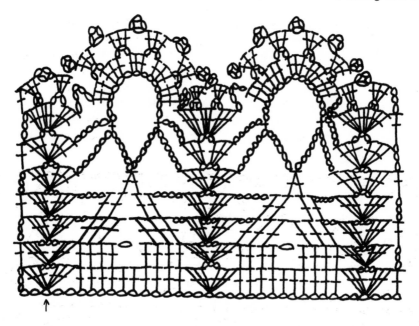

·15·
Puff Stitch

262. Chain multiples of 9 plus 2.

Row 1: Sc in the 2nd ch and in each ch all across the row, ch 5 and turn.
Row 2: Work 3-looped puff stitch in the 1st sc, * work 3-ch picot, 3-looped puff stitch in the 4th sc, work 3-ch picot, 3-looped puff stitch in the 4th sc, ch 5, sl st, ch 5, work 3-looped puff stitch in the sc just used, rep from *, ending row with 5 chs and a sl st in the last sc.

263. Chain multiples of 3 plus 2.

Row 1: Sc in the 2nd ch and in each ch all across the row, ch 4 and turn.
Row 2: Work 3-looped puff stitch in the 1st sc, *finish together with a 3-looped puff stitch in the 3rd sc, ch 2, work 3-ch picot, ch 1, work 3-looped cluster in the sc just used, rep from *, ending row after last set with 2 chs and 1 dc in the same sc as the last puff stitch.

264. Chain multiples of 3 plus 4.

Row 1: Dc in the 4th ch and in each ch all across the row, ch 8 and turn.
Row 2: Finish 3 2-looped puff stitches together, 1 in the middle of the 8-ch, 1 in the top of the 1st dc and 1 in the 2nd dc, *ch 4, work 3 2-looped puff stitches together, one in the 1st of the 4-ch, 1 in the next dc and 1 in the 2nd dc, rep from *, ending row with last set and 1 dc in the turning ch.

265. Chain multiples of 8 plus 10.

Row 1: Sc in the 14th ch, *ch 4 and trc in the 4th ch, ch 4 and sc in the 4th ch, rep from *, ending row with last trc, ch 1 and turn.

Row 2: * sc in the trc, ch 3 and work 2-looped puff stitch in the sc, ch 3 and rep from *, ending row with sc in the turning ch, ch 1 and turn.

Row 3: * sc in the sc, ch 3 and sc just before the puff stitch, ch 6 and sc just after the puff stitch, ch 3 and rep from *, ending row with sc in the last sc.

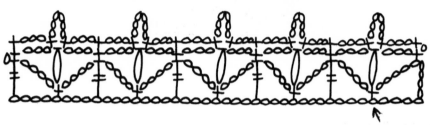

266. Chain multiples of 5 plus 2.

Row 1: Sc in 2nd ch, * ch 9, work 3-looped puff stitch back in sc just made, sc in 5th ch, rep from *, ending row with last sc, ch 4 and turn.

Row 2: * work 2 sc around the middle of the 9-ch, ch 3, work 2 sc around the middle of the same 9-ch, work 1 3-looped puff stitch in the sc, ch 1, rep from *, ending row with last set and 1 dc in the last sc.

267. Chain multiples of 4 plus 2.

Row 1: 1 sc in the 2nd ch, *ch 6, work 3-looped puff stitch back in the sc, sc in the 4th ch, rep from *, ending row with last sc, ch 5 and turn.

Row 2: Work 2-looped puff stitch in the base of the 5-ch, ch 1, * sc in the middle of the 5-ch, ch 6, work 3-looped puff stitch in the middle of the 6-ch, rep from *, ending row with last puff stitch finished together with a dc in the last sc, ch 1 and turn.

Row 3: Sc in the dc, ch 5, work 3-looped puff in the 3-ch of the row below, ch 1, *sc in the middle of the 6-ch, ch 5, work 1 3-looped puff stitch in the middle of the 6-ch, ch 1, rep from *, ending row with sc in the turning ch.

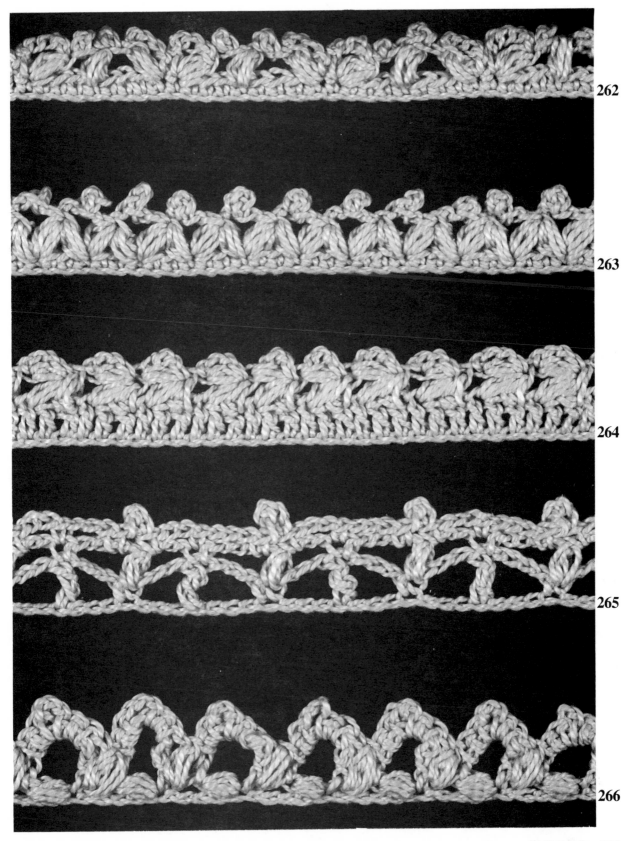

262

263

264

265

266

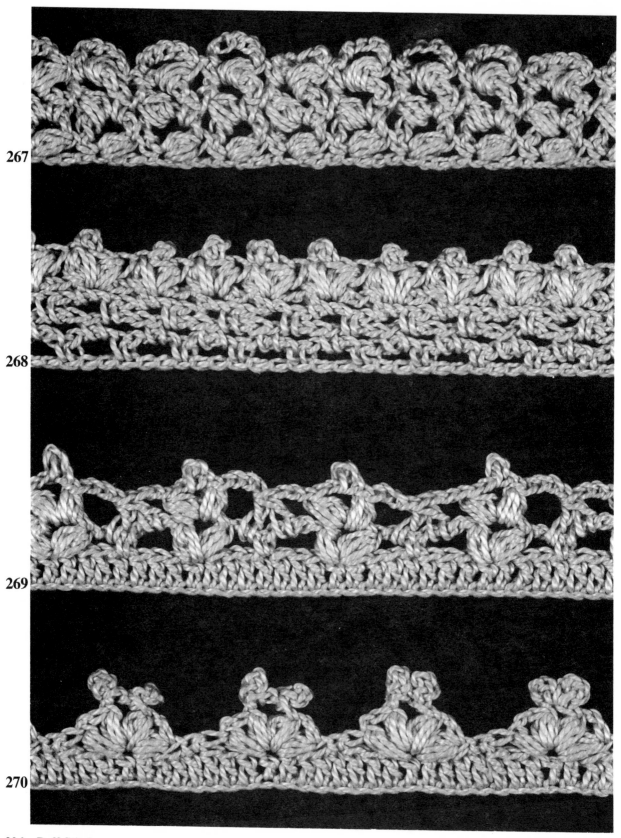

267

268

269

270

206   Puff Stitch

268. Chain multiples of 3 plus 2.

Row 1: Sc in the 2nd ch, *ch 3 and sc in the 3rd ch, rep from *, ending row with sc in the last ch, ch 4 and turn.
Row 2: * sc around the 3-ch, ch 3 and rep from *, ending row with last sc, ch 1 and dc in the last sc, ch 1 and turn.
Row 3: Sc in the 1st dc, *ch 3, sc around the 3-ch, rep from *, ending row with sc in the turning ch, ch 4 and turn.

Row 4: * sc around the 3-ch, ch 3, rep from *, ending row with sc in the last 3-ch, ch 1 and dc in the last sc, ch 3 and turn.
Row 5: Work 3-looped puff stitch in the sc, *ch 3, work 3-looped puff stitch in the last sc, finish together with 3-looped puff stitch in the next sc, rep from *, ending row with last puff stitch and 1 dc in the turning ch.

269. Chain multiples of 8 plus 4.

Row 1: Dc in the 5th ch and in each dc all across the row, ch 1 and turn.
Row 2: Sc in the 1st dc, * ch 3 and work 3-looped puff stitch in the 4th dc, ch 3 and work 3-looped puff stitch in the same dc, ch 3 and sc in the 4th dc, rep from *, ending row with sc in the turning ch, ch 3 and turn.

Row 3: Dc in the beginning of the 3-ch, *ch 3 and work 3-looped puff stitch in the next 3-ch, ch 1 and work 3-ch picot, ch 1 and work 3-looped puff stitch in the same 3-ch, ch 3 and finish 2 dc together in the next 3-ch, and the 3-ch after that, rep from *, ending row with 2 dc finished together in the last 3-ch and the sc.

270. Chain multiples of 8 plus 5.

Row 1: 1 dc in the 5th ch and in each ch all across the row, ch 1 and turn.
Row 2: Sc in the 1st dc, *ch 1, work 3-looped puff stitch in the 4th dc, ch 2, work 3-looped puff stitch in the dc just used, ch 1, work 1 4-ch picot, ch 1, work another 4-ch picot, ch 1 and attach to base of 1st picot, work 3-looped puff stitch in the dc just used, ch 2, work another 3-looped puff stitch in the same dc, sc in the 4th dc, rep from *, ending row with sc in the turning ch.

271. Chain multiples of 8 plus 2.

Row 1: Sc in the 2nd ch, *ch 2, work 3-looped puff stitch in the 4th ch, ch 3, work 3-looped puff stitch in the same ch, ch 3, sc in the 4th ch, rep from *, ending row with sc in the last ch, ch 3 and turn.

Row 2: Dc in the middle of the 3-ch, *ch 2, work 3-looped puff stitch in the middle of the next 3-ch, ch 3, work 3-looped puff stitch in the middle of the same 3-ch, ch 3, finish 2 dc together in the last 2-ch and the next 3-ch, rep from *, ending row with 2 dc finished together.

Rows 3–4: Repeat row 2.

Row 5: Dc in the 1st 3-ch, *ch 2, work 3-looped puff stitch in the next 3-ch, ch 1 and work 4-ch picot, ch 1 and work another 3-looped puff stitch in the same stitch used for 1st puff, ch 3 and finish 2 dc together in the next 2-ch and the 3-ch after that, rep from *, ending row with 2 dc finished together.

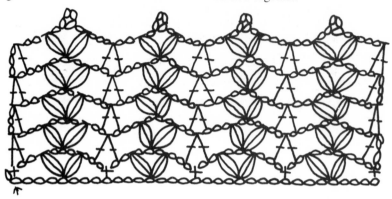

272. Chain multiples of 14 plus 4.

Row 1: 1 dc in the 5th ch, *ch 1, dc in the 2nd ch, rep from *, ending row with dc in 2nd ch and an additional dc in the next ch, ch 1 and turn.

Row 2: Sc in the 1st dc, ch 3, sc in the next 1-ch, ch 3, sc in the next 1-ch, * ch 7, 1 sc in the 3rd 1-ch, ch 3, sc in the next 1-ch, ch 3, sc in the next 1-ch, ch 3, sc in the next 1-ch, rep from *, ending row with sc, 3 chs, sc, 3 chs and 1 sc in the turning ch, ch 4 and turn.

Row 3: Sc in the 3-ch, ch 3, sc in the next 3-ch, * ch 3, work 1 2-looped puff stitch in the middle of the 7–ch, ch 3, work 2-looped puff stitch in the same 7-ch, ch 3, sc in the 3-ch, ch 3, sc in the next 3-ch, ch 3, sc in the next 3-ch, ch 3, sc in the next 3-ch, rep from *, ending row with sc in the last 3-ch, ch 1 and 1 dc in the last sc, ch 1 and turn.

Row 4: Sc in the 1st dc, ch 3, sc in the next 3-ch, * ch 4, work 2-looped puff stitch in the ch after the puff from the row below, ch 4, work puff stitch in the ch just before the puff stitch in the row below, ch 4, sk next 3-ch, sc in the next 3-ch, ch 3, sc in the next 3-ch, ch 3, sc in the next 3-ch, rep from *, ending row with sc in the turning ch, ch 4 and turn.

Row 5: Sc in 3-ch, * ch 5, work 2-looped puff in 4-ch after puff stitch of row below, work 3-ch picot, ch 3, work another 3-ch picot, 2-looped puff stitch in the same 4-ch, ch 3, work another 2-looped puff stitch in the 4-ch, work 3-ch picot, ch 3, work 2-looped puff stitch in the 4-ch, work 3-ch picot, ch 5, sc in the next 3-ch, ch 3, sc in the next 3-ch, rep from *, ending row with last set, ch 1 and dc in last sc.

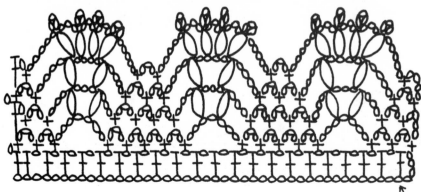

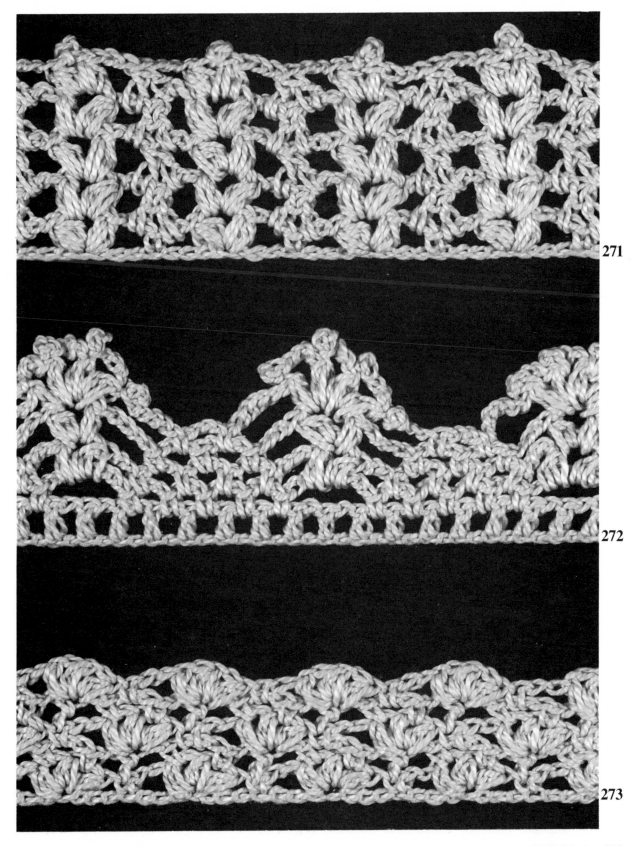

271

272

273

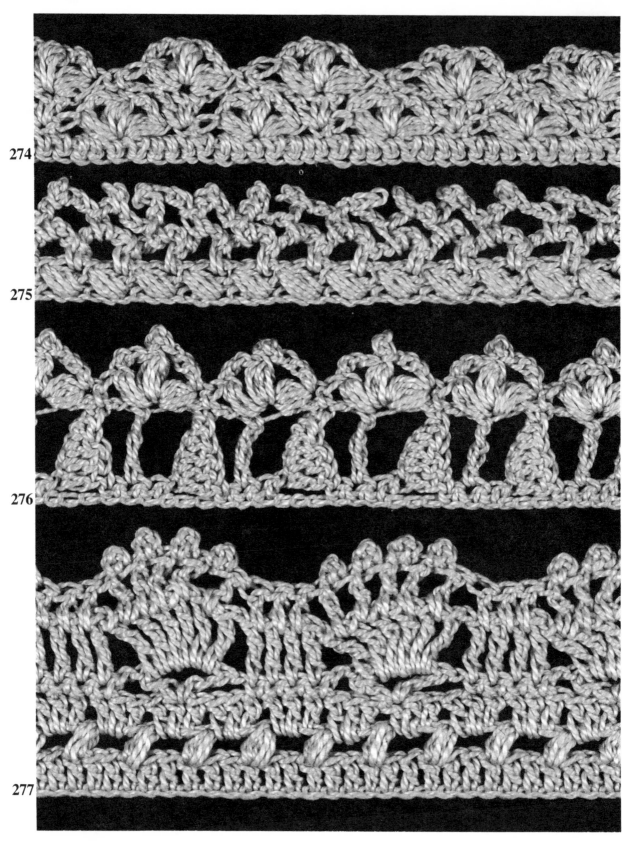

274

275

276

277

210 **Puff Stitch**

273.   Chain multiples of 8 plus 2.

Row 1: Sc in the 2nd ch, * ch 1 and work 2-looped puff stitch in the 4th ch, ch 1 and work another 2-looped puff stitch in the same ch, ch 1 and work another 2-looped puff stitch in the same ch, ch 1, sc in the 4th ch, rep from *, ending row with sc in the last ch, ch 5 and turn.
Row 2: * sc in the 2nd 1-ch, ch 3, sc in the next 1-ch, ch 1 and dc in the next sc, ch 1, rep from *, ending row with last sc, ch 2 and dc in the last sc, ch 3 and turn.
Row 3: Dc in the 1st dc, * ch 1, work 2-looped puff stitch in the same spot, ch 1 and sc in the middle of the 3-ch, ch 1 and 2-looped puff stitch in the next dc, ch 1 and work

another 2-looped puff stitch in the same dc, rep from *, ending row with 1 puff, 1 ch and another puff in the turning ch, ch 3 and turn.
Row 4: * sc in the 1-ch, ch 1 and dc in the sc, ch 1, sc in the 1-ch, ch 3, rep from *, ending row with last sc, ch 1 and 1 hdc in the last dc, ch 1 and turn.
Row 5: Sc in the hdc, * ch 1, work 2-looped puff stitch in the next dc, ch 1, and 2-looped puff stitch in the same dc, ch 1 and work another 2-looped puff stitch in the same dc, ch 1 and sc in the middle of the 3-ch, rep from *, ending row with sc in the turning ch.

274.   Chain multiples of 8 plus 2.

Row 1: Sc in the 2nd ch, * work 3-looped puff stitch in the 4th ch, ch 3, work another 3-looped puff stitch in the same ch, ch 3, work another 3-looped puff stitch in the ch just used, sc in the 4th ch, rep from *, ending with 2-looped puff stitch in the last ch, ch 1 and turn.
Row 2: Sc in the 2-looped puff stitch, * ch 2, work 3 dc in the sc, ch 2, work 1 sc in the top of the 2nd puff stitch,

rep from *, ending row with 2 dc in the last sc, ch 3 and turn.
Row 3: 1 dc in the 1st dc, * ch 3, work 3-looped puff stitch in the dc just used, sc in the sc, work 3-looped puff stitch in the 2nd dc, ch 3, work another 3-looped puff stitch in the same dc, rep from *, ending row with sc in the last sc.

275.   Chain multiples of 3 plus 4.

Row 1: Dc in the 7th ch, ch 2, work 3-looped puff stitch back in the 3rd ch from the dc just formed, * dc in the 3rd ch, ch 2, work 3-looped puff stitch in the ch where the previous dc was formed, rep from *, ending row after last puff stitch with 1 dc in the same ch where the last dc was formed, ch 5 and turn.

Row 2: * sc in the middle of the 2-ch, ch 5, rep from *, ending row with sc in the last 2-ch, ch 2 and 1 dc in the top of the turning ch, ch 1 and turn.
Row 3: Sc in the dc, * ch 2, work 3-ch picot, ch 2, sc around the middle of the 5-ch, rep from *, ending row with sc in the turning ch.

276. Chain multiples of 6 plus 2.

Row 1: Sc in the 2nd ch and sc in the next ch, * ch 6 and turn, work sc in the 2nd ch from the end, hdc in the next ch, work 1 dc in each of the next 3 chs, sc in the 4th ch, and sc in each of the next 2 sc, rep from *, ending row with sc in each of the last 2 chs, ch 7 and turn.

Row 2: * sc in the last ch made of the set, ch 2 and double trc in the middle of the 3 sc, ch 2 and rep from *, ending row with last double trc, ch 3 and turn.

Row 3: Work dc in the top of the double trc, * work 3-ch picot, ch 3 and work 3-looped puff stitch in the place just used, sc in the next sc, work 3-looped puff stitch in the top of the next double trc, ch 3 and work 3-looped puff stitch, rep from *, ending row with 2-looped puff stitch in the turning ch and 3-ch picot.

277. Chain multiples of 12 plus 4.

Row 1: Dc in the 5th ch and dc in each ch all across the row, ch 4 and turn.

Row 2: Work 3-looped puff stitch in the 3rd dc, * ch 2 and work another 3-looped puff stitch in the 3rd dc, rep from *, ending row with 3-looped puff stitch in the turning ch, ch 3 and turn.

Row 3: * work 1 dc in each of the 2-ch, dc in the top of the puff stitch, and rep from *, ending row with 2 dc in the turning ch, ch 1 and turn.

Row 4: Sc in the 1st dc and the next dc, * ch 1 and trc in the 4th dc, ch 4 and work another trc in the dc just used, ch 1 and sc in the 4th dc and in each of the next 3 dc, rep from *, ending row with sc in the last dc and sc in the turning ch, ch 4 and turn.

Row 5: Work double trc in the 2nd sc, * ch 1 and trc in the 4-ch, rep ch 1 and trc in the 4-ch 5 more times, ch 1 and double trc in each of the next 4 sc, rep from *, ending row with double trc in each of the last 2 sc, ch 3 and turn.

Row 6: Dc in between the 1st 2 double trc, * sk next 1-ch, trc in next 1-ch, work 3-ch picot, trc in next 1-ch 4 times, work dc after the 2nd double trc, work dc after each of the next 2 double trc, and rep from *, ending row with dc in the turning ch.

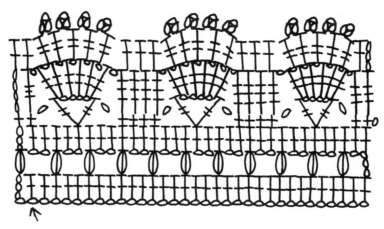

·16·
Popcorn Stitch

278. Chain multiples of 6 plus 7.

Row 1: Sc in the 10th ch, *ch 3, work 4-looped popcorn stitch in the 3rd ch, ch 3, sc in the 3rd ch, rep from *, ending row with last sc, ch 3 and dc in the 3rd and final ch, ch 3 and turn.

Row 2: Dc in the 1st dc, *ch 5, dc in the top of the popcorn stitch, ch 1, dc in the top of the same popcorn stitch, rep from *, ending row with 2 dc in the turning ch.

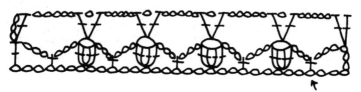

279. Chain multiples of 4 plus 2.

Row 1: Sc in the 2nd ch, * ch 3, work 5-looped popcorn stitch in the 2nd ch, ch 3, sc in the 2nd ch, rep from *, ending row with last sc, ch 5 and turn.
Row 2: * sc in the top of the popcorn stitch, ch 3, rep from *, ending row with last sc, 2 chs and 1 dc in the last sc, ch 1 and turn.
Row 3: Sc in the 1st dc, * work 3-ch picot, ch 1, sc in the sc, work 3-ch picot, ch 1, sc in the middle of the 3-ch, rep from *, ending row with sc in the turning ch.

280. Chain multiples of 4 plus 2.

Row 1: Sc in the 2nd ch and in each ch all across the row, ch 1 and turn.
Row 2: Sc in each sc all across the row, ch 1 and turn.
Row 3: Sc in the 1st sc, dc in the 2nd sc, *ch 3, dc in the sc just used, sc in the 2nd sc, dc in the 2nd sc, rep from *, ending row with sc in the last sc, ch 5 and turn.
Row 4: Dc in the 1st sc, * sc in the middle of the 3-ch, dc in the next sc, ch 3, dc in the sc just used, rep from *, ending row with a dc in the last sc, 1 ch, and 1 trc in the last sc, ch 1 and turn.
Row 5: Sc in the trc, * ch 3, work 1 5-looped popcorn stitch in the sc, ch 3, sc in the middle of the 3-ch, rep from *, ending row with sc in the turning ch.

281. Chain multiples of 14 plus 4.

Row 1: Dc in the 5th ch and the next ch, * ch 2, sc in the 3rd ch, ch 1, dc in the 3rd ch, ch 1 and dc in the same ch, ch 1 and dc in the same ch, ch 1 and sc in the 3rd ch, ch 2, and dc in the 3rd ch and dc in each of the next 2 chs, rep from *, ending row with 1 dc in each of the last 3 dc, ch 3 and turn.

Row 2: Dc in the 2nd dc and the next dc, * work 5-looped popcorn stitch in the 1st 1-ch, ch 4, and work 5-looped popcorn stitch in the next 1-ch, ch 4 and work 5-looped popcorn stitch in the next 1-ch, ch 4 and work 5-looped popcorn stitch in the next 1-ch, dc in each of the next 3 dc, rep from *, ending row with dc in each of the last 2 dc and 1 in the turning ch, ch 3 and turn.

Row 3: Dc in the 2nd dc and the next dc, * ch 2, sc in the 4-ch, ch 3, sc in the next 4-ch, ch 3, sc in the next 4-ch, ch 2, dc in each of the next 3 dc, rep from *, ending row with dc in the turning ch.

282. Chain multiples of 12 plus 2.

Row 1: Sc in the 2nd ch, *ch 5, sc in the ch just used, * ch 5, work a 5-looped popcorn stitch in the 6th ch, ch 6, 1 sc in the 6th ch, ch 5, 1 sc in the same ch, ch 5, 1 sc in the same ch, rep from *, ending row with 1 sc in the last ch, ch 8 and turn.

Row 2: * 1 sc in the top of the popcorn stitch, ch 5, 1 sc in the same ch, ch 5, 1 sc in the same stitch, ch 5, work a 5-looped popcorn in the middle of the 3 sc, ch 6, rep from *, ending row with 5 chs and 1 dc in the last sc, ch 1 and turn.

Row 3: Sc in the 1st sc, ch 5, sc in the same sc just used, * ch 5, work 5-looped popcorn stitch in the middle of the sc, ch 6, sc in the top of the popcorn stitch, ch 5, sc in the same stitch, ch 5, sc in the same stitch, rep from *, ending row with sc in the turning ch, ch 5 and sc in the same stitch.

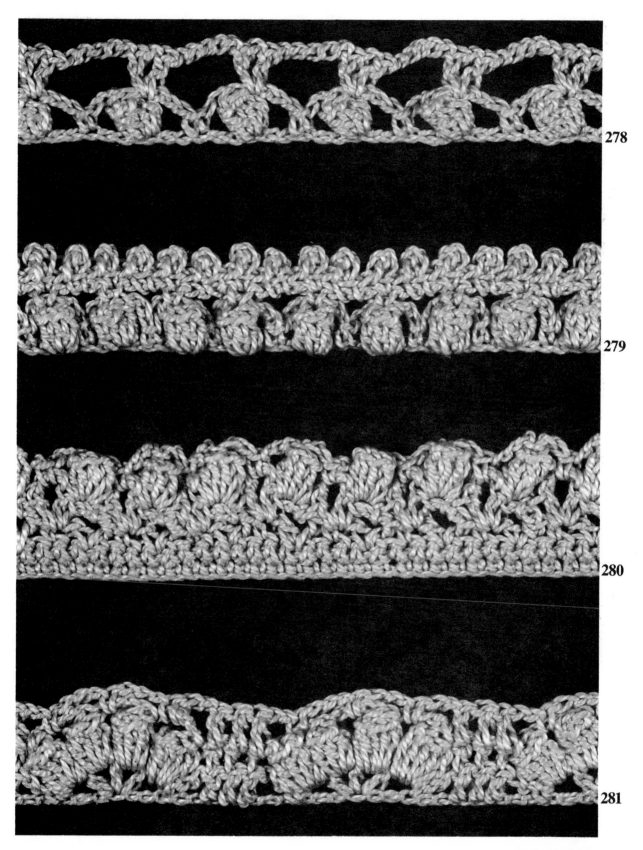

278

279

280

281

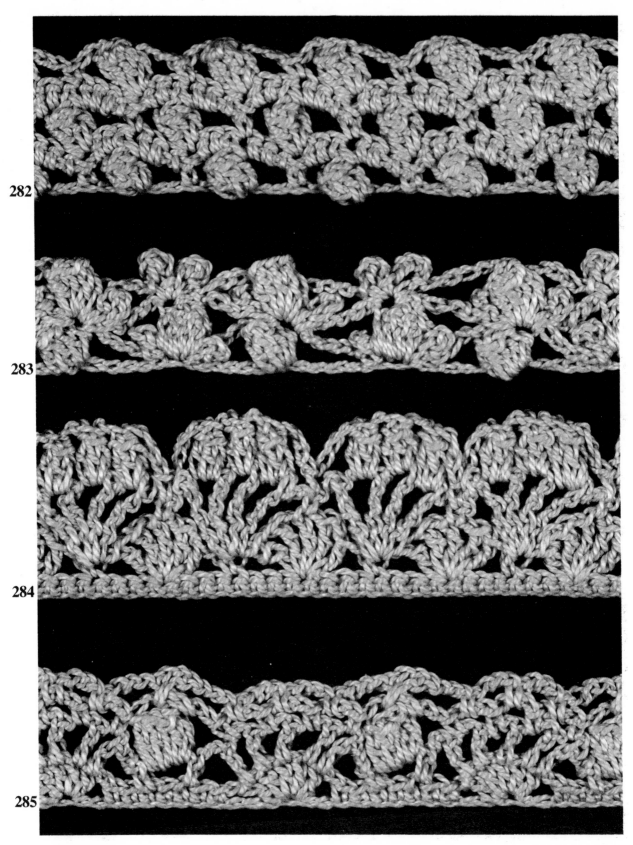

282

283

284

285

216   Popcorn Stitch

283. Chain multiples of 6 plus 2.

Row 1: Sc in the 2nd ch, * ch 3, work 4-looped popcorn stitch in the 3rd ch, ch 3, sc in the 3rd sc, rep from *, ending row with sc in the last ch, ch 1 and turn.

Row 2: Sc in the 1st sc, * 3 sc in the 3-ch, 3 sc in the next 3-ch, rep from *, ending row with sc in the last sc, ch 3 and turn.

Row 3: Dc in the 1st sc, * ch 3, sc in the top of the popcorn stitch, ch 3, work 4-looped popcorn stitch be-tween the 3rd and next sc, rep from *, ending row with 2-looped popcorn stitch, ch 1 and turn.

Row 4: Sc in the 1st popcorn stitch, * 3 sc in the 3-ch, rep from *, ending row with sc in the turning ch, ch 1 and turn.

Row 5: Sc in the 1st sc, * ch 3, work 4-looped popcorn stitch between the 2 sc over the sc of the row below, ch 3, sc above next popcorn stitch, rep from *, ending row with sc in the last sc.

284. Chain multiples of 8 plus 2.

Row 1: Sc in the 2nd ch and in each ch all across the row, ch 1 and turn.

Row 2: Sc in the 1st sc, * ch 1 and trc in the 4th sc, ch 1 and trc in the sc just used 4 more times, ch 1 and sc in the 4th ch, rep from *, ending row with sc in the last sc, ch 8 and turn.

Row 3: Double trc in the 1st sc, * ch 2, sc in the 3rd trc, ch 2, double trc in the next sc, ch 2 and double trc in the same sc 3 more times, rep from *, ending row with 2 chs, 1 double trc in the last sc, ch 2 and 1 more double trc in the same sc, ch 3 and turn.

Row 4: Work 3-looped popcorn stitch in the 1st 2-ch, * ch 5, sc in the sc, ch 5, work 3-looped popcorn stitch in the next 2-ch, ch 2, work another 3-looped popcorn stitch in the next 2-ch, ch 2, work another 3-looped popcorn stitch in the next 2-ch, rep from *, ending row with 3-looped popcorn stitch, 2 chs and 1 dc in the turning ch.

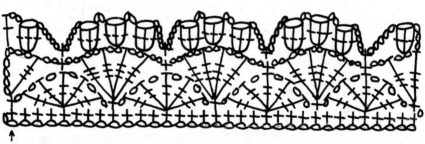

285. Chain multiples of 12 plus 4.

Row 1: 3 dc in the 4th ch, * ch 1, sc in the 3rd ch, sc in each of the next 6 chs, ch 1, work 5 dc in the 3rd ch, rep from *, ending row with 3 dc in the last ch, ch 5 and turn.

Row 2: Dc in the 2nd dc, ch 2, dc in the next dc, * ch 3, sc in the 3rd sc, ch 3, sc in the 2nd sc, ch 3, dc in the next dc and 2 chs 4 times, dc in the next dc, and rep from *, ending row with dc in the turning ch, ch 1 and turn.

Row 3: Sc in the 1st dc, ch 1, sk next 2-ch, * sc in the 2-ch, ch 3, sc in the next 2-ch, ch 3, work 6-looped pop-corn stitch in the 2nd 3-ch, ch 3, sc in the next 2-ch, ch 3, sc in the next 2-ch, ch 3, rep from *, ending row with 1 ch and sc in the turning ch, ch 1 and turn.

Row 4: Sc in the 1st sc, ch 3, sc in the next 3-ch, * ch 3, work 1st part of small X-stitch just after the popcorn stitch, ch 2, and 2nd part just before the popcorn stitch, ch 3, sc in the 2nd 3-ch, ch 3, sc in the next 3-ch, ch 3, sc in the next 3-ch, rep from *, ending row with sc in the last sc.

286. Chain multiples of 16 plus 5.

Row 1: Dc in the 5th ch, * ch 3, work 4-looped popcorn stitch in the 4th ch, ch 1 and popcorn stitch in the 2nd ch 4 times, ch 3, dc in the 4th ch, rep from *, ending row with dc in each of the last 2 chs, ch 3 and turn.

Row 2: Dc in the 2nd dc, * dc in the 1st ch, ch 3, work 4-looped popcorn in the next 1-ch, ch 1, 4-looped popcorn stitch in the next 1-ch, ch 1, 4-looped popcorn stitch in the next 1-ch, ch 1, 4-looped popcorn in the next 1-ch, ch 3, dc in the last of the 3-ch, dc in the dc, rep from *, ending row with dc in the turning ch, ch 3 and turn.

Row 3: Dc in the 2nd dc and the next dc, * dc in the 1st of the 3-ch, ch 3, work 4-looped popcorn in the 1-ch, ch 1, work another 4-looped popcorn in the next 1-ch, ch 1 and work another popcorn stitch in the next 1-ch, ch 3, dc in

the last of the 3-ch, dc in each of the next 3 dc, rep from *, ending row with 3 dc and 1 dc in the turning ch, ch 3 and turn.

Row 4: Dc in the 2nd dc, and dc in each of the next 2 dc, * dc in the beginning of the 3-ch, ch 3, work 4-looped popcorn stitch in the 1-ch, ch 1, work 4-looped popcorn stitch in the next 1-ch, ch 3, dc in the last of the 3-ch, dc in each of the next 5 dc, rep from *, ending row with 4 dc and 1 dc in the turning ch, ch 3 and turn.

Row 5: Dc in the 2nd dc and each of the next 3 dc, * dc in the beginning of the 1-ch, ch 3, work 4-looped popcorn stitch in the 1-ch, ch 3, dc in the last of the 1-ch, dc in each of the next 7 dc, rep from *, ending row with 5 dc and 1 dc in the turning ch.

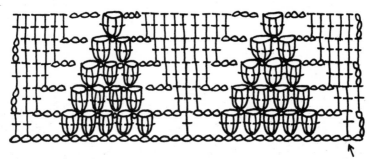

287. Chain multiples of 6 plus 2.

Row 1: Sc in the 2nd ch, * ch 3, work 5-looped popcorn stitch in the 3rd ch, ch 3, 1 sc in the 3rd ch, rep from *, ending row with last sc, ch 3 and turn.

Row 2: Dc in the 1st sc, work 3-ch picot, * sc in the top of the popcorn stitch, work dc in the sc and work 3-ch picot

4 times, rep from *, ending row with 1 dc, 1 picot and 1 dc in the last sc.

Bottom Row: Sc in the 2nd ch and in the next 2 chs, * ch 5, sc in the 2nd ch and in each of the 4 following chs, rep from *, ending row with 3 sc.

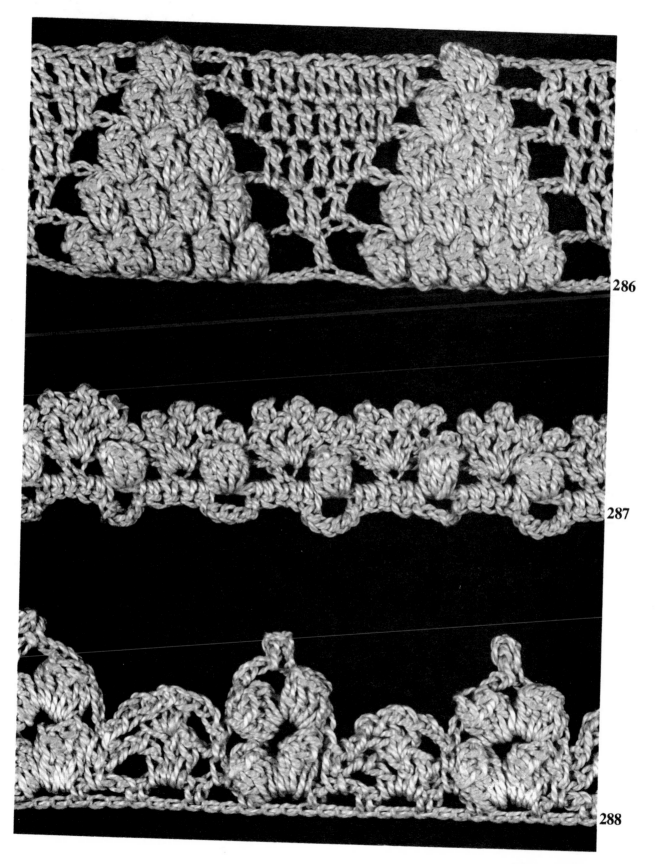

286

287

288

288.   Chain multiples of 12 plus 2.

Row 1: Sc in the 2-ch, * ch 3 and sc in the 3rd ch, rep from *, ending row with last sc, ch 1 and turn.
Row 2: Sc in the sc, and 2 in the 3-ch, * ch 2 and work 5-looped popcorn stitch in the next 3-ch, ch 5 and work another 5-looped popcorn stitch in the same 3-ch, ch 2 and sc in the next 3-ch, ch 3 and dc in the next 3-ch, ch 1 and dc in the same 3-ch, ch 1 and dc in the same 3-ch, ch 3 and sc in the next 3-ch, rep from *, ending row with 2 sc in the last 3-ch and 1 sc in the last sc, ch 1 and turn.
Row 3: Sc in each of the 3 sc, * ch 3 and dc in the 2nd dc, ch 2 and dc in the same dc, ch 2 and dc in the same dc, ch 3 and sc in the next sc, ch 3 and work 5-looped popcorn stitch in the 5-ch, ch 3 and work 4-ch picot, ch 4 and work another 5-looped popcorn stitch in the same 5-ch, ch 3 and sc in the next sc, rep from *, ending row with sc in each of the last sc.

289.   Chain multiples of 8 plus 2.

Row 1: Sc in the 2nd ch and the next 4 sc, * ch 7 and attach to 1st ch, ch 7 and sc in the next ch, ch 7 and sc in the next ch, sc in each of the next 6 chs, rep from *, ending row with last sc, ch 4 and turn.
Row 2: * work 5-looped popcorn stitch in the top of the 1st 7-ch, ch 4, work another 5-looped popcorn stitch in the top of the next 7-ch, ch 4, work another 5-looped popcorn stitch in the top of the next 7-ch, rep from *, ending row with last set and 1 double trc in the last sc, ch 7 and turn.
Row 3: * sc in the middle of the 4-ch, ch 5, rep from *, ending row with last sc, ch 2 and work 1 double trc in the turning ch, ch 1 and turn.
Row 4: Sc in the 1st double trc, * ch 5 and sc around the 5-ch, rep from *, ending row with sc in the turning ch, ch 5 and turn.
Row 5: * sc around the 5-ch, ch 5, rep from *, ending row with last sc, ch 2 and dc in the last sc.

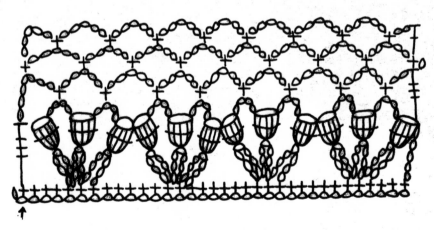

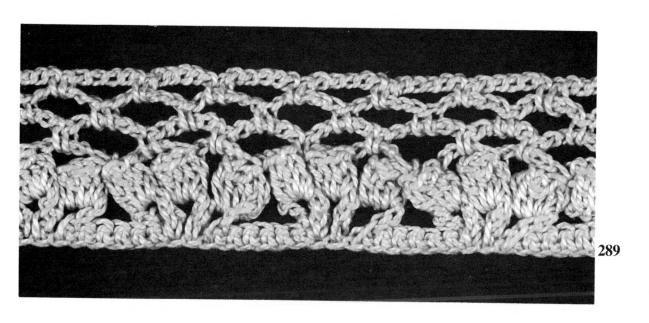

289

·17·
Cluster Stitch

290. Chain multiples of 5 plus 6.

Row 1: Work 1 3-looped triple cluster in the 6th ch, together with 3-looped triple cluster in the 5th ch, * ch 5, work 3-ch picot, ch 5, work 3-looped triple cluster in the ch just used, together with the next triple cluster in the 5th stitch, rep from *, ending row with triple cluster in the 5th and last ch, ch 2 and 1 trc in the same last ch.

291.

Pattern: * work 1 5-ch picot, work 2nd 5-ch picot into the base of the 1st, work 5-ch picot into the base of the other 2, ch 4, work 3-loop triple cluster into the base of the 3 picots just formed, rep from *, ending row with last pattern.

292.

Row 1: Chain 5, * ch 7 and sl st last of the 7-ch into the 1st, ch 1, sc in the 7-ch ring, ch 4, work 2-looped triple cluster into the 7-ch, ch 4, work sc in the 7-ch, ch 4, work 2-looped triple cluster into the same 7-ch, ch 4, work sc into the same 7-ch, ch 4, work another 2-looped triple cluster into the same 7-ch, ch 4, sc into the 7-ch, ch 4, work 2-looped triple cluster into the 7-ch, ch 4, sc into the 7-ch, ch 4, 2-looped triple cluster into the same 7-ch, ch 4, sc into the same 7-ch, there should be a total of 5 triple clusters formed, ch 10 and repeat pattern until desired length is formed.

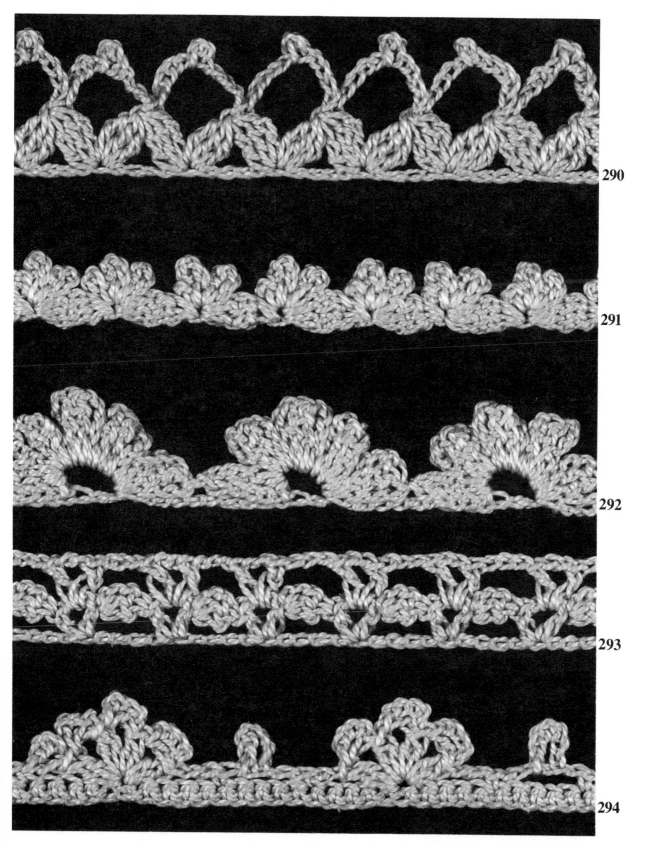

290

291

292

293

294

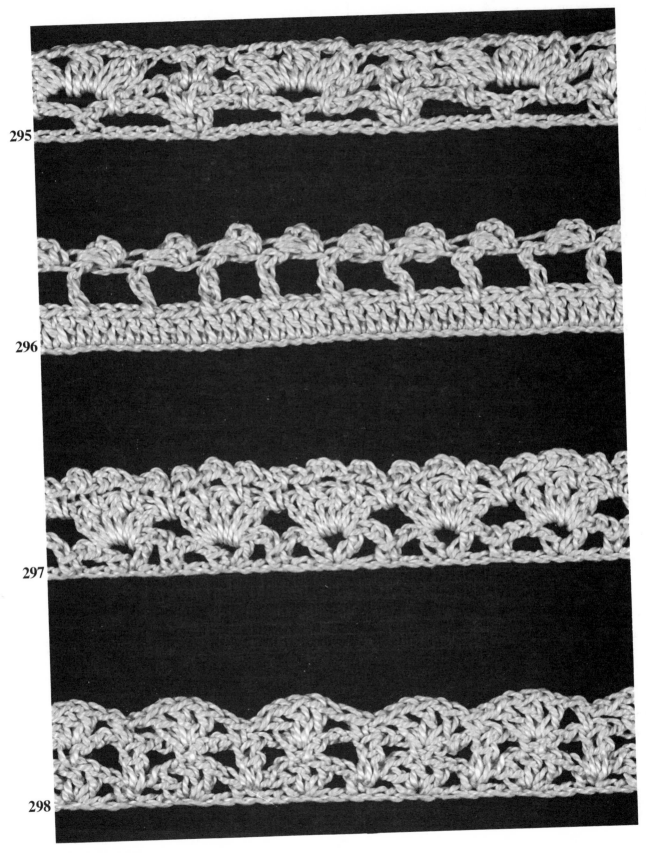

295

296

297

298

293. Chain multiples of 5 plus 4.

Row 1: Dc in the 4th ch, * ch 3, work 2-looped cluster back in the top of the dc, dc in the 5th ch, ch 2, dc in the ch just used, rep from *, ending row with last set and dc in the last ch, ch 3 and turn.

Row 2: Dc in the 1st dc, * ch 3, dc in the 2-ch, ch 2 and dc in the same 2-ch, rep from *, ending row with 2 dc in the turning ch.

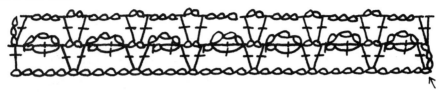

294. Chain multiples of 18 plus 2.

Row 1: Sc in the 2nd ch, *ch 2, work 2-looped cluster in the 6th ch, ch 5 and dc back in the 1st ch, work another 2-looped cluster in the same ch, ch 5 and dc back in the 1st ch formed, work another 2-looped cluster in the same ch, ch 5 and dc back in the 1st ch formed, work another 2-looped cluster in the same ch, ch 2, sc in the 6th sc, ch 2, work 7-ch picot, ch 2 and sc in the 6th ch, rep from *, ending row with sc in the last ch.

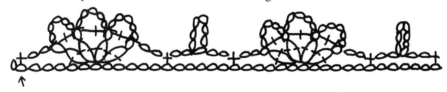

295. Chain multiples of 12 plus 4.

Row 1: Dc in the 4th ch, * ch 5, sc in the 6th ch, ch 5, dc in the 6th ch, ch 1, dc in the ch just used, rep from *, ending row with 2 dc in the last ch, ch 3 and turn.
Row 2: Dc in the 1st dc, * ch 3, sc around the 5-ch, ch 4, sc around the middle of the next 5-ch, ch 3, dc in the 1-ch, ch 1, dc in the same 1-ch, rep from *, ending row with 2 dc in the turning ch, ch 3 and turn.

Row 3: Dc in the 1st dc, *ch 1, work 3-looped cluster in the beginning of the 4-ch, ch 3, work another 3-looped cluster in the middle of the 4-ch, ch 3, work another 3-looped cluster in the end of the 4-ch, dc in the 1-ch, ch 1, dc in the same 1-ch, rep from *, ending row with 2 dc in the turning ch.

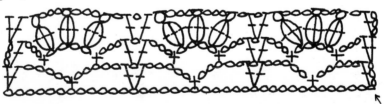

296. Chain multiples of 4 plus 4.

Row 1: Dc in the 5th ch and in each ch all across the row, ch 8 and turn.
Row 2: Work 2-looped cluster in the 5th ch back just formed, trc in the 5th dc, * ch 4, work 2-looped cluster in the top of the trc just formed, work trc in the 4th dc, rep from *, ending row with trc in the turning ch.

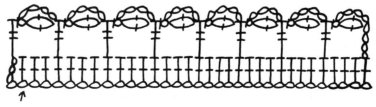

297. Chain multiples of 6 plus 2.

Row 1: Sc in the 2nd ch, * ch 2, dc in the 3rd ch, ch 2, dc in the same ch just used, ch 2, sc in the 3rd ch, rep from *, ending row with sc in the last ch, ch 4 and turn.
Row 2: * work 2-looped cluster in the 2 chs between the 2 sides of the V-stitch, ch 1, work another 2-looped clus-ter in the same 2-ch, ch 1, work another 2-looped cluster in the same 2-ch, ch 1, rep from *, ending row with last set and a trc in the last sc, ch 1 and turn.
Row 3: Sc in the trc, * ch 3, sc in the next 1-ch, rep from *, ending row with sc in the turning ch.

298. Chain multiples of 6 plus 5.

Row 1: Dc in the 5th ch, * ch 1, sc in the 3rd ch, ch 1, dc in the 3rd ch, ch 1, dc into the same ch, ch 1, dc in the same ch, rep from *, ending row with dc in the last ch, ch 1, and dc in the same ch, ch 1 and turn.
Row 2: Sc in the 1st dc, * ch 3, work 2-looped cluster in the sc, ch 3, sc in the 2nd dc, rep from *, ending row with sc in the turning ch, ch 4 and turn.
Row 3: Dc in the 1st sc, * ch 1, sc in the top of the cluster, ch 1, dc in the sc, ch 1, dc in the same sc, ch 1, dc in the sc, rep from * ending row with dc in the last sc, ch 1, dc in the same sc.

299. Chain multiples of 4 plus 4.

Row 1: Dc in the 5th ch and dc in each of the next 2 chs, * ch 1, dc in the 2nd ch and dc in each of the next 2 chs, rep from *, ending row with last set and 1 additional dc in the ch following, ch 3 and turn.
Row 2: Work 3-loop cluster in the 3rd dc, * ch 4, work 3-looped cluster in the dc just used, work 3-looped cluster in the 3rd dc (2nd dc of the next group), rep from *, ending row with last cluster and dc in the turning ch, ch 4 and turn.
Row 3: * Sl st in the middle of the 4-ch, ch 5, rep from *, ending row with last sl st, ch 3 and sc in the turning ch.

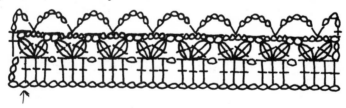

300. Chain multiples of 3 plus 2.

Row 1: Sc in the 2nd ch and in each ch all across the row, ch 3 and turn.
Row 2: Dc in the 2nd sc, ch 1 and dc in the sc just used, * dc in the 3rd sc, ch 1, dc in the same sc, rep from *, ending row with last set and 1 dc in the last sc, ch 3 and turn.
Row 3: * work 3-looped cluster in the 1-ch, ch 2, rep from *, ending row with last cluster and 1 dc in the turning ch, ch 1 and turn.
Row 4: sc in the dc, * sc in the top of the cluster, ch 3, sc in each of the next 2 chs, rep from *, ending row with sc in the turning ch.

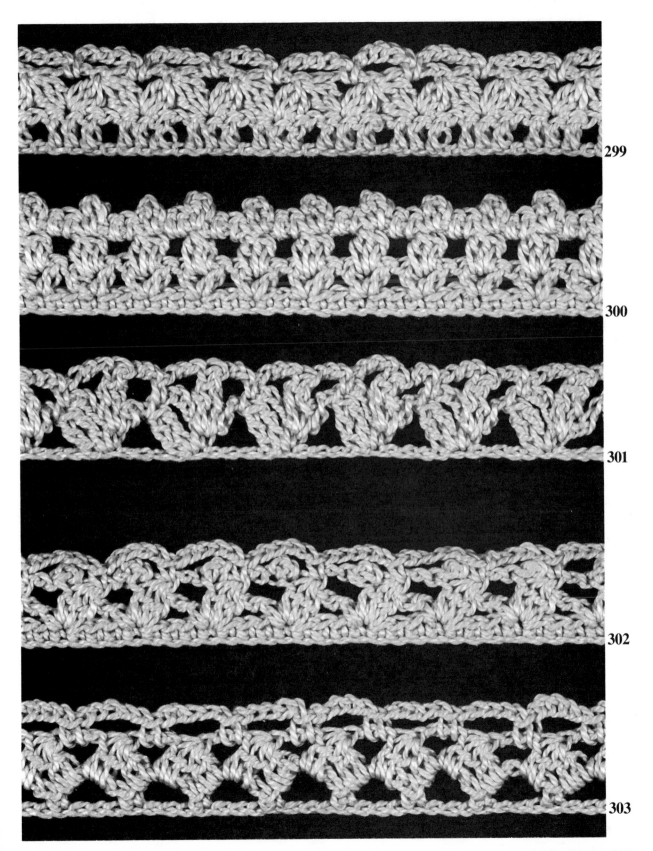

299

300

301

302

303

304

305

306

307

228   Cluster Stitch

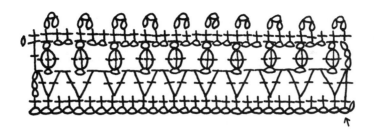

301. Chain multiples of 5 plus 2.

Row 1: Sc in the 2nd ch, * ch 4, work 2-looped triple cluster in the sc just formed, ch 4, sc in the 5th ch, rep from *, ending row with sc, ch 7 and turn.

Row 2: * sc in the top of the cluster, ch 3, work 2-looped triple cluster in the sc, ch 3 and rep from *, ending row with 3 chs and 1 trc in the last sc.

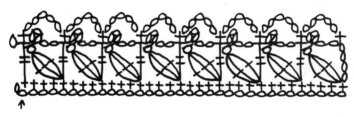

302. Chain multiples of 4 plus 2.

Row 1: Sc in the 2nd ch and in each ch all across the row, ch 6 and turn.
Row 2: Work 3-ch picot, work 3-looped cluster back in the base of the 1st sc, * trc in the 4th sc, ch 2, work 3-ch picot, work 3-looped cluster back in the base of the trc, rep from *, ending row with last trc, ch 1 and turn.
Row 3: * sc in the trc, ch 5 and rep from *, ending row with last sc in the turning ch.

303. Chain multiples of 4 plus 2.

Row 1: Sc in the 2nd ch, * ch 5 and sc in the 4th ch, rep from *, ending row with sc in the last ch, ch 3 and turn.
Row 2: Work 2-looped cluster in the beginning of the 5-ch, * ch 3, work 2-looped cluster towards the end of the same 5-ch, together with 2-looped cluster in the beginning of the next 5-ch, rep from *, ending row with cluster in the last 5-ch finished together with 1 dc in the last sc, ch 2 and turn.
Row 3: Sc in the top of the 1st cluster, * ch 5, sc towards the end of the 3-ch, rep from *, ending row with sc in the turning ch.

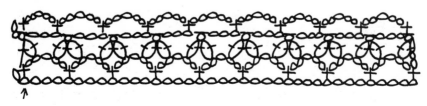

304. Chain multiples of 12 plus 7.

Row 1: Sc in the 10th ch, * sc in each of the next 6 chs, ch 7, sc in 6th ch, rep from *, ending row with sc in each of the last 4 chs, ch 1 and turn.

Row 2: Sc in the 1st sc, * ch 1, work 3-looped cluster around the beginning of the 7-ch and ch 2, work another 3-looped cluster and 2 chs 3 times, work another 3-looped cluster around the end of the 7-ch and ch 1, sc in the 4th sc, rep from *, ending row with a cluster, 2 chs, a cluster, 2 chs and a dc in the turning ch, ch 1 and turn.

Row 3: Sc in the dc, * sc in the 2-ch, ch 3, sc in the next 2-ch, ch 3, sc in the 1-ch, sc in the next 1-ch, ch 3, sc in the 2-ch, ch 3, and sc in the next 2-ch, ch 3 and rep from *, ending row with sc in the last sc.

305. Chain multiples of 10 plus 2.

Row 1: Sc in the 2nd ch, * ch 5, work 4-looped cluster in the 5th ch, ch 5, sc in the 5th ch, rep from *, ending row with sc in the last ch, ch 7 and turn.

Row 2: * work 4-looped cluster in the last of the 5-ch before the cluster of the row below, ch 5, and sc in the middle of the next 5-ch, ch 5, and rep from *, ending row with sc in the last 5-ch, ch 3 and double trc in the last sc, ch 1 and turn.

Row 3: Sc in the top of the trc, * ch 5, work 4-looped cluster in the last of the 5-ch, ch 5, sc in the middle of the 5-ch, rep from *, ending row with sc in the turning ch.

306. Chain multiples of 17 plus 8.

Row 1: Sc in the 12th ch, * ch 4, sc in the 3rd ch, ch 4, sc in the third ch, ch 4, sc in the 3rd ch, ch 4, dc in the 4th ch, ch 4, sc in the 4th ch, rep from *, ending row with dc in the last ch, ch 3 and turn.

Row 2: 2 dc in the 1st dc, * ch 2, sc around the 4-ch, ch 4, sc around the 4-ch, ch 4, sc around the 4-ch, ch 2, 5 dc in the dc, rep from *, ending row with 3 dc in the turning ch, ch 3 and turn.

Row 3: Dc in the 1st dc, * work 3-picot, ch 1, work 2-looped cluster in the next dc, work 3-ch picot, ch 1, work 2-looped cluster in the next dc, work 3-ch picot, ch 2, sc in the next 4-ch, ch 4, sc in the next 4-ch, ch 2, work 2-looped cluster in the next dc, work 3-ch picot, ch 2, work 2-looped cluster in the next dc, work 3-ch picot, ch 2, work 2-looped cluster in the next dc, 3-ch picot, ch 1, work 2-looped cluster in the next dc, rep from *, ending row with cluster in the turning ch.

307.   Chain multiples of 16 plus 2.

Row 1: Sc in the 2nd ch and in each ch all across the row, ch 5 and turn.

Row 2: Sc in the 3rd sc, * ch 5 and sc in the 4th sc, rep from *, ending row with sc in the last sc, ch 5 and turn.

Row 3: * sc around the middle of the 5-ch, ch 5, rep from *, ending row with sc in the turning ch, ch 5 and turn.

Row 4: Sc around the middle of the 5-ch, ch 5, * sc around the middle of the next 5-ch, ch 8, dc back into the 4th ch made and ch 3, sc around the middle of the next 5-ch, ch 5 and sc in the next 5-ch, ch 5 and sc in the middle

of the next 5-ch and ch 5, rep from *, ending row with sc in the turning ch, ch 9 and turn.

Row 5: * work 2-looped cluster in the end of the next 5-ch, work 2-looped cluster in the middle of the next 5-ch, work another 2-looped cluster in the beginning of the next 5-ch, ch 1 and work 3-looped triple cluster in the 5-ch, ch 4, and work another 3-looped triple cluster in the same 5-ch, ch 4 and work another 3-looped triple cluster in the same 5-ch, ch 4 and work another 3-looped triple cluster in the same 5-ch, ch 1, rep from *, ending row with 2-looped cluster in the turning ch.

308.   Chain multiples of 25 plus 2.

Row 1: Sc in the 2nd ch, * ch 5, sc in the 5th ch, rep from *, ending row with last sc, ch 2 and dc in the 3rd ch, ch 3 and turn.

Row 2: Work 4 dc in the 2-ch, * sc in the middle of the 5-ch, ch 5, sc in the middle of the next 5-ch, ch 5, sc in the middle of the next 5-ch, ch 5, sc in the middle of the next 5-ch, work 9 dc in the middle of the next 5-ch, rep from *, ending row with sc in the last 5-ch, ch 2 and dc in the last sc, ch 1 and turn.

Row 3: Sc in the 1st dc, * ch 5, sc in the middle of the next 5-ch, ch 1, work 3-looped cluster in the next dc, ch

3, work another 3-looped cluster in the 2nd dc, ch 3, work another 3-looped cluster in the 2nd dc, ch 3, work 3-looped cluster in the dc just used, ch 3, work 3-looped cluster in the 2nd dc, ch 3, work 3-looped cluster in the next dc, ch 1, sc around the 5-ch, ch 5, sc around the next 5-ch, rep from *, ending row with last cluster, 1 ch and 1 trc in the turning ch, ch 1 and turn.

Row 4: Sc in the trc, * ch 5, sc in the 2nd 3-ch, ch 5, sc around the 5-ch, ch 5, sc around the 5-ch, ch 5, sc in the next 3-ch, ch 5, sc around the 2nd 3-ch, rep from *, ending row with sc, 2 chs and dc in the last sc.

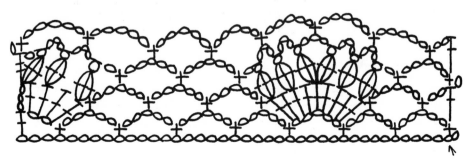

309.   Chain multiples of 8 plus 4.

Row 1: Dc in the 4th ch, *ch 2, sc in the 2nd ch, ch 3, sc in the 4th ch, ch 2, work 3-looped cluster in the 2nd ch, rep from *, ending row with 2 chs and 2-looped cluster in the 2nd ch, ch 1 and turn.

Row 2: Sc in the 1st cluster, * ch 1, 2 dc in the 3-ch, ch 2, 2 dc in the same 3-ch, ch 1, sc in the top of the cluster, rep from *, ending row with sc in the last dc, ch 1 and turn.

Row 3: Sc in the sc, ch 2, * sc in the 1st dc, ch 2, work 3-looped cluster in the 2-ch, ch 2, sc in the 2nd dc, ch 3, rep from *, ending row with last set, 2 chs and 1 sc in the last sc.

310.   Chain multiples of 8 plus 6.

Row 1: Work 3-looped cluster in the 10th ch, * ch 1, work 3-looped cluster in the same ch, ch 2, dc in the 4th ch, ch 2, work 3-looped cluster in the 4th ch, rep from *, ending row with dc in the 4th ch.

Row 2: * work 3-looped cluster in the 1-ch, ch 1, work 3-looped cluster in the same 1-ch, ch 2, dc in the next dc, ch 2, rep from *, ending row with dc in the turning ch, ch 5 and turn.

Row 3: * work 3-looped cluster in the 1-ch, ch 1, work 3-looped cluster in the same 1-ch, ch 2, dc in the next dc, ch 2, rep from *, ending row with dc in the turning ch.

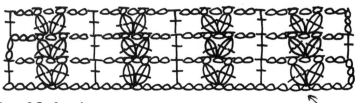

311.   Chain multiples of 5 plus 4.

Row 1: Work 3-looped cluster in the 4th ch, * ch 5 and 3-looped cluster in the 5th ch, rep from *, ending row with last cluster, 1 ch and dc in the next ch, ch 7 and turn.

Row 2: * work 1 sc in the middle of the 5-ch, ch 6, work 1 dc in the 2nd ch and 1 dc in the 2nd ch, ch 6, rep from *, ending row with sc, 3 chs and dc in the turning ch, ch 1 and turn.

Row 3: Sc in the dc, work 3-ch picot, work another 5 sc around the 3-ch, * work 5 sc around the beginning of the 6-ch, work 3-ch picot, work another 4 sc around the same 6-ch, sc in each of the 2 dc, work 4 sc in the next 6-ch, work 3-ch picot, work another 5 sc in the same 3-ch, rep from *, ending row with 6 sc in the turning ch and 3-ch picot.

312.   Chain multiples of 3 plus 2.

Row 1: Sc in the 2nd ch, * ch 3 and sc in the 3rd ch, rep from *, ending row with sc in the last ch, ch 4 and turn.

Row 2: * sc in the 3-ch, ch 4, rep from *, ending row with last sc, ch 1 and dc in the last sc, ch 1 and turn.

Row 3: Sc in the dc, * ch 5 and sc in the middle of the 4-ch, rep from *, ending row with last sc in the turning ch, ch 5 and turn.

Row 4: * work 2-looped cluster in the 5-ch, ch 2, rep from *, ending row with last cluster, ch 1 and dc in the sc, ch 1 and turn.

Row 5: Sc in the dc, sc in the 1-ch, * sc in the next 2-ch, ch 3 and sc in the same 2-ch, rep from *, ending row with last set and 1 extra sc in the turning ch.

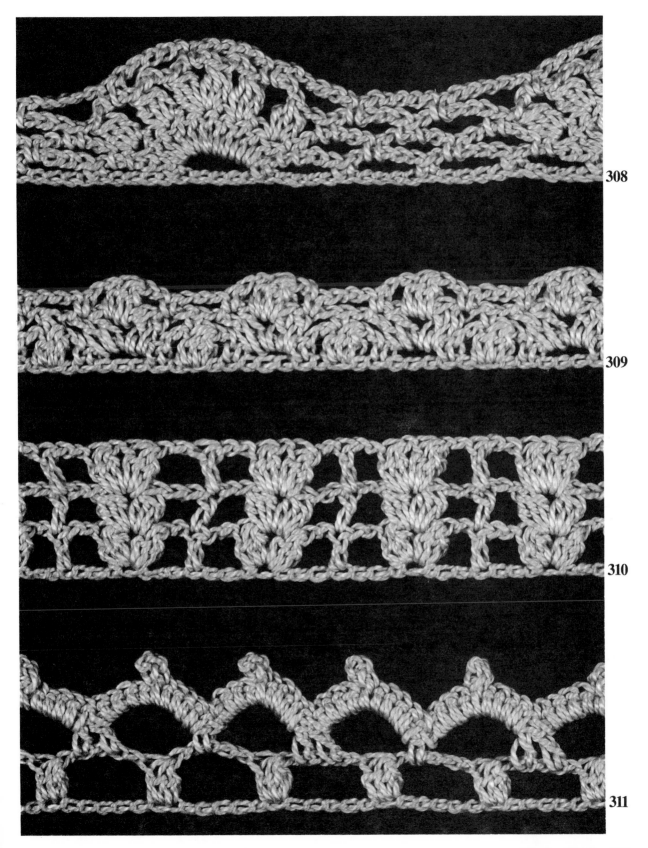

308

309

310

311

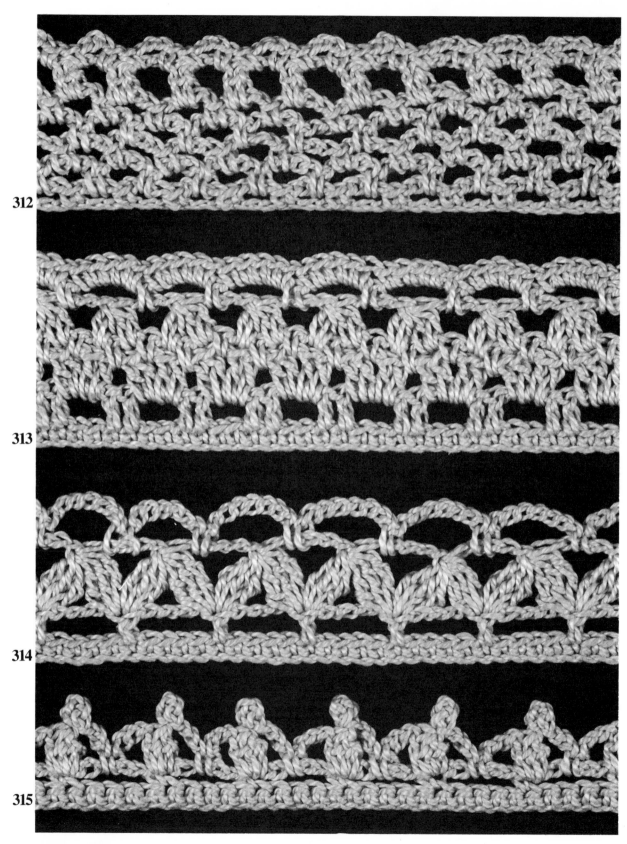

312

313

314

315

234   Cluster Stitch

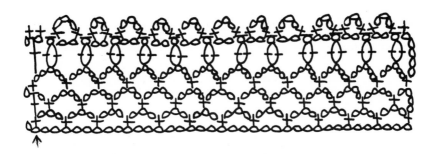

313. Chain multiples of 4 plus 2.

Row 1: Sc in the 2nd ch and in each ch all across the row, ch 3 and turn.

Row 2: Dc in the 2nd sc, * ch 2 and dc in the 3rd sc, dc in the next sc, and rep from *, ending row with dc in each of the last 2 sc, ch 3 and turn.

Row 3: * work 2 dc in the 2-ch, ch 1 and 2 dc in the same 2-ch, rep from *, ending row with last set and 1 dc in the turning ch, ch 1 and turn.

Row 4: Sc in the 1st dc, * ch 1, sc in the 1-ch, ch 1 and sc between the dc of the 2 sets, rep from *, ending row with sc in the turning ch, ch 5 and turn.

Row 5: * finish 2 2-looped cluster together, 1 in the last 1-ch and in the next 1-ch, ch 3, rep from *, ending row with last set and 1 dc in the last sc, ch 1 and turn.

Row 6: Sc in the dc, * ch 4, sc in the middle of the 3-ch, rep from *, ending row with sc in the turning ch, ch 1 and turn.

Row 7: * work 5 sc in the 4-ch, and rep from *, ending row with last set.

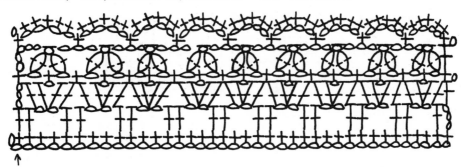

314. Chain multiples of 5 plus 2.

Row 1: Sc in the 2nd ch and in each ch all across the row, ch 7 and turn.

Row 2: Dc in the 6th sc, *ch 4, dc in the 5th sc, rep from *, ending row with last dc, ch 7 and turn.

Row 3: * work 3-looped triple cluster in the dc, finish it together with 3-looped triple cluster in the next dc, ch 4, rep from *, ending row with last cluster, ch 2 and trc in the same spot on the turning ch, ch 1 and turn.

Row 4: Sc in the trc, * ch 7, sc around the middle of the 4-ch, rep from *, ending row with sc in the turning ch.

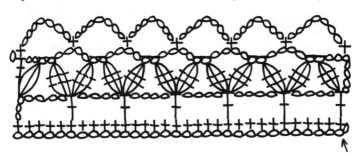

315. Chain multiples of 5 plus 2.

Row 1: Sc in 2nd ch and in each ch all across the row, ch 4 and turn.

Row 2: Sc in 3rd sc, *ch 5, sc in the 5th sc, rep from *, ending row with sc, 2 ch and 1 hdc in the 2nd sc, ch 1 and turn.

Row 3: Sc in hdc, * ch 3, work 3-looped cluster in sc, 3-ch picot, ch 3, sc in the middle of the 5-ch, rep from *, ending row with sc in the turning ch.

316. Chain multiples of 4 plus 2.

Row 1: 1 sc in the 2nd ch and in each ch all across the row, ch 3 and turn.

Row 2: 1 dc in the 2nd sc, * ch 1, 1 dc in the 2nd sc and in the next 2 sc, rep from *, ending row with 1 dc in each of the last 2 sc, ch 1 and turn.

Row 3: 1 sc in the 1st dc, * ch 3, work 3-ch picot, work 3-looped cluster in the 1-ch, work another 3-ch picot, ch 3, 1 sc in the 2nd dc, rep from *, ending row with sc in the turning ch.

317. Chain multiples of 8 plus 2.

Row 1: 1 sc in the 2nd ch and in each ch all across the row, ch 1 and turn.

Row 2: Work 1 sc in the 1st sc, * ch 4, work 3-looped cluster in the 4th sc, ch 4, 1 sc in the 4th sc, rep from *, ending row with last sc, ch 3 and turn.

Row 3: Work 2-looped cluster in the 1st sc, * ch 4, work 1 sc in the top of the cluster, ch 4, work 3-looped cluster in the sc, rep from *, ending row with last cluster, ch 1 and turn.

Row 4: * sc in the cluster, ch 4, work 3-looped cluster in the sc, ch 4, rep from *, ending row with sc in the turning ch, ch 1 and turn.

Row 5: * sc in the sc, sc in each of the 4 chs, sc in the cluster, work 3-ch picot, sc in each of the next 4 chs, rep from *, ending row with sc in the last sc.

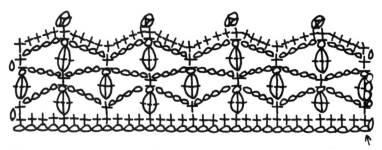

318. Chain multiples of 3 plus 2.

Row 1: 1 sc in the 2nd ch and in each ch all across the row, ch 1 and turn.

Row 2: 1 sc in the 1st sc, *ch 5, 1 sc in the 3rd sc, rep from *, ending row with sc, ch 4 and turn.

Row 3: * work 2-looped cluster in the middle of the 5-ch, work 3-ch picot, ch 1, work 2-looped cluster in the middle of the same 5-ch, ch 1, rep from *, ending row after last set with a trc in the last sc.

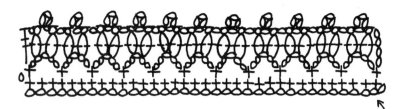

319. Chain multiples of 9 plus 6.

Row 1: 1 dc in the 9th ch, * ch 2, 1 dc in the 3rd ch, rep from *, ending row with last dc, ch 3 and turn.

Row 2: Work 1 double triple 3-looped cluster in the 2nd 2-ch, * ch 5, work 1 dc in the 1st of the 5-ch, ch 5, work 1 dc in the 1st of the 5-ch, ch 5, work 1 dc in the 1st of the 5-ch, work 1 double triple 3-looped cluster in the same 2-ch as the double triple cluster just formed, work 1 double triple 3-looped cluster in the 3rd 2-ch, rep from *, ending row after last double triple 3-looped cluster with 1 dc in the turning chain.

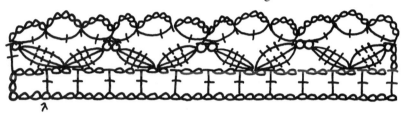

320. Chain multiples of 10 plus 2.

Row 1: Sc in the 2nd ch and in each ch all across the row, ch 1 and turn.

Row 2: Sc in the 1st sc, * ch 3, dc in the 5th sc, ch 3, dc in the sc just used, ch 3, dc in the sc just used, ch 3, sc in the 5th sc, rep from *, ending row with sc in the last sc, ch 6 and turn.

Row 3: * work 3 dc in the 2nd 3-ch, ch 3, sc in the 2nd dc, ch 3, 3 dc in the next 3-ch, ch 3, dc in the next sc, ch 3, rep from *, ending row with dc in the last sc, ch 3 and turn.

Row 4: Sk 1 dc, * dc in the next dc, ch 3, sc in the top of the 3-ch, ch 4, sc in the top of the next 3-ch, ch 3, dc in the last of the 3 dc of the set, dc in the next dc, rep from *, ending row with dc in the turning ch, ch 3 and turn.

Row 5: Sc in the 2nd dc, * ch 3, work 3-looped cluster in the 4-ch, ch 3, work 3-looped cluster in the same 4-ch, ch 3, work 3-looped cluster in the same 4-ch, ch 3, sc in the next dc, ch 3, sc in the 2nd dc, rep from *, ending row with sc in the last dc, ch 2, 1 dc in the turning ch.

321. Chain multiples of 5 plus 4.

Row 1: Dc in the 5th ch and in each ch all across the row, ch 4 and turn.

Row 2: 1 dc in the 3rd dc, * ch 3, 1 dc in the dc just used, ch 3, dc in the 5th dc, rep from *, ending row with last set, ch 1 and work 1 dc in the turning ch, ch 8 and turn.

Row 3: Work 2-looped double cluster in the 1st 3-ch, * ch 5, work another 2-looped double cluster in the same 3-ch, ch 4, work 2-looped double cluster in the 2nd 3-ch, rep from *, ending row with last set, ch 2, 1 double trc in the turning ch, ch 1 and turn.

Row 4: Sc in the 1st double trc, * ch 1, work 1 hdc, 1 dc, 3 trc, 1 dc and 1 hdc in the 5-ch, ch 1, 1 sc in the 4-ch, rep from *, ending row with last set and 1 sc in the turning ch.

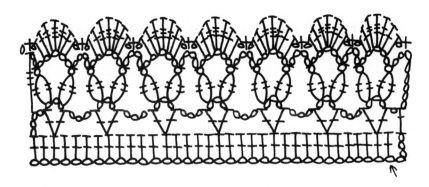

322. Chain multiples of 11 plus 2.

Row 1: Sc in the 2nd ch and in each ch all across the row, ch 1 and turn.

Row 2: Sc in the 1st sc, * ch 6, work 3-ch picot, ch 6 and sc in the 11th sc, rep from *, ending row with sc in the last sc, ch 7 and turn.

Row 3: * work 3-looped double triple cluster in the 3-ch picot, ch 5 and work another 3-looped double triple cluster in the same picot, ch 5 and work another 3-looped double triple cluster in the same picot, finish 2 double trc together near the end of the last 6-ch, and near the beginning of the next 6-ch, rep from *, ending row with 7 chs.

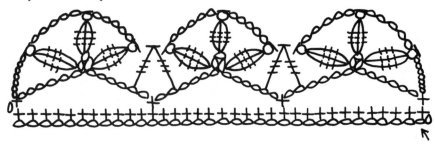

323. Chain multiples of 6 plus 5.

Row 1: Work 2-looped cluster in the 6th ch, * ch 3 and work 2-looped cluster in the 6th ch, ch 2 and work another 2-looped cluster in the same ch, rep from *, ending row with cluster in the last ch, ch 1 and dc in the ch just used for the cluster, ch 5 and turn.

Row 2: Work 3-looped triple cluster in the 1st dc, * work 5-ch picot, ch 5 and sc in the middle of the 3-ch, ch 5 and work 3-looped triple cluster in the 2-ch, rep from *, ending row with cluster in the turning ch, 5-ch picot and trc in the same stitch.

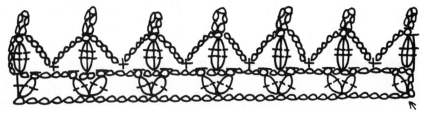

324. Chain multiples of 5 plus 2.

Row 1: Sc in the 2nd ch and in each ch all across the row, ch 7 and turn.

Row 2: Sc in the 4th sc, * ch 7 and sc in the 5th sc, rep from *, ending row with last sc, ch 4 and dc in the 4th sc, ch 4 and turn.

Row 3: Ch 5 and work 2-looped triple cluster back in the last of the 4-ch, * dc in the middle of the next 7-ch, ch 5 and work 2-looped triple cluster back in the top of the dc, rep from *, ending row with dc in the turning ch, ch 9 and turn.

Row 4: * dc backwards in the 4th from the last ch, ch 2, finish 2 trc together in the top of the last dc and the next dc, ch 7, rep from *, ending row with dc back in the 4th ch of the last set, ch 1 and double trc in the turning ch.

238 Cluster Stitch

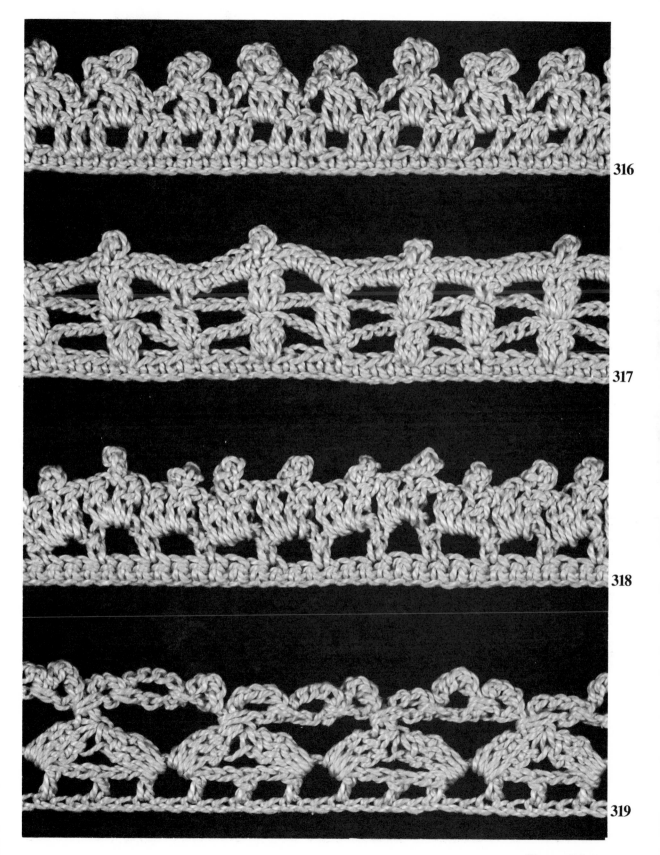

316

317

318

319

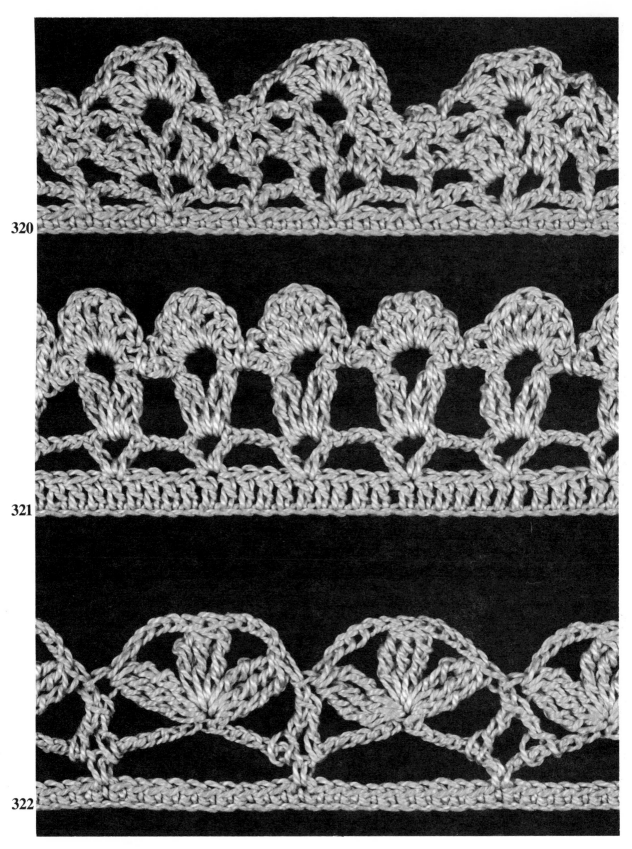

320

321

322

240 Cluster Stitch

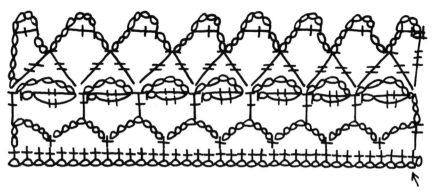

325.   Chain multiples of 6 plus 2.

Row 1: Sc in the 2nd ch and in each ch all across the row, ch 6 and turn.

Row 2: Work 1 trc in the 5th sc, * ch 1 and trc in the sc just used, ch 1 and trc in the same sc, ch 1 and trc in the 6th sc, rep from *, ending row with last set and double trc in the 2nd sc, ch 6 and turn.

Row 3: Finish together 1 double trc in the double trc, with 3-looped cluster in the 2nd trc and 1 double trc in the 2nd 1-ch, * ch 5 and work 1 double trc in the 1-ch just used, finished together with 1 3-looped cluster in the 2nd trc, and 1 double trc in the 2nd 1-ch, rep from *, ending row with last set, ch 3 and trc in the turning ch, ch 1 and turn.

Row 4: Sc in the trc, work 6-ch picot, sc in the 1st of the 3-ch, * ch 5 and sc in the middle of the 5-ch, work 6-ch picot, work another 6-ch picot and sl st into 1st picot, sc in the same ch, rep from *, ending row with last set, 1 sc in the turning ch and 6-ch picot.

326.   Chain multiples of 8 plus 2.

Row 1: Sc in the 2nd ch, *ch 5 and work 3-looped triple cluster in the 4th ch, ch 5 and sc in the 4th ch, and rep from *, ending row with last sc, ch 3 and turn.

Row 2: * sc in the beginning of the 5-ch, ch 10, and sc towards the end of the next 5-ch, ch 3, rep from *, ending row with the last sc and 1 hdc in the last sc, ch 1 and turn.

Row 3: * work 5 sc around the beginning of the 10-ch, work 3-ch picot, work another 3 sc around the middle of the 10-ch, 3-ch picot, 3 sc around same 10-ch, another 3-ch picot, work another 5 sc around the same 10-ch, work 1 sc in each of the 3-chs, rep from *, ending row with last set.

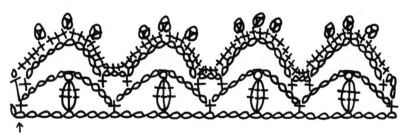

327. Chain multiples of 9 plus 2.

Row 1: Sc in the 2nd ch and in each ch all across the row, ch 5 and turn.

Row 2: Dc in the 4th sc, * ch 2 and dc in the 3rd sc, rep from *, ending row with dc in the last sc, ch 3 and turn.

Row 3: Work 3-looped cluster in the 2nd dc, *ch 9, finish 2 3-looped clusters together, 1 in the next dc and 1 in the 2nd dc, rep from *, ending row with last cluster and trc in the turning ch, ch 5 and turn.

Row 4: Work 3-looped cluster in the middle of the 9-ch, ch 7, and work another 3-looped cluster in the same ch, ch 3 and rep from *, ending row with last cluster, ch 1 and trc in the last cluster, ch 1 and turn.

Row 5: Sc in the trc, *ch 4 and sc in the middle of the 7-ch, ch 3 and sc in the middle of the same 7-ch, ch 4 and sc in the middle of the next 3-ch, rep from *, ending row with sc in the turning ch.

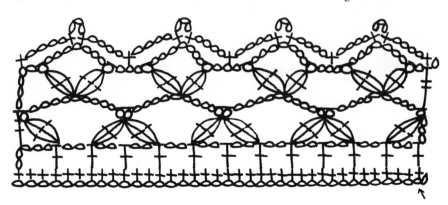

328. Chain multiples of 6 plus 2.

Row 1: 1 sc in the 2nd ch, sc in the next ch, * ch 1, sc in the 2nd ch, rep from *, ending row with sc, ch 1 and turn.

Row 2: Sc in the 1st sc, * sc in 1-ch, ch 5, sc in the 2nd 1-ch, ch 1, rep from *, ending row with sc in last sc, ch 3 and turn.

Row 3: 1 dc in 1st sc, * ch 3, sc in the middle of the 5-ch, ch 2, work 3-looped cluster in the 1-ch, rep from *,

ending row with 2-looped cluster in the last sc, ch 6 and turn.

Row 4: * sc in 2-ch, ch 5, sc in 3-ch, ch 5, rep from *, ending row with 2 chs and 1 dc in the turning ch, ch 1 and turn.

Row 5: Sc in the dc, * ch 5, sc in 5-ch, rep from *, ending row with sc in the turning ch.

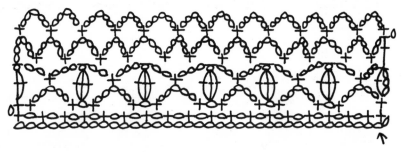

329. Chain multiples of 6 plus 4.

Row 1: Dc in the 5th ch and in each ch all across the row, ch 4 and turn.

Row 2: Dc in the 3rd dc and the next dc, * ch 2, dc in the 2nd dc and the dc after that, ch 1, dc in the 2nd dc and the dc after that, rep from *, ending row with 2 chs and 1 dc in the turning ch, ch 3 and turn.

Row 3: * work 3-looped cluster in the 2-ch, ch 3, work 2-looped cluster back in the top of the 2-looped cluster, rep

from *, ending row with last set and dc in the turning ch, ch 6 and turn.

Row 4: * work 3-looped cluster in the top of the 3-looped cluster, ch 4, rep from *, ending row with last cluster and dc in the turning ch, ch 1 and turn.

Row 5: Sc in the dc, * work 2 sc in the 1st part of the 4-ch, work 4-ch picot, work another 2 sc in the 2nd part of the 4-ch, rep from *, ending row with last set in the turning ch.

242 **Cluster Stitch**

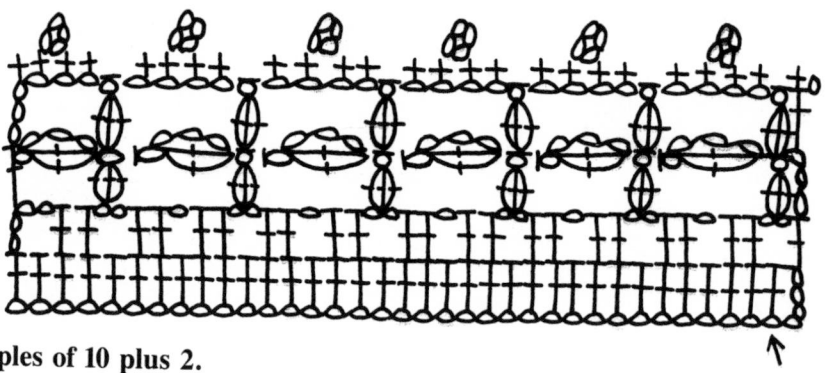

330. Chain multiples of 10 plus 2.

Row 1: Sc in the 2nd ch and in each ch all across the row, ch 1 and turn.

Row 2: Sc in each of the 1st 3 sc, * ch 5, sc in the 5th sc, rep from *, ending row with last sc in sc and 1 in the turning ch, ch 4 and turn.

Row 3: * work 3-looped triple cluster in the beginning of the 5-ch, ch 3, work another 3-looped triple cluster in the middle of the same 5-ch, ch 3, work another 3-looped triple cluster towards the end of the 5-ch, rep from *,

ending row with last cluster and 1 dc in the last sc, ch 1 and turn.

Row 4: Sc in the top of the 1st cluster, * ch 11, sc in between the 2 sets of 3 triple clusters, rep from *, ending row with sc in the turning ch, ch 1 and turn.

Row 5: Sc in the 1st sc, * work 6 sc around the 1st half of the 11-ch, work 5-ch picot, work 6 sc around the last half of the 11-ch, rep from *, ending row with sc in the last sc.

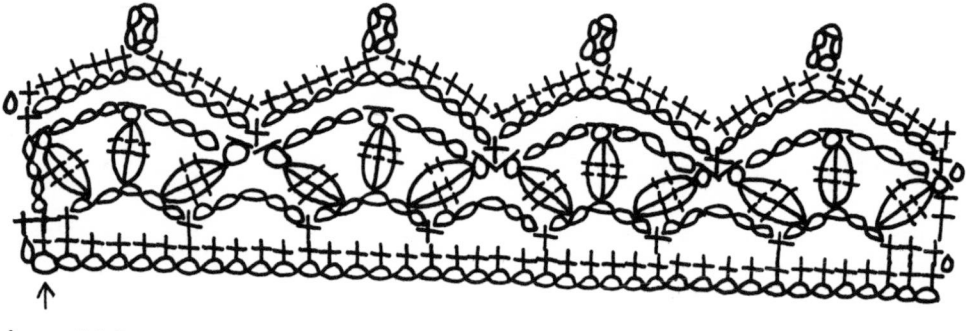

331. Chain multiples of 7 plus 5.

Row 1: Work 3-looped triple cluster in the 8th ch, * ch 7 and work another 3-looped triple cluster in the same ch, finished together with 3-looped triple cluster in the 7th ch, rep from *, ending row with last set and trc in the 4th ch, ch 1 and turn.

Row 2: Sc in the trc, * work 11 sc around the 7-ch, rep from *, ending row with last set and an extra sc in the turning ch, ch 4 and turn.

Row 3: * work 1 trc in the middle of the 11 sc, ch 1 and trc in the same sc 5 times, rep from *, ending row with last set and dc in the last sc, ch 1 and turn.

Row 4: Sc in the 1st trc, * ch 5 and sc in the next 1-ch 5 times, rep from *, ending row with last set, ch 5 and sc in the turning ch.

332. Chain multiples of 16 plus 9.

Row 1: Trc in the 6th ch, trc in each of the next 3 chs, * ch 5, trc in the 6th ch, ch 5, trc in the 6th ch, trc in each of next 4 chs, rep from *, ending row with trc in each of the last 5 chs, ch 3 and turn.

Row 2: Dc in the 2nd trc, dc in each of the next 2 trc, * ch 5, trc in the 2nd trc, ch 5, trc in the same trc, ch 5, dc in the 2nd trc, dc in each of the next 2 trc, rep from *, ending row with dc in the turning ch, ch 1 and turn.

Row 3: Sc in the 1st and next dc, * ch 5, dc in the trc, ch 1 and dc in the 5-ch 5 times, ch 1 and dc in the trc, ch 5, sc in the next dc and the next dc, rep from *, ending row with sc in each of the last dc and the turning ch, ch 1 and turn.

Row 4: Sc in the 1st sc, * ch 5, work 3-looped triple cluster in the 1-ch, ch 1, work 4-ch picot and ch 1 5 times, work another triple 3-looped triple cluster in the next 1-ch, ch 5 and sc in the next sc, rep from *, ending row with sc in the last sc.

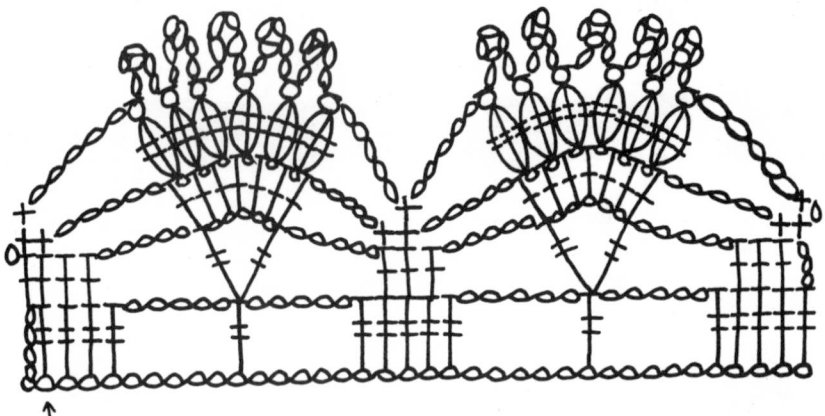

333. Chain 1.

Row 1: * ch 8 and sl st end to the ch before, ch 7, rep from *, ending row with last 8 chs, sl st and ch 1, break thread.

Row 2: Attach thread to middle of 8-ch, ch 5, * work 3-looped cluster in the middle of the 8-ch, ch 3 and rep 3 more times, sc in the middle of the next 8-ch, ch 3 and make another sc in the same ch, ch 3, rep from *, ending row with sc, ch 3 and sc, ch 2 and turn.

Row 3: * sc in the 3-ch, ch 3 and sc in the same 3-ch, ch 3 and sc in the next 3-ch, ch 3 and sc in the next 3-ch, ch 3 and sc in the same 3-ch, ch 3, sc in the next 3-ch, ch 3 and sc in the same 3-ch, ch 3 and sc in the next 3-ch, ch 3 and sc in the same 3-ch, ch 3 and sc in the next 3-ch, ch 3, rep from *, ending row with sc.

Bottom Row: Sc in the 1st ch, * ch 3, sc in the next ch, work another sc in each of the next 7-chs, rep from *, ending row with last sc.

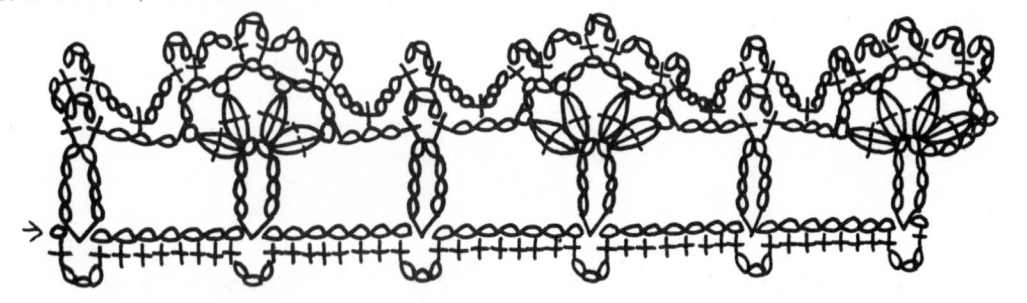

334. Chain multiples of 4 plus 4.

Row 1: Dc in the 4th ch and in each ch all across the row, ch 1 and turn.

Row 2: Sc in the 1st dc, *ch 3 and work 3-looped cluster back in the dc after the sc, sc in the 2nd dc, rep from * ending row with sc in the turning ch, ch 4 and turn.

Row 3: Dc in the 1st sc, finished together with dc in the next sc, * ch 3, dc in the sc just used, dc in the next sc, rep from *, ending row with dc in the last sc, ch 1 and dc in the same sc, ch 3 and turn.

Row 4: Work 4 dc in the 3-ch, * work 4-ch picot, work 4 dc in the 3-ch just used, work 4 dc in the 2nd 3-ch, rep from *, ending row with 4 dc, 4-ch picot and 1 dc in the turning ch.

246 Cluster Stitch

330

331

332

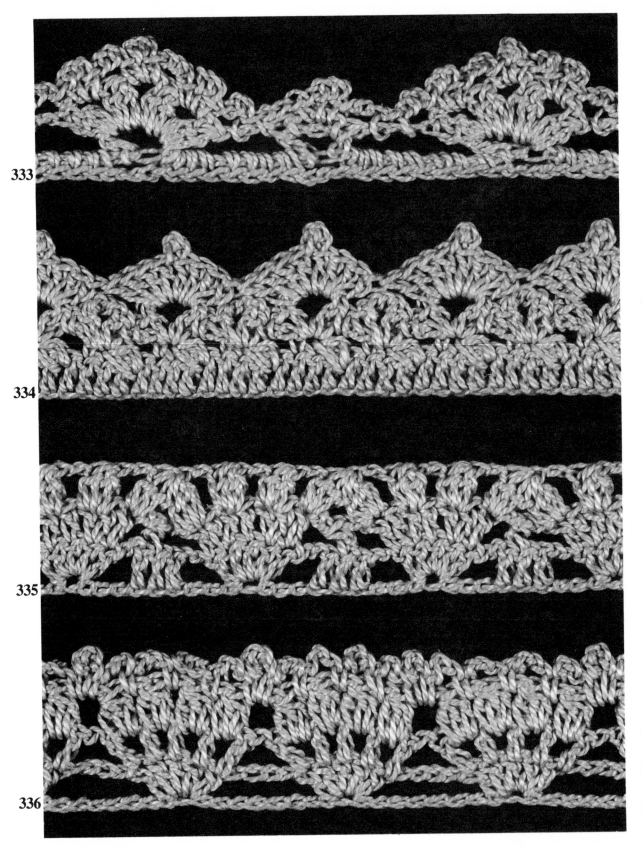

333

334

335

336

248   Cluster Stitch

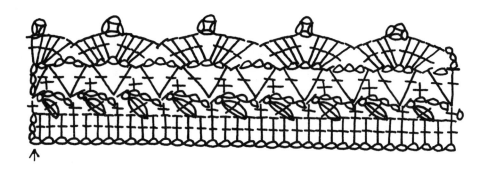

335.   Chain multiples of 10 plus 4.

Row 1: Dc in the 5th ch, * ch 2, work 5 dc in the 4th ch, ch 2, dc in the 4th ch, dc in each of the next 2 chs, rep from *, ending row with 2 dc, ch 5 and turn.

Row 2: Sk 1st 2 dc, * dc in next dc, 2 dc in the next dc, dc in the next dc, 2 dc in the next dc, dc in the next dc, ch 2, dc in the 2nd dc, ch 2, rep from *, ending row with dc in the turning ch, ch 3 and turn.

Row 3: * work 3-looped cluster in the next 2nd dc, ch 2, work 3-looped cluster in the 2nd dc, ch 2, work 3-looped cluster in the 2nd dc, ch 2, work 3-looped cluster in 2nd dc, rep from *, ending row with dc in the turning ch.

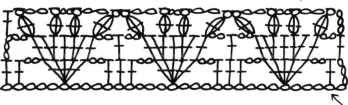

336.   Chain multiples of 9 plus 5.

Row 1: Work 5 dc in the 9th ch, * ch 4, work 5 dc in the 9th ch, rep from *, ending row with last set, 1 ch and dc in the 4th ch, ch 3 and turn.

Row 2: Sk 1st dc, * dc in next dc and 1 ch, 5 times, rep from *, ending row with last set and 1 dc in the turning ch, ch 3 and turn.

Row 3: * work 3-looped cluster in the next 1-ch, ch 1 3 times, work another 3-looped cluster in the next 1-ch and ch 2, rep from *, ending row with last cluster and dc in the turning ch, ch 1 and turn.

Row 4: Sc in the 1st dc, * ch 3 and sc in the next 1-ch 3 times, ch 3 and sc in the 2-ch, ch 4, sc in the same 4-ch, rep from *, ending row with last sc in the turning ch.

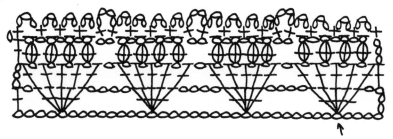

337.   Chain multiples of 7 plus 2.

Row 1: Sc in 2nd ch and in each ch all across the row, ch 1 and turn.

Row 2: Sc in 1st sc and in the next 3 sc, * ch 7, sl st in 1st ch, ch another 7, sl st, sc in next sc, ch 7, sl st back into 1st 7-ch, sc in next sc and in the following 7 sc, rep from *, ending row with sc, ch 5 and turn.

Row 3: * Work 3-looped cluster in the middle of the 1st 7-ch, ch 5, work 3-looped cluster in the middle of the next 7-ch, ch 5, work a 3-looped cluster in the middle of the next 7-ch, rep from *, ending row after last set with a double trc, ch 7 and turn.

Row 4: * sc in the middle of the 5-ch, ch 7, rep from *, ending row with sc in the middle of the last 5-ch, ch 3, and trc in the turning chain.

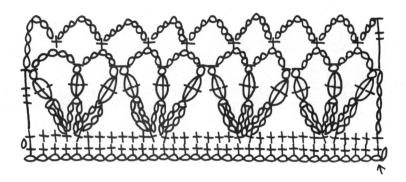

338. Chain multiples of 8 plus 4.

Row 1: Dc in the 5th ch, * ch 1 and dc in the 2nd ch, rep from *, ending row with last dc and 1 dc in the next ch, ch 6 and turn.

Row 2: Sk 1st dc, * dc in the 2nd dc, dc in the 1-ch and dc in the next dc, work 2-looped cluster in the 2nd 1-ch, ch 4 and work another 2-looped cluster in the same 1-ch, rep from *, ending row with 2-looped cluster in the turning ch, ch 2 and dc in the turning ch, ch 1 and turn.

Row 3: Sc in the dc, ch 3, * sc in the next dc, ch 3 and sc in the 2nd dc, ch 3 and sc in the 4-ch, ch 3 and another sc in the same 4-ch, ch 3, rep from *, ending row with sc in

the turning ch, ch 1 and work 1 hdc in the turning ch, ch 1 and turn.

Row 4: Sc in the hdc, * ch 1 and work 2-looped cluster in the 2nd 3-ch, ch 3 and work another 2-looped cluster in the same 3-ch, ch 3 and work another 2-looped cluster in the same 3-ch, ch 1 and sc in the 2nd 3-ch, rep from *, ending row with sc in the last sc, ch 1 and turn.

Row 5: * sc in the sc, ch 3 and sc in the next 3-ch, ch 3 and sc in the same 3-ch, ch 3 and sc in the next 3-ch, ch 3 and sc in the same 3-ch, ch 3, rep from *, ending row with last set.

339. Chain multiples of 9 plus 6.

Row 1: Dc in the 5th ch, and dc in the next ch, * ch 9 and dc in the 7th ch, dc in each of the next 2 chs, rep from *, ending row with dc in each of the last 3 chs, ch 3 and turn.

Row 2: Sk 1st dc, dc in each of the next 2 dc, * ch 3 and sc around the middle of the 7-ch, ch 3 and dc in each of the next 3 dc, rep from *, ending row with dc in each of the last 2 dc and dc in the turning ch, ch 3 and turn.

Row 3: Sk 1st dc, dc in each of the next 2 dc, * ch 4 and sc in the next sc, ch 4 and dc in each of the next 3 dc, rep from *, ending row with dc in each of the last 2 dc and dc in the turning ch, ch 3 and turn.

Row 4: Sk 1st dc, dc in each of the next 2 dc, * ch 9 and

dc in each of the next 3 dc, rep from *, ending row with dc in each of the last 2 dc and dc in the turning ch, ch 3 and turn.

Row 5: Same as row 2, ch 3 and turn.

Row 6: Same as row 3, ch 3 and turn.

Row 7: Same as row 4, ch 4 and turn.

Row 8: * work 3-looped cluster in the next dc, ch 1 and work 3-ch picot, work another 3-looped cluster in the next dc, ch 1 and work 3-ch picot, work another 3-looped cluster in the next dc, ch 1 and work 3-ch picot, sc in the middle of the 9-ch, rep from *, ending row with last cluster.

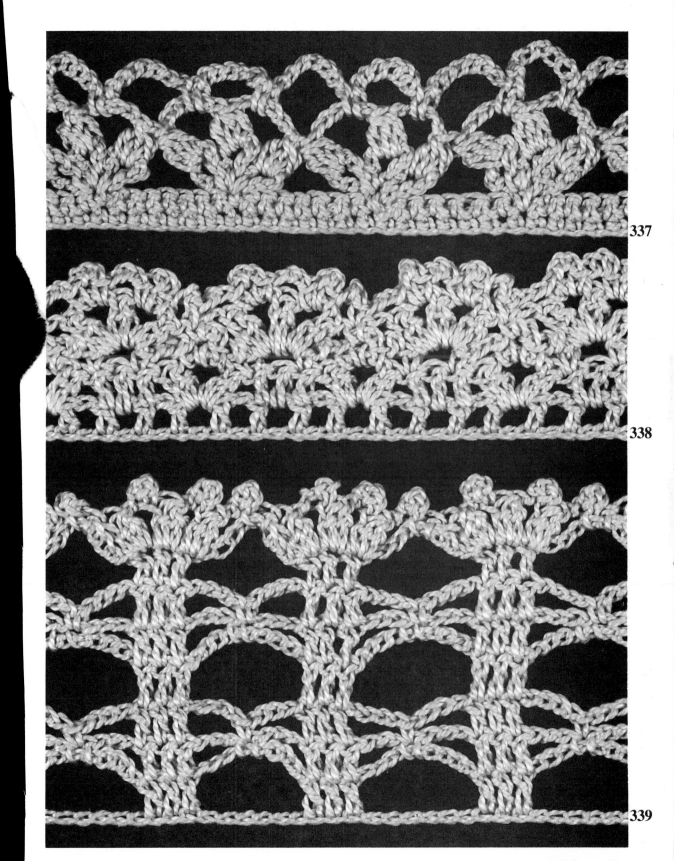

337

338

339

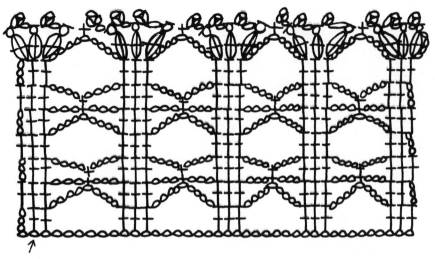

340. Chain multiples of 12 plus 6.

Row 1: Dc in the 9th ch, * ch 2 and dc in the 3rd ch, rep from *, ending row with last dc, ch 9 and turn.

Row 2: Work 3-looped double triple cluster in the 3rd dc, * ch 3 and work 3-looped double triple cluster in the same dc, ch 4 and work double triple stitch in the 2nd dc, ch 4 and work 3-looped double triple cluster in the 2nd dc, rep from *, ending row with last set and double triple stitch in the turning ch, ch 9 and turn.

Row 3: * work 3-looped double triple cluster in the 3-ch, ch 3 and work another 3-looped double triple cluster in the same 3-ch, ch 4 and double triple stitch in the next double triple stitch, ch 4, rep from *, ending row with double triple stitch in the turning ch, ch 9 and turn.

Row 4: Same as row 3, ch 1 and turn.

Row 5: Sc in the double triple stitch, ch 5, * sc in the 4-ch, ch 6 and sc in the 3-ch, ch 6 and sc in the next 4-ch, ch 6, rep from *, ending row with sc in the turning ch.

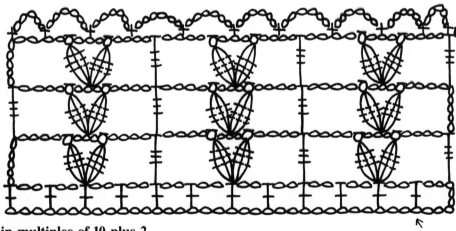

341. Chain multiples of 10 plus 2.

Row 1: Sc in the 2nd ch, * ch 7 and sc in the 5th ch, rep from *, ending row with sc in the last set, ch 8 and turn.

Row 2: * sc around the 7-ch, ch 7, rep from *, ending row with sc in the last 7-ch, ch 3 and work trc in the last sc, ch 1 and turn.

Row 3: Sc in the 1st trc, * ch 7 and sc around the next 7-ch, rep from *, ending row with sc in the turning ch, ch 7 and turn.

Row 4: * sc around the 7-ch, ch 7, rep from *, ending row with sc, ch 3 and trc in the last sc, ch 1 and turn.

Row 5: Sc in the trc, * ch 7 and sc around the next 7-ch, rep from *, ending row with sc in the turning ch, ch 7 and turn.

Row 6: * sc around the 7-ch, ch 7 and sc around the next 7-ch, work 3 trc in the next sc, ch 3 and work another 3 trc in the same sc, rep from *, ending row with sc in the last 7-ch, ch 3 and trc in the last sc, ch 1 and turn.

Row 7: Sc in the trc, ch 3 and 3 dc in the 2nd 3-ch, * ch 3 and work another 3 dc in the same 3-ch, ch 3 and sc in the next 7-ch, ch 3 and work 3 dc in the next 3-ch, rep

252 Cluster Stitch

from *, ending row with sc in the turning ch, ch 7 and turn.

Row 8: Work 1 trc in the 1st of the 7 turning ch formed, ch 1 and trc twice in the same ch, ch 7 and trc in the 2nd 3-ch, * ch 1 and trc in the same 3-ch 5 more times, ch 7 and trc in the 3rd 3-ch, rep from *, ending row with last set, ch 3 and double trc inn the last sc, ch 1 and turn.

Row 9: Sc in the double trc, * ch 3 and work 1 3-looped triple cluster in the 2nd trc, ch 3 and work another 3-looped triple cluster in the next trc, ch 3 and work another 3-looped triple cluster in the next trc, ch 3 and work another 3-looped triple cluster in the next trc, ch 3 and sc in the middle of the 7-ch, ch 3 and rep from *, ending row with 1 trc in the turning ch, ch 6 and turn.

Row 10: Work 3-looped triple cluster in the 3-ch, * ch 3 and sl st in the next sc, ch 3 and work 3-looped triple cluster in the 3-ch between the 2 cluster, ch 3 and work another 3-looped triple cluster in the 3-ch between the next 2 clusters, ch 3 and work another 3-looped triple cluster between the next 2 clusters, rep from *, ending row with sl st in the last sc.

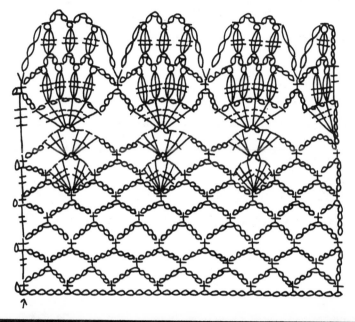

340

341

342.   Chain multiples of 14 plus 2.

Row 1: Sc in the 2nd ch and in each ch all across the row, ch 4 and turn.

Row 2: Work 2-looped cluster in the 1st sc, * ch 3, sc in the 4th sc, ch 5, sc in the 6th sc, ch 3, work 2-looped cluster in the 4th sc, ch 3, work another 2-looped cluster in the same sc, rep from *, ending row with 2-looped cluster, 1 ch and 1 dc in the last sc, ch 4 and turn.

Row 3: Work 2-looped cluster in the 1st dc, * ch 3, work 7 trc around the 5-ch, ch 3, work 2-looped cluster in the 2nd 3-ch, ch 3, work another 2-looped cluster in the same 3-ch, rep from *, ending row with 2-looped cluster, 1 ch and 1 dc in the turning ch, ch 4 and turn.

Row 4: Work 2-looped cluster in the dc, * ch 3, work trc in each trc, ch 3, work 2-looped cluster in the 2nd 3-ch, ch 3, work 2-looped cluster in the same 3-ch, rep from *, ending row with 2-looped cluster in the turning ch, ch 1, 1 dc, ch 4 and turn.

Row 5: Work 2-looped cluster in the 1st dc, * ch 4, work dc in the 2nd trc, and dc in each of the next 4 trc, ch 4, work 2-looped cluster in the 2nd 3-ch, ch 3, work another 2-looped cluster in the same 3-ch, rep from *, ending row with 2-looped cluster, 1 ch and dc in the turning ch, ch 4 and turn.

Row 6: Work 2-looped cluster in the 1st dc, * ch 2, work dc in the last of the 4-ch, ch 1, dc in the 2nd dc and each of the next 2 dc, ch 1 and dc in the 1st of the next 4-ch, ch 2, work 2-looped cluster in the 3-ch, ch 3, work another 2-looped cluster in the same 3-ch, rep from *, ending row with 2-looped cluster, 1 ch and 1 dc in the turning ch, ch 4 and turn.

Row 7: Work 2-looped cluster in the dc, * ch 3, sc in the 1-ch, ch 2, dc in the 2nd dc, ch 2, sc in the next 1-ch, ch 3, 2-looped cluster in the 3-ch, ch 3, work another 2-looped cluster in the same 3-ch, rep from *, ending row with the last 2-looped cluster, ch 1 and the dc in the turning ch, ch 4 and turn.

Row 8: Work 2-looped cluster in the 1st dc, * ch 3, work 2-looped cluster in the sc, ch 1, work another 2-looped cluster in the same sc, ch 1, and work another 2-looped cluster in the next dc, ch 1 and another 2-looped cluster in the same dc, ch 1 and work 2-looped cluster in the next sc, ch 1 and work another 2-looped cluster in the same sc, ch 3 and work another 2-looped cluster in the 2nd 3-ch, ch 3 and work another 2-looped cluster in the same 3-ch, rep from *, ending row with 2-looped cluster, 1 ch and dc in the turning ch, ch 3 and turn.

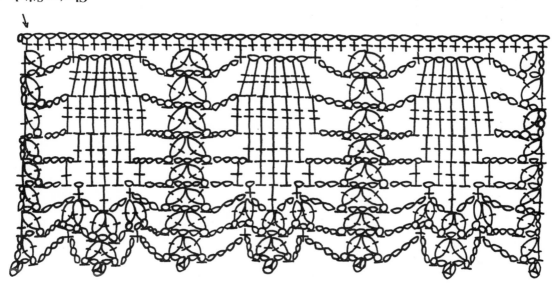

Row 9: * work 3-ch picot, ch 1, and work a 2-looped cluster in the 2nd 1-ch, ch 3, work 2-looped cluster in the 2nd 1-ch, ch 1, work 3-ch picot, ch 1 and work another 2-looped cluster in the same 1-ch, ch 3, sc in the 2nd 1-ch, ch 4, work 3-ch picot, ch 1, work another 2-looped cluster in the same 3-ch, ch 1, rep from *, ending row with 2-looped cluster, 1 ch, 3-ch picot and 1 dc in the turning ch.

342

Photo Index

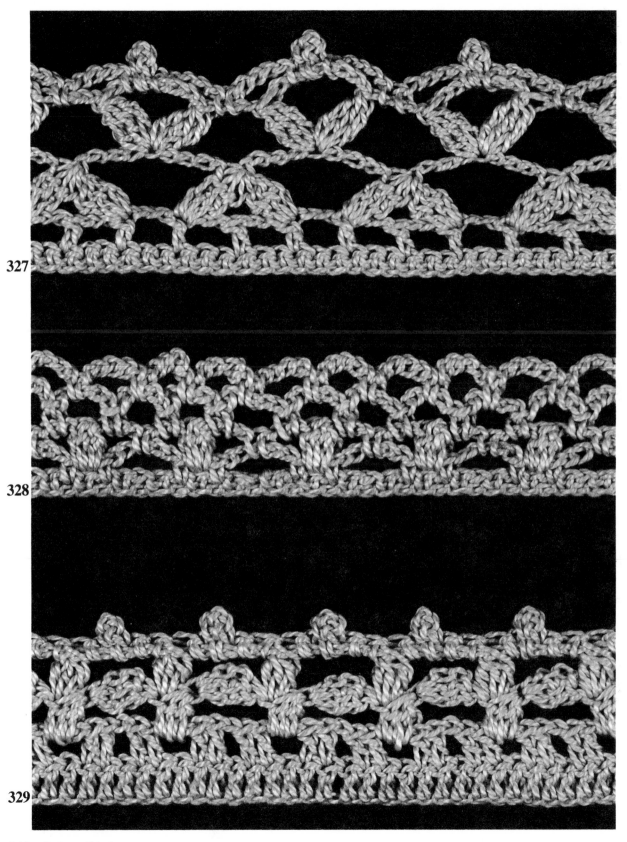

327

328

329

244 Cluster Stitch

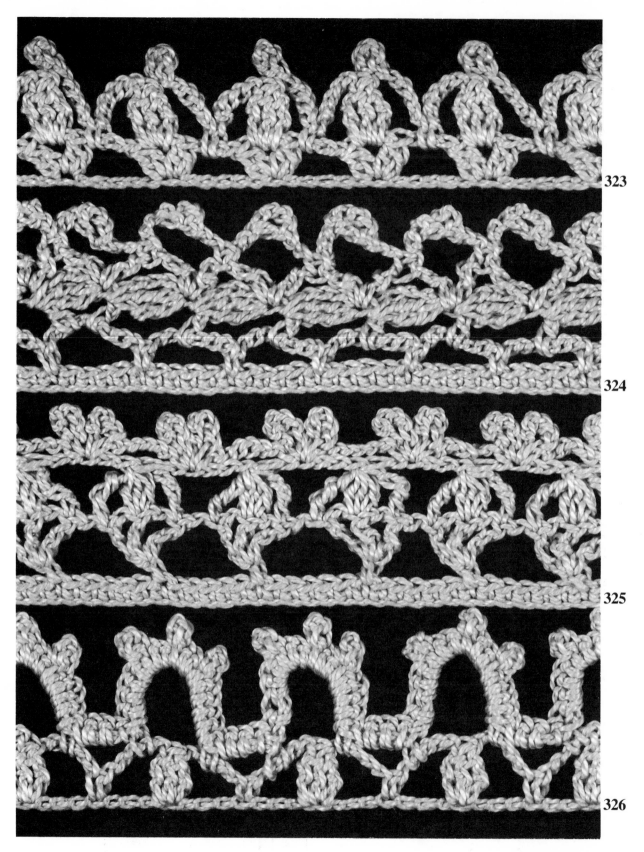

323

324

325

326

Cluster Stitch   243